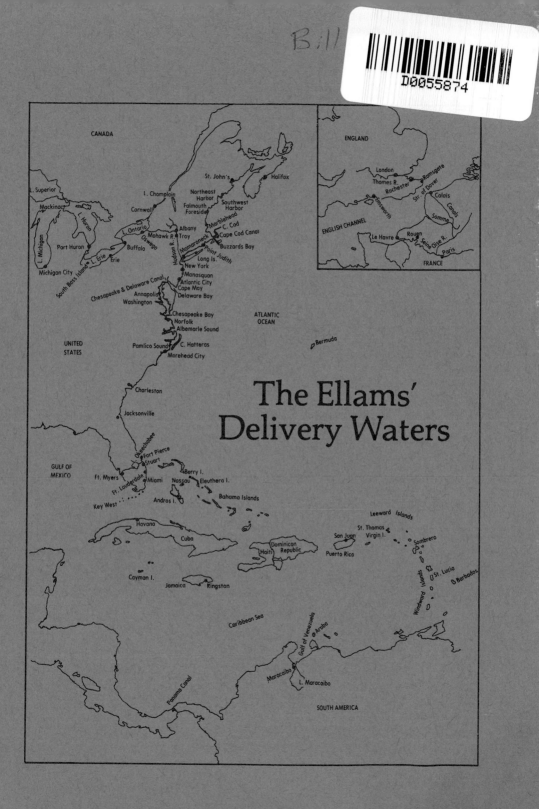

The Ellams'
Delivery Waters

WIND SONG

WIND SONG

Our Ten Years in the Yacht Delivery Business

by Patrick and June Ellam

International Marine Publishing Company
Camden, Maine

For all those who worked with us.

Map drawn by Deena Stearns

CONTENTS

WIND SONG

1   FIRST ONE

It was hot that day. *Wind Song* lay becalmed in the Sargasso Sea, midway between the Virgin Islands and Bermuda, heaving and rolling on the slight swell but not moving forward an inch. June was on watch at the tiller, Bob was dozing on the foredeck in the shade of the sails, and I was below in my bunk.

Suddenly there was a bump and the whole boat shook as though she had run into something hard. In the few seconds that it took me to go up on deck, I went over the possibilities in my mind. We could not have run into anything, since we were not moving. And we could hardly have touched bottom, as the water was about fifteen thousand feet deep. So something must have run into us.

Outside I found Bob and June looking out to starboard, watching a large shark as he swam lazily away. Then he made a tight turn and came back, gathering speed until he was rushing straight at us like a torpedo. In the last few yards he rolled on his back and opened his mouth. Then he disappeared and a moment later we felt him hit the boat. He probably weighed half a ton and he must have been doing the best part of 30 knots. And when he hit, *Wind Song* shuddered from stem to stern.

She was well built but she was not young and wooden boats can easily spring leaks if they are treated like that. In fact she had been leaking so badly, earlier in the passage, that we had seriously considered putting back into port while we could. So I had better do something about that shark right away. But for an instant I stopped to wonder how we got into that situation.

And so did I. When we first met, Patrick told me he was a writer. One book had been published before we were married and he was hard at work on a second. But getting involved in sailing was something I wasn't sure about. And so far, the passage in Wind Song *had only heightened my doubts.*

I thought that sailing involved donning a floppy hat, grabbing some tanning lotion and probably rowing ashore for lunch. With each day, I realized that it was more a serious struggle for survival. And yet I was constantly reminded by the others that "Gentlemen consider 'yachting' a sport." *

I was six years old when I got my first boat. She was an old sailing dinghy that my father gave me as soon as I could swim across the Thames River in England with my clothes and shoes on. He had all kinds of yachts, from a 30-foot yawl to an 84-foot power boat, and as I grew up, I did the same sort of thing. I had a 16-foot day sailer called *Nigella*, a 23-foot sloop called *Girouette* and a 52-foot schooner called *Magnet* in which I cruised the English Channel, the North Sea and the Bay of Biscay.

But after World War II, the cost of running any yacht was so high that people began to wonder how large a boat one really needed to make long cruises safely.

So I had *Theta* built to my specifications by Kenneth Gibbs of Sunbury. She was 20 feet long by 4 feet 8 inches beam, decked over so as to be completely watertight. Lightly built, with a large sloop rig, she was very fast and made some interesting passages, including nine crossings of the English Channel in all weather. But she provided no shelter, not even a place to lie down, so that we could not go for more than four days without putting into port for some sleep and that limited her cruising range.

Then I went to Laurent Giles, the leading designer of ocean racing yachts in England and asked him to draw me a boat the same size, still very light but with room for a few more comforts. And in due course he came up with *Sopranino*.

She was 19 feet 8 inches long by 5 feet 4 inches beam and her all-up weight, including two men and supplies for a week, was around

*June Ellam's comments are in italic type to distinguish them from Patrick Ellam's narrative, which is in roman type.

half a ton, as compared with a small cruising yacht of that time that weighed about five tons. And since the cost of any boat is geared closely to her weight, that was quite a step forward. Still she had everything we needed: two bunks, a galley, a chart table and room for plenty of water, food and sails. But no motor or radio or other unnecessary gadgets.

She sailed very well and I started a club called the Junior Offshore Group that was soon putting on regular long distance races for similar boats. But there were people who said it was not safe, so I took Colin Mudie, a young naval architect, and we sailed *Sopranino* ten thousand miles to show that it was. From England we sailed south to Spain, Portugal, Africa and the Canary Islands, then across the Atlantic Ocean to the Windward and Leeward Islands, the Virgin Islands, Jamaica and Cuba before cruising up the east coast of America from Miami to New York.

Colin went back to England while I wrote a book about the cruise and, liking it in America, decided to stay. So first I married June and then I went looking for a job. But my background was in management and though I was quite willing to do whatever was needed, nobody would hire a 35-year-old foreigner, inexperienced in anything but running a factory.

We were both at loose ends. He didn't really want to go back to a factory and I had been wandering from one job to another, without much interest in any. We wanted to do something together but we had no capital. How does one start?

Then we had a piece of luck: We met a man with a problem. He had left his boat at Palladian Bridge in upstate New York to go back to work after his vacation and now he wanted someone to take her from there to Martha's Vineyard.

He explained that she was a single-engined motor boat, about 40 feet long, that had been built many years ago for duck hunting. She was quite beamy but only drew a foot or so of water, and everything needed to make the trip, including charts, was aboard. So I agreed to move her for him and left the next day with John Miles, a former lieutenant in the Canadian navy, as my crew.

The train followed the east bank of the Hudson River to Albany, then headed northwest along the Mohawk River to our destination and we found the boat lying at the old concrete dock by the Beech-Nut factory.

She was indeed unusual. Outside she had a level deck, running almost her entire length, where people once stood to shoot at ducks, and right aft there had been a small cockpit but that was now enclosed by a pilot house that stuck straight up, giving her something of the look of an early steam locomotive. Inside we found one large cabin, wide open, with bunks along both sides and a gasoline engine in a wooden box standing in the middle of the linoleum-covered floor, while forward there was a simple galley and a bathroom.

It did not take us long to check her out, for there was not much to check. The engine looked serviceable, the steering gear seemed to be okay and there was a bilge pump that one worked by hand, which produced a little water but not much. For navigation she had a compass and a roll of charts. And that was it.

She was on the Mohawk River, which at that point is a part of the New York State Barge Canal, and we headed southeast toward Albany, increasing our speed as the engine warmed up until she was doing her full nine knots. Soon the little town dropped away behind us and the old brick buildings gave way to a pastoral scene of fields and trees as the river ran through rich farm land. Then we came to our first lock.

We were following the chart of course, so we knew that it was coming, but you could not miss it, for there is a line of steel girder work that looks like a very low bridge right across the river. And over to one side you can see the long concrete training wall along the bank, with a shorter wall on the dam side and the gates of the lock in between them.

As you get closer, you can see a large white building and a couple of smaller ones, standing on well-kept lawns beside the lock. There are several interesting black boxes dotted around. If you look closely, you can make out a traffic light. Usually it is red when first you get there so you hang well back, a couple of hundred yards from the gates, and give three blasts of your horn to let the operator know that you are waiting.

If the lock is already set for traffic going your way, it does not take the operator long to open the gates for you. But if the water in the lock is at the next level, he has to close the valves at that end, open the ones at your end and wait for the water to get to your level before he can open them. Which can take a quarter of an hour, so there is no point in getting impatient. If the gates don't open right away, they probably won't for a while. And in that case you nuzzle gently up to the end of the training wall, toss a line over a bollard, lie down on the grass and watch the clouds go by. Unless you prefer to do something more enterprising, like wondering how a duck swims. It is all very relaxing and sensible.

In due course the gates will open and the traffic light will turn green. Then you go into the lock, very slowly, and make fast to the wall on the same side as the operator's little hut, to save him from having to walk around the lock to speak to you. While you are doing that, you hear a thump as the gates come together and a few moments later you notice that the water level is going down.

Locking down is a silent, almost eerie business, with no sign of motion in the water. Rather the walls seem to go up, exposing large areas of wet, slimy concrete. Standing on deck, slacking off your lines, you notice that the grass lawn comes up to your eye level, then suddenly disappears and soon you are at the bottom of a dark, dank canyon. Behind you there is a small waterfall coming from the leaks in the gates, which are now high up on a ledge.

On each side the walls rise up, pitted with great holes caused by countless barges, tiny jets of water spurting from seams here and there to fall clear down into the black water below. And ahead the gates that once looked low and harmless now seem huge and somehow menacing until with a groan and a creak they swing open and let the world back in, with the next section of river. And off you go, giving her a little kick of rudder to counteract the swirls in the water as you pass the gates, reaching for the chart to see what lies ahead.

Quite soon we found a dock on the chart and as we came around a bend, there it was on the left bank of the river. Slowing down, we made a long, easy, curving approach to it against the current. John went up forward with a line and I pulled the gear lever back.

Nothing happened. She continued to plow resolutely on toward the dock, 20 tons or so of runaway boat.

I turned off the ignition and called out: "The gear's stuck. I've killed her." John understood immediately and leaped off the bow onto the dock, spun around and handed her off before she could touch. Meanwhile I took the stern line, led it amidships, jumped from there to the dock, ran astern and helped him stop her.

So we arrived, safe and sound, without a scratch on the paint. But it was lucky that we had been making a slow, careful approach instead of blasting in fast and relying on the engine to stop us, as many people do.

Soon we had fixed the gearshift, filled her up with gas and were under way again, winding down the river, following the chart and using the navigation aids to help us stay in the deep channel.

The aids on the Barge Canal in those days were fun. In the wider reaches there were buoys that sat low and flat in the water, each with a piece of pipe forming an inverted V maybe three feet high, from which hung a large oil lantern. In the narrower reaches you would find the same lanterns hung on pieces of pipe sticking out from the bank or on long wires beneath a bridge.

They were great to work with, for their light was yellowish and easy to distinguish from the blueish white of the casual lights along the shore. And to maintain them was a fleet of jolly little motor boats, all glass windows and bright colors, that chuffed busily from one to the next like bees looking for pollen.

But most of the traffic moved by day and for it there was an assortment of equally attractive day marks. On each bridge there were diamond-shaped signs, painted in red on one side and in black on the other, to show the preferred span. The same symbols appeared in prominent places along the banks and when the channel was in doubt they would just paint a rock red or black to give you an extra clue.

So with the chart and the aids, it was an easy job for the navigator. Until we ran out of charts.

In those days they were separate sheets and when I reached for the next one, it was not there. By then it was mid-afternoon. John was asleep below and I was alone on deck. But she was an easy boat to handle, it was flat calm and the river was well marked. So I decided to carry on until we either came to a place to buy the missing chart or went on to the next one.

After a while it seemed to be rather a long time since we last came to a lock but one could hardly miss those, with their girder work right across the river, so I did not worry. Then we came to a place wider than usual and we were steaming right down the middle of it when I noticed, quite close ahead, a low, dark line, maybe six inches high, sticking out of the water. And above it were hills. Something was not right.

Looking to the left, I followed the dark line over to the bank and there was a building that looked like some sort of power station. Then I looked to the right and almost abeam was a lock. We were about to go over a dam.

Taking no chances with the gearshift, I put the rudder hard over and the boat spun around to head upstream. And since the water level was down, she could easily beat the current and draw away from the dam. At which point I called down to John and casually suggested that he come on deck, as we were approaching a lock.

Leaving the lock 20 minutes later, we looked back. The dam stretched clear across the wide river but was of a different type from the previous ones, having no girder work over it. And at nine knots that boat, with her shallow draft, might well have gone clear over it. In which case we would both have died in a shipwreck on the Mohawk River, which would have been humiliating.

After that, we both stood in the pilot house, looking anxiously ahead, keeping a sharp eye out for anything unusual. And soon we found something. The river swept around a bend to the right, with the buoys spaced quite far apart, then it opened out into a wide round lake, and we could not find the next buoy. Over to our right were a couple of small islands and between them was a low, dark line of another dam. So we must be approaching a lock. But there was no sign of a channel to it.

On our left was a high rock wall and ahead was what looked like the channel to a power station: a narrow gap in the rock wall with some sort of machinery across it and a small white house nearby. I did not feel much like approaching that too closely, having read stories of small boats that were sucked into them by the current and swept down into the turbines. But the more we looked, the more there appeared nowhere to go, except back the way we had come. And we were both reasonably sure that we had not passed any side channel in the last several miles.

If we had had a chart, it would have been easy to fix our position and we would have known which way to go. But we were still in the section covered by the missing chart, so we slowed right down and searched the banks for any possible clues.

On our left we found a patch of paint on the rock wall. Evidently that marked the left-hand side of the channel. But how about the other side? There was no sign of any gap in the wall until you came to the one ahead, with the machinery across it. Then just to the right of that, we found another mark of the opposite color and close by the machinery we found a red light.

As we looked at it, something began to happen. Wheels turned and a great rectangular gate rose slowly out of the water to stop, dripping, about 15 feet above the surface. And the light turned green.

John and I looked at each other in silence, then back at the gate. I slipped her into gear and we moved slowly forward. There was no great rush of water into the channel beyond, so maybe it was all right. I decided that it must be and we slid under the gate, drops of water pattering along the deck from bow to stern as we went.

We had hardly cleared it when there was a loud rumbling noise and it came down into the water behind us, surprisingly fast. Then we went around a sharp curve and found another one like it waiting for us, open and dripping. And beneath it we could see the lock.

Chatter broke out in the pilot house, as it does on such occasions. Those must have been guard gates, put there to safeguard the town below in case a lock gate should fail. So this must be more than just an ordinary lock. And soon we found out that it was, indeed. It was a flight of five locks with a total drop of about 170 feet and it took us the rest of the day to get through them.

It was the summer of 1955 and the temperature that day was 104 degrees. Everybody was feeling hot and cross. We were the only boat going through and we really must have been something of a nuisance, making them open and shut all those huge gates. But as evening came, it cooled a little and everyone felt better. Until we left the last lock, in the pitch dark, and turned through 360 degrees just outside the gates.

Perhaps the gates opened a little faster than usual, making more of a swirl in the water. Perhaps we left a little sooner than usual. Anyway, a swirl caught her and turned her quite sharply, so that she looked like she would run into the concrete wall. I reacted by putting her hard astern, and, having a single engine, she spun around, making a neat 180 and giving the lock operator the impression that we had changed our minds and wanted to go back through all those locks. But before he could comment on the matter I backed her around, completing the 360 since she preferred to go that way and took her out into the Hudson River, to tie up for the night at the Troy Motor Boat and Canoe Club on the opposite bank.

The next day, we went down through the Federal Lock that separates the canal system from the tidal waters and there, right on the lock, was a large notice warning us not to go over the dam. We could have done with one of those six locks earlier.

Passing through Albany, you begin to see big seagoing ships lying at docks and steaming up the river, looking very large by comparison with the buildings ashore, and regular navigation aids, buoys and beacons, of the kind that you see along the coast. And if you are lucky, you carry your tide down toward the sea.

The tidal current in the Hudson makes quite a difference to a nine-knot boat, for it runs at around three knots each way. When it is running against you, it cuts your speed down to six knots but when it is going with you, it brings it up to 12. Of course it tends to average out in the 130-mile passage down to New York but still it is nice to have a fair tide to take you swiftly down past the drab commercial area into the pleasant countryside below, with its low hills and green fields and interesting old houses.

Going down the river, you see more traffic than there was on the canal: little coastwise tankers laden to their gunwales with oil, a few pleasure craft and later on towboats struggling along, each hauling four or five great barges full of sand.

The river gets wider and the hills on each side get higher until you come to West Point, where they become mountains, so close together that the river has to narrow sharply to fit between sheer cliffs on either side. Then just as suddenly, it widens out into the Tappan Zee, where you have to use binoculars to see the next buoy. Over on the left is Sing Sing prison (how easy it is in this life for one man to fetch up in there while another steams past in a yacht) and soon you come to the Harlem River.

There you have to sound three blasts on your horn and wait while the operator gets up enough steam to open the old swing bridge. But the run through the Harlem is easy and it saves you the long trip around Manhattan Island by taking you directly across the Hell Gate.

That did not give us the trouble we had expected, partly because the boat was relatively fast and partly because she drew so little water that she slid over the top of the deep eddies, and before long we came to City Island, where John had to leave to go back to his business, while I carried on alone.

Going down Long Island Sound was pleasant at first. The weather was calm and clear and it was easy to run from buoy to buoy, using the chart and the compass. But in the eastern part, there were strong currents and patches of fog, which was tiresome. For with no other navigational equipment, your dead reckoning has to be right every time in those conditions; otherwise, you would soon be lost in the fog off the unseen coast of Connecticut, and it is not easy to do mathematical calculations with one hand while steering a boat on a compass course with the other.

But in due course Race Rock lighthouse appeared, quite close ahead. Fortunately the tide was slack at that moment so that the Race itself, which can be quite nasty at times, was no more than a patch of rough water, maybe half a mile across. And soon we were through it and heading down outside Fisher's Island.

The wind had been increasing steadily all day and out in the open sea there was a swell running. But the boat did not seem to be riding over it as she should. Rather, she would go up in a series of jerky movements, as though a large weight inside her was moving to and fro. Which means one thing: water.

Leaving the steering for a moment, I went below to find that there was quite a bit of water in the bilges. Evidently she had been in calm water for some time and her planking above the water line had dried out and shrunk, opening her seams. That happens quite often with wooden boats, so I was not greatly surprised. But dealing with the situation presented problems.

The only pump aboard was hand-operated and was located so that I could not steer while pumping. And clearly it would take half an hour or so to get that lot out. But I did not feel like stopping the elderly engine, in case it would not start again. So I waited until we came up to the buoy off Watch Hill lighthouse, then put the wheel hard over and left her going around in circles while I pumped the water out.

That way she was still within sight of the buoy when I had finished and I was able to take a position from it, from which to make the run down to Point Judith.

There I repeated the procedure, circling by the red buoy while getting all the water out of her before making the 20-mile run across to Vineyard Sound. That took a couple of hours and by the time I had a landfall and reached the first buoy it was high time to do it again, for the old girl was shimmying like my sister Kate on every swell and the wind was rising all the time.

We learned something from each delivery job. From this one we became determined that a man should never be expected to sail alone. The owner of a boat always assured us that his craft was in good condition, ready to sail. But you were never really sure until it was too late.

Still the engine kept running steadily, in spite of having a bit of water slopping around it, and I was able to get the worst of it out of her before she wandered too far from the buoy. After which it was only a matter of pilotage to run down the Sound and into Vineyard Haven, for the course is well marked all the way.

I was just finishing cleaning the boat when her owner appeared, happy to have her safely in her home port. He gave me a lift to the ferry and late that night I was home at our apartment in New York City, eating June's cooking, which was an improvement on mine.

Pat returned tanned and relaxed. Instead of pacing the floor of our one-room apartment like a caged cat, he happily retraced every minute of the passage. There had been problems, of course, but nothing we couldn't handle. Perhaps you did get wet and tired but you came home with enough to pay the rent and with a certain sense of accomplishment. You hadn't spent the whole day sitting behind a desk or waiting on tables, or struggling for a place on a subway, or running to punch a time clock. If sailing was what he really wanted to do, then we'd have to find a way of doing it.

The next morning we were discussing the trip and decided that we should go into the yacht delivery business. So through that fall and winter I went around to the various naval architects, yacht brokers, yards and so on, handing out literature and letting them know that we were available.

2   WIND SONG

Early next spring we had a telephone call from Bob Garland at Sparkman & Stephens. A client of his had just bought a 38-foot ketch that was lying in St. Thomas and wanted her brought up to New York right away. She was not young but she was well built by Kretzer of City Island and he considered her a good, sound boat. So I said that we would get right on it, put the phone down and called Bob Sheckley.

He was a science fiction writer, already well known, but, like most writers, not averse to going off on a trip, especially if it helped to pay the rent. I outlined the project to him and he agreed to meet June and me at Idlewild Airport the next morning.

It took six hours to fly down there in those days and every time we looked out of the windows of the airplane, there was more ocean below us. Seventeen hundred nautical miles of it to be exact (about 1,945 statute miles), over which we should not expect to average more than a hundred miles a day. So it would be half a day's ride down and two and a half weeks' journey back.

Stepping out in St. Thomas after flying from New York at that time of the year is like going from winter to summer in a few seconds. Suddenly it is no problem to keep warm but rather a problem to stay cool. The windows of the taxi are wide open as you go down into the town of Charlotte Amalie, then along the coast road to the Yacht Haven. Palm trees rustle in the wind and the sun glints harshly off the deep blue sea. There is no doubt that you are in the tropics.

The Yacht Haven had only one dock in those days and most of

the boats were anchored out in the harbor, so we borrowed a din-ghy, loaded our duffel bags into it and rowed out to look around. It was a deep, U-shaped bay, sheltered on the windward side by high, green mountains and looking southwest toward the distant town with its large buildings and commercial docks.

There were a couple of dozen boats out there but it did not take us long to find the right one. She was a fine, beamy vessel with high topsides and short ends, a small bowsprit and a ketch rig, ideal for making a long passage. In fact, if she had had any other rig I might have taken a crew of four people for that trip, but as it was, three were enough. She was painted white, with varnished upperworks, and across her transom was her name: *Wind Song*.

When you step aboard a strange boat, the first thing you do is to look inside the binnacle, for nine times out of ten that is where you will find the key. And there it was, lying underneath the compass as usual.

Going below, we first opened all the ports and hatches, for she had been lying all closed up and it was truly hot down there. Then we made a thorough inspection from bow to stern, to see what we would need to do before we sailed. First we checked all her sails, found two that needed repairing and took them to a sailmaker. Next we tried the engine but could not get it to start and sent a message to a mechanic to come and look at it as soon as he could. Then we opened up her bilges, to find them full of shavings and odds and ends that would surely clog up the bilge pump if we had to use it. So Bob and I spent a happy day on our hands and knees, cleaning them out while June was doing mysterious things of her own devising in the galley and cabin areas. And each evening we would all sit in the cockpit making baggywrinkle.

Wooden hulled boats and cotton canvas sails. How different the odors were from those of today's boats, which are all fiberglass and dacron.

When you first opened the hatch of a sailboat that had been sitting for weeks or months in the hot sun with only a tiny port or two open, it was wise to stand a little to the side. Waiting below were the musty, rotting canvas, the intense heat, the smells from the old gas engine, the oil spills floating on top of the rancid bilge water.

Hold your breath, rush down the companionway and open every port, ventilator and hatch possible. Then back on deck for a breath of fresh air.

Now for the hammer and screwdriver. Look under the steps that lead to the galley—or in a locker near the engine. Grab any tool that looks vaguely useful and tackle the hatches and ports that wouldn't open on the first go around. And back on deck for another breath of fresh air.

The boat lies to her anchor, heading into the wind, bobbing gently. Slowly the air funnels through the cabin and the terrible heat and the foul smells lessen. Armed with a swatter and a bug bomb, you start at the forepeak and move everything out that you can, squirting the scurrying roaches as you go.

Then, carefully stepping over the other crew, who by this time are half in the bilges or have what looks like the engine strewn across the cabin sole, you carry anything that can be dislodged onto the deck. Drape the sails over the booms, tie them so they won't blow overboard. Take out drawers, bunk squabs, anything loose and give it its day in the sun.

Clean the head, be sure the toilet is operational. Better start on the galley soon. Someone will be wanting lunch.

Food! Make a list. There is some cleanser under the galley stove but that's about all. Is there a coffee pot? Fuel for the stove. What can you cook with a two-burner stove and one saucepan? And where's the can opener? Open the ice box. Now there's a smell! That box will need boiling water plus! Better let those wooden racks air, too. If you can get them out.

And then the men call down for lunch. Impossible. How about a quick hamburger ashore on the way to a store? You need cleaning materials, food for tonight and tomorrow. No more now—just enough to get you started. And ice.

Now to get the galley cupboards clean. Wash all the dishes and utensils, so they are ready for use at dinner time. Get the bunks into shape. Spray around each one to kill the roach that is surely hiding behind that crack.

Stow the gear you had draped all over the deck before it gets too dark. Get the lamps working. Start dinner. A good smell for a change. Better have a sweater handy. The cool night air is such a sharp contrast to the heat of the day.

A drink and dinner in the cockpit, sitting around the binnacle. A cushion for your back. Talk of the problems uncovered today and the things that must be started tomorrow.

Tired. So very tired and the gentle rolling of the boat lulls you below to your bunk. The oil lamps glow dimly, emitting a homey smell. You smooth the blanket over your bunk. Another damned roach scurries across the floor.

Tomorrow. You'll find it tomorrow.

The new owner had asked that we put baggywrinkle on her rigging and knowing no better, I had blithely agreed. But it turned out to be miserable stuff to make, taking hours of work for a few inches of finished product and sending little ends of twine blowing all through the accommodations that took us weeks to get out. And it really was not necessary with that rig. But it looked as salty as Hell and probably impressed his neighbors no end.

The water temperature was in the 80's, so we swam around the boat to check her bottom and found that it was very foul, with grass all over it, long enough to cut her speed down quite a bit. So I rented an aqualung and gave it to Bob, with a scrub brush.

He disappeared under the boat and for the best part of an hour we saw nothing of him except bubbles rising to the surface here and there, then he climbed back aboard and said that he had finished. I asked him how it had gone and he said: "Oh, not too bad. Except for that fool fish."

It turned out that a large barracuda had come up to him while he was working and being a city boy, he had simply hit it on the nose with his scrub brush. And that had gone on for half an hour. The barracuda would come in, get hit on the nose and go away. And Bob would go on scrubbing, never even realizing that the thing might be dangerous.

Later we found out that there was one barracuda who lived under the dock at the Yacht Haven who was quite harmless. In fact the local children would jump off the dock on top of him. He must have been well fed and happy with all the garbage that was thrown overboard from the yachts, and possibly Bob's barracuda was a relative of his. But in general, hitting a large barracuda with a scrub brush is about as safe as giving a cop the razz.

It has been said that in any expedition, 90 percent of the work is finished the day you start out, and there is a great deal of truth in that when it comes to a long passage in a small boat. For the preparation is critically important and if that is really well done, the rest is often relatively easy. That passage was not atypical. Altogether it was nine days before we set sail for New York, for after getting *Wind Song* into shape, we had to provision her for three weeks, put fuel and water aboard, then clear with the customs and immigration people. All of which takes time in a small tropical island where nothing moves very fast.

That was my first ocean passage and Patrick did the major provisioning. He had spent months on the ocean, so we trusted to his judgment when it came to exactly what it was possible to prepare in a rolling boat.

St. Thomas had the beginnings of a supermarket when we arrived to provision Wind Song. *An old warehouse sort of building on a waterfront street had been lined with shelves. And on them we found an assortment of canned goods from various parts of the world. Through the center of the building ran a long case of frozen meats and poultry—mostly unidentifiable and of little use to us.*

Patrick pushed the shopping cart toward the tinned meat section. The selection was slim. Vienna sausage, Spam and three brands of Argentine corned beef. He stopped the cart in front of the corned beef and counted out 48 tins.

"Three people for three meals a day for 20 days," he mumbled. "That should just about do it."

He added a few cans of vegetables, some baked beans, cans of fruit and juice, and a goodly supply of tinned crackers. Then a few bags of fresh onions and carrots and potatoes and we headed back to Wind Song *with our shopping finished for the next three weeks. With that lesson behind us, on all future passages I did the provisioning.*

So you do not try to hustle but neither do you dawdle. You set a middle pace, doing everything you can yourselves and persuading the local people to do their parts, calling by to encourage them every day. And for a short while you fall into a routine. Each day you do your work and make your rounds ashore, then in the evening you relax and visit with friends from the other boats.

That spring there were a few charter yachts in port, some local boats and a couple of ocean voyagers. One of those, a nice red cutter about 30 feet long with no engine, was on her way from Sweden to New York, while the other was the 25-foot *Marco Polo* on her way around the world. She had been built in New Zealand by her crew of three men, one of whom was Brian Loe (called Tig) who later came up to New York to work with us. They were a wild bunch. They had a dinghy about eight feet long by four feet wide but scarcely six inches deep that they claimed to have built while drunk. In fact, it was very practical for it stowed on deck, offering a minimum of windage, but it would only carry one man and the groceries, while the other two swam along beside it. And they got so used to swimming around that they would come to visit that way, each swimming with one hand and holding his cigarettes in the air with the other.

Our dinghy was in the way on the cabin top and rather too high up for my ideas of safety, so we turned it upside down and lashed it on the foredeck, with a life line running from the forestay to the mainmast above it.

And suddenly one day we found that everything was finished. We were ready to go. So we said our goodbyes and sailed away.

We always filled the ice chest just before sailing on a long passage. The ice wouldn't last more than three or four days but the chilled cans of juice and a bit of fresh meat softened for a few days the harshness of life at sea after the ease of port life.

In the harbor, under the lee of the mountains, it was always hot and still but as we drew away from the island we began to feel the weight of the trade wind and by the time we were clear of the Virgins we were booming along, lee rail under, heaving and dipping in quite a heavy sea.

Since we were not familiar with *Wind Song*, I had set our course due north. That way we would later have two choices: If things went well, we could bear off halfway and head straight for New

York without losing much distance. But if anything went wrong we could put into Bermuda, only a thousand miles away.

The trade wind blows from the east northeast in those parts, which put the true wind a little forward of our beam and the apparent wind (including our motion) forward of that, giving us a fast ride but a wet and bumpy one. And what with the heeling and the motion and all those fine meals that June had cooked for us in port, Bob and I both felt a little queasy, while June was just plain sick. But all that is quite normal for the first three or four days. The problem is that there is a strong tendency for everyone to hang on and stare out to sea, which must be firmly discouraged.

For if you were to let it go, everyone would tire out at the same time, which would be ridiculous. So you must set watches right away, put one person on watch and make one go below and try to sleep. He won't, of course, but he'll get some rest and by his next watch off he'll be so tired that he'll be asleep before his head hits the pillow.

With a crew of three I like to have one person on watch, steering and keeping a lookout, one below in his bunk and the third on standby: cooking, cleaning, doing odd jobs but ready in a moment if needed on deck. And we preferred the Swedish system that gives you two watches of four hours each by night, two of five hours each in the morning and evening, and one of six hours by day. That way you get a good, long sleep of six hours every second day, yet the night watches are not too long.

It was becoming apparent to me that I was not a born sailor. I had never even learned to swim. The ocean was a new world and I was quite honestly afraid of it.

But it was fascinating as it was frightening and the lonely watches became hours to treasure. We stood watches, four to six hours on deck alone, day and night. There was plenty of time to think and wonder.

I remember the thunderous quiet of a busy sea. The working of the hull and the constant whine of the rigging. And always around us were the reminders of life, the weed and fish and birds. Then the men aboard, who had somehow come to terms with the life of the sailor. They bent to the demands of the ocean and the boat and believed that they were masters of it. But I wonder if anyone ever has been or will be. There is an unfathomable quality about the sea and the life it does permit to exist. You're kidding yourself if you ever think you have the upper hand.

We were carrying all plain sail (jib, staysail, mainsail and mizzen) and making good progress. The sea was a deep, clear blue, flecked with white foam from the occasional breaker, heaving in long swells that had come clear across the Atlantic Ocean. The sky was a lighter blue, dotted with neat little white clouds, spaced as evenly as you can imagine. The wind hummed in the rigging and *Wind Song* was muttering to herself, creaking and sighing as a sailboat will in a seaway. Once in a while, a small wave would slap against her topsides, drenching the man on watch with spray, but the hot sun soon dried him out again, leaving a layer of salt on his hands that tasted good when licked off.

But as the Virgin Islands fell away astern and the darkness of our first night at sea approached, we handed the jib and took a reef in the mainsail, snugging her down in case we should be hit by a squall. Then we pumped her bilges dry, made sure that everything was secure on deck, checked the running lights and got out the flashlights.

There is very little twilight on the open sea in those latitudes. The sun goes down to the horizon, almost as hot as ever, and disappears below it. Immediately the moon and all the stars come out, shining so brightly that you can soon see by their light. The compass glows red in the cockpit and from the hatch comes the warm, friendly light of the cabin.

Surprisingly, you can make out the clouds quite well. The little trade wind clouds stand out clearly against the background of stars, but those clouds are no problem. The ones you have to watch out for are the larger ones, big enough to have squalls in them. Those are big and black and blot out a sizeable patch of sky, but they come down on the wind, so if you keep an eye lifting to windward every few minutes, you can see them coming.

The first one came in June's watch. Bob was asleep and I was making some coffee when she called down the hatch: "Patrick, I think you'd better come and take a look at this."

Going on deck, I glanced to windward and there was a dark cloud, bearing down on us. Having already snugged the boat down, we were ready for it. All we had to do was lower the mizzen, which was right there in the cockpit, and stow it securely. Then I closed the hatch and took over the tiller, since it was June's first night at sea.

The cloud was moving toward us at the speed of the wind and as it loomed overhead, we could see a line of white on the surface of the water below it: the sea churned up by the wind, white with foam and spray. So while June eased the sheets, I bore off down wind, to bring it on our starboard quarter. That meant going west, which was out of our way, but there was nothing to run into for several hundred miles in that direction and I knew that she would ride out the squall more comfortably on that heading.

As it overtook us we felt a gust of cold air, then a strong, blustery wind. *Wind Song* heeled a little and her wake increased as her speed built up. Then a dark gray wall of rain swept over us and blotted out everything except the red light of the compass and the breaking tops of the seas immediately around us.

For several minutes we went on like that, sitting in the teeming rain, watching the compass, keeping her on her heading and looking out for any signs of trouble, while the wind tugged and pulled at the sails and *Wind Song* churned and wound through the waves.

The noise was alarming, for the wind was strong enough to whistle and whine in the rigging in ever-changing keys, to send the rain drumming against the boat and to shake and rattle anything loose on deck, while the sea made loud hissing noises in the dark, as though we were surrounded by a thousand angry snakes.

Then, just as quickly as it had arrived, it passed over. The rain moved away, the wind eased off, and we could see a patch of starry sky below the clouds to windward.

For a while the sea was confused in the wake of the squall and we bounced around in an erratic fashion. But by the time we were on our proper course, with the sheets trimmed and the mizzen set, it was back to normal. Soon the sky cleared and the stars came out, the rain water gurgled down the scuppers, the hatch opened and Bob's head appeared.

He had managed to get some sleep but was awakened by the jumpy motion of the boat just after the squall passed and came up to see what was going on. So I made soup for us all, while he sat on deck and became accustomed to the sights and sounds of night sailing and June gave him her version of how to steer by a star.

For when stars are available, they are much more relaxing to steer by than the compass. All you have to do is get the boat on her proper course, according to the compass, then find a convenient star that you can line up with something like the end of a spreader or the top of the mainmast. And for the next quarter of an hour you can sail along, keeping the two in line and looking out around you. But since the earth rotates and the stars do not, you have to find a fresh star every 15 minutes or so.

However that works out well, as it is the proper interval at which to stand up and look all around the horizon. A ship can come out of nowhere and be close up to you inside 20 minutes, and it would be most unwise to assume that anyone on her bridge will notice your little boat. So it is up to you to see her coming in good time and change course, if necessary, so that she misses you.

It is pleasant to sit in the cockpit of a small boat after a squall at sea, drinking hot soup and enjoying the comparative peace of trade wind sailing. But it was Bob's watch so he took over, while June went below and I climbed around, checking everything. Up forward we were in pretty good shape; nothing had come adrift and all our gear seemed to be holding up well. But back in the cockpit I tried the bilge pump and it brought up a great deal more water than I expected. We had better keep an eye on that.

At four in the morning I took over the watch, Bob went below and I sat alone on deck. That always seems to be the longest watch: two hours sitting alone in the dark, then two more to wait before you can decently wake up the others and demand breakfast.

For like the sunset, the dawn itself takes very little time. The sun comes up out of the sea and hardly clears the horizon before you can feel its heat on your face, as though you were standing close to an electric fire. You look around: the stars are all gone and it is full daylight. The night has vanished as though it had never been. Then you settle back and wait for breakfast.

Wind Song's *galley stove had a mind of its own. No matter*

which lighting routine we used, it would manage to flare up at least once during a workout.

We would try to keep the flames down but more often than not they became a serious threat. The constant rolling and lurching of the boat would dispatch the flames to odd corners. I stood tied to a bulkhead, leaving one hand free for the fire extinguisher, while the other held the pot on the stove.

The CO₂ extinguisher was very effective. Flames out in an instant. And because it's nothing but carbon dioxide, all we had to do was stir the food in the pot and serve it. Any other extinguisher would have ruined our dinner. We couldn't take chances like that with our limited food supply.

After breakfast I started to pump the bilges but half an hour later the pump was still drawing water, so Bob had a go. He was a former athlete and in pretty good shape but by the time he finished the job, he had had enough. Evidently we had a problem there.

For several hours Bob and I searched all through *Wind Song's* hull, looking for the source of the leak, while June steered and kept watch on deck. But eventually it became clear that there was no one source. She was weeping all along her seams. We really did have a problem. A leak in one place can generally be stopped but an over-all condition like that is virtually impossible to fix at sea. And if ever the water starts to come in faster than you can pump it out, more seams will be exposed. Which is the beginning of the end, for a boat like that has enough lead on her keel to send her to the bottom like a stone if you lose the game.

Wind Song *had no life raft and her little dinghy would not have lasted 10 minutes in that sea—even I could see that.*

I sat on deck, considering the matter. Theoretically the planking should begin to swell up soon, closing the seams. If that happened, the leaking would get steadily less and within a few days we would have no more problem on that account. But if it did not; if for some reason it got worse? I looked over the side at the water rushing past the hull as we went barrelling along in a good, stiff trade wind, straight away from the nearest land.

Still it was hard to think of turning back, one day out, after all the work that had gone into preparing for the passage.

I decided to give it another hour.

When we pumped her again, it was about the same, maybe a couple of strokes more but hardly enough to justify turning back. And so it went on, all through the afternoon and all through the night. Each hour we would pump the bilges and count the strokes. And each hour there would be a few more, until it reached 300.

But though the strokes per hour were more, the increments were getting smaller. It was not getting worse as fast as it had been. And there were signs in the sky that the wind might ease before long. So I went on giving her another hour. And another hour.

Next morning, when I woke up and went on deck, Bob was grinning happily. Which is unreasonable before breakfast, so I asked him why.

"Two hundred and seventy," he said. Period.

I considered that for a moment, then caught on.

"Strokes?" I asked.

"Yes," he said, "I think we're winning."

June was already up and looking cheerful; so she must have heard the news. Which being so, I turned to and cooked breakfast.

Slowly, all through the day, the number of strokes each hour shrank. And just after dark the wind eased a little, leaving us sailing comfortably along, no longer wet and hanging on but able to relax and look around us, to admire the stars and enjoy a casual chat in the cockpit without having to shout.

Less heeling and less motion meant fewer strakes of planking immersed. Meanwhile the planks themselves were swelling, tightening the seams, and the total effect was a sharp reduction in the leakage. No longer need we pump every hour. Every four hours would do. A pleasant little ceremony at the change of watches.

I slept better that night and was just waking up when I heard a voice call out: "Pigeon." Then a pause. Then: "Here, pigeon." A female voice. June's voice. I went on deck.

It was her watch and we were becalmed, heaving gently on the swell left over from yesterday's wind. She had abandoned the tiller and was sitting on the stern, her feet dangling over the transom, feeding bread to a bird. Not a pigeon, of course, but enough like one to make a city girl feel at home.

There was no wind at all. The surface of the sea was smooth and unruffled. And all over it, as far as you could see, was yellowish brown seaweed, so closely packed that we might have been in a vast field of freshly reaped corn, with little patches of water showing here and there like blue lakes. I leaned over the side and picked up a handful of the weed. It felt springy and quite firm and was maybe four inches thick, floating in the water with perhaps an inch sticking out and the rest below the surface.

Evidently we had run out of the trade wind, into the Sargasso Sea, an oval patch of ocean about 200 miles from north to south by 300 from west to east that lies midway between the Virgin Islands and Bermuda.

With no wind, we were rolling gently on the swell and all our sails were slatting to and fro, the booms banging from side to side. If we let that go on for long, the sails would begin to come apart at the seams. But if we took them down, we might never get out of the Sargasso Sea. For though we had an engine, the tank only held about 15 hours' fuel. We had used a little leaving St. Thomas and we were using an hour's worth each day to keep the batteries charged. We would need some to enter New York Harbor and the rest we should keep for emergencies. Which did not leave any for motoring out of calms.

With all due respect, I can't think of an emergency when 15 hours of fuel would be worth a tinker's damn. Unless, of course, you consider blowing yourself up an emergency.

The emergencies I learned to cope with were things like the forestay breaking, the galley stove on fire, the stuffing box springing a leak or a fire in the engine room. Not the sort of times when a tank of gasoline would matter much. One day I must remember to ask Patrick about those other emergencies and why motoring out of a calm 400 miles offshore was not one of them.

Many stories have been written about the days when sailing ships would lie in the Sargasso Sea for weeks on end, becalmed under the blazing tropical sun, running out of food and water, mutiny breaking out among their crews. And it is easy to see how it could have been. For those ships were big and heavy and it would take them quite a while, after a breeze came along, to get moving. By which time the breeze would have left them.

In a small, modern yacht it is different. She is light enough to get moving on the slightest breeze, but it is hard work.

First you take down all the working sails. Then you get out the lightest sails you can find — the number one Genoa, the mizzen staysail and the spinnaker — and rig them, all ready to go up at a moment's notice. Then you wait for a breeze.

The first sign that one is coming is a patch of tiny ripples, moving toward you across the smooth surface of the sea. As soon as you see one of those, you light a cigarette and call the rest of the crew to stand by on deck. Then you all watch the smoke rising vertically from the cigarette and if you are lucky it will bend a little, showing you which way the breeze is coming from.

Immediately you set as much sail as you can, as fast as you can, and trim it to catch the breeze. And if you are still lucky, the boat will begin to ease forward, slowly at first but soon fast enough to leave a tiny wake. Then the breeze will usually die away, so that all the sails will go aback, due to her forward motion. Then you take them all down, carefully prepare them for the next time and go back to watching and waiting.

Of course you will not be lucky every time. Maybe once in every three or four times. But each time you have to go through the procedures, first of standing by, then of setting all the sails, then of taking them down and preparing them for the next time. Sometimes you may get two nice breezes within half an hour and gain as much as a mile. Other times you may lie so still that when you throw your garbage overboard after a meal, you find the garbage from the meal before right there, beside the boat. You have not moved a yard.

In those conditions it is hot. The sun beats down on your head and reflects back up from the glassy sea, catching you coming and going. With the sails down there is no shade, except in the cabin and that is like an oven. If you rig an awning, it may hinder your getting the sails up in a hurry and you can not afford that, for the name of the game is to sail her out of the Sargasso Sea before you run out of water. So you stick with it, day after day and look forward to the nights.

As soon as the sun goes down, everything changes. Suddenly it is cool, even chilly, and soon the cabin cools off, so that you can face going below to cook a meal. You still have to go through your procedures at every sign of a breeze, but the waiting is quite pleasant, sitting around in the cockpit, chatting and watching the reflections of the stars in the water for signs of ripples.

Then the sun comes up and you have to face another day.

We learned to wash everything in sea water. The salt-water soap was never successful as far as I was concerned but liquid detergents, especially hair shampoo, worked very well. And still do, if you can find a patch of ocean clean enough to wash in.

We kept a bucket handy with a long line for dipping over the side. We'd carry the dishes onto the deck and wash them in the warm sea and let them dry in the sun.

We cooked potatoes in sea water. In fact, anything that needed salt. Or diluted it with some fresh water for oatmeal. So our precious fresh water was available for the occasional drink.

We carried canned fruits and juices and used all the liquid from the canned vegetables. Water was never really a problem, but being without it could have been if something major were to go wrong. We guarded our supply.

There are ways of breaking a calm that are known to all seamen and they come in various degrees of severity. The mildest is to stick a knife in the mast and while we have tried that, we never felt that it did much good. The next is to throw a penny overboard and that we did quite often, on the grounds that at that price we could hardly afford not to. But if you are very brave, you throw a penny into the sea and say: "Black Pig."

We never had the nerve to try that. In fact the only person we know who ever did was Shorty Trimmingham in Bermuda. As he told it to us, he had been becalmed for several hours near the island when he did it and within minutes he was in a howling gale that blew for a week. Luckily he was under a lee and made it back home. But we were certainly not about to try it in the open sea.

We were busy with other things, mainly cleaning, cooking, and checking chafe. Calm periods are the easiest times to clean the oatmeal off the overhead, fish rotting sausages out from behind the galley stove and generally make your living quarters more habitable. They are the only times when you can cook up large, elaborate meals and hope to keep them down. They are the best times to check everything aboard, from the mastheads to the bilges. And they are the worst times for chafe.

Any ocean voyager will tell you that chafe is the number one enemy of a small boat on the open sea. It is sneaky and often silent, and it can do remarkable damage. When I crossed the Atlantic Ocean in my own boat *Sopranino*, a whole set of brass jib hanks chafed clear through on the stainless steel forestay in a couple of weeks. A friend of ours in another yacht hung his best suit on a hanger in a locker. A month later he found the top part, down to the shoulders, on the hanger and the rest lying in the bottom of the locker.

So you prowl around, looking and listening, peering into corners and closely examining anything that might possibly move the least bit. Then you either secure it, or if that is not practical, you cut a small piece of white rubber to a suitable shape and glue it in place so as to act as a buffer. Or at least so as to wear away instead of the part that you are trying to protect.

For five days we lay in the Sargasso Sea, sometimes moving but mostly not, four or five hundred miles from the nearest land and far from any shipping lane. It was a lonely and desolate place. Soon after we entered it, our bird deserted us. We saw no fish. Just great areas of weed and smaller patches of clear, blue water. We told June that if she threw any garbage overboard at midnight, a black hand would rise out of the water and throw it back. I think she believed us.

It was on the fifth day that the shark attacked the boat, going off maybe 50 yards, turning and rushing in to ram her at his full speed. Evidently he was trying to break in and that was one time when we were glad that we were not in a very lightly-built boat. As it was, I had to stop him before he started a leak. So I fetched a long boathook with a sharp pointed end and lay in wait for him.

He was a large shark, gray on top and white underneath. Coming in to attack, he rolled over and we could see red smears on his head where he had rubbed some paint off the bottom of the boat.

I waited until he was close, then hit him as hard as I could on the nose. The boathook jarred and bounced back through my hands as though it had struck a rock. But the shark vanished immediately and we never saw him again. For a while we waited anxiously in case he should come back with his friends to fix us up but he never did.

Then we noticed his pilot fish. There were five of them and evidently they decided that we were a larger fish who had just won a battle with their shark. So they transferred to us, doubtless assuming that we would provide them with bigger and better scraps to eat. They hung around for a couple of days, then came to the conclusion that we were lousy providers and went off to look for another shark.

Meanwhile we got a breeze. Not one of those miserable little puffs that we had been getting, but an honest, steady breeze that stayed in one direction while we set all our sails and *Wind Song* gathered speed, her wake chuckling in her lee, her crew grinning like idiots on her deck. We were under way again.

As the sun went down, the breeze came up a little. Soon it was cool enough to cook supper and we all sat around in the cockpit, eating corned beef hash and discussing the various methods of getting rid of sharks.

Ernest Hemingway once told me that he kept a box of hand grenades aboard *Pilar* for the purpose. He would lob one in front of a shark and as it went down, trailing bubbles through the water, the shark would swallow it. A few seconds later there would be a muffled explosion and the shark would be dead. Immediately all the rest would set upon it, while *Pilar* steamed away to fish in peace for a while.

But my favorite method, when I had the time, was that given me by a Chinese sea cook. You take a slice of bread and spread it with hot Chinese (or English) mustard, about a quarter of an inch thick. Then you put another slice of bread on top of it, to make a sandwich. Feed that to your shark and he will rush off into the far distance with his mouth open. And I doubt that he will ever come back.

By breakfast time the next morning, the breeze had increased to a steady wind out of the southeast, on our port quarter. Once again we were able to set all plain sail, but this time, with the wind lighter and farther aft, we were much more comfortable than we had been in the trade wind.

That was a pleasant day, sailing along, making good time, warm without being too hot. But the sky was clouding over a little, so I took a couple of sun sights while I could and figured our position. We were about 250 miles south of Bermuda.

I took stock of the situation. Our leaks had died away to a mere trickle. The crew was doing well. We had plenty of food and water. Our gear was in good shape. I decided to change course for New York, aiming for a point 50 miles west of it, to allow for the effect of the Gulf Stream. That brought the wind onto our beam and by the time we had trimmed the sheets, we were heeling more than before. But we were making good progress and staying reasonably dry and very happy to have the Sargasso Sea behind us.

Now we were coming into northern waters and could expect to encounter different kinds of weather, so I kept an eye on those clouds and sure enough they continued to make up in the west. Something large was brewing out there and since most systems move from west to east in those latitudes, it would probably be with us in a day or so. Meanwhile we had another pleasant night's sail.

But in the morning the sky was definitely threatening. Gray clouds extended from horizon to horizon, darker in the west. And more ragged around the edges over that way. The wind was rising steadily and the sea was building up, the waves becoming larger and more solid.

In a situation like that it is important to stay ahead of the game, to be ready for things before they happen, rather than to try to cope with them after they have happened. So we took in the jib, put it in its bag and stowed it below. Then while June steered, Bob and I took a deep reef in the mainsail. Now *Wind Song* was slightly under-canvassed and inclined to bobble around but that would not last for long, the way things were going.

By lunch time the wind was beginning to moan in the rigging, the sky was a darker gray, and we had all the canvas we needed. The boat was going like a train, putting her lee rail under water in the stronger puffs, throwing up sheets of spray. But the motion was getting wild. It was time to go to work again.

Carefully we checked all through the boat, securing anything that could move, ramming cushions into lockers to keep the plates and dishes from sliding around, making sure that the flashlights were working and filling the galley stove while we could. On deck, we put an extra lashing on the dinghy, checked the rigging and took in all loose gear. Then we rigged life lines between the main and mizzen shrouds, on either side.

Patrick had slowly and carefully explained the problems that would arise if one of us were to be foolish enough to fall overboard. I had the distinct impression that although he would make every attempt to pick us up, he would not necessarily feel compelled to endanger the vessel.

In fact, I think his words were something like: "If any damned fool falls overboard he'd better plan on swimming to shore."

I was suitably cautious, seldom ventured onto the foredeck in a seaway unless necessary, and Bob would gallantly tackle the jib when it had to come in.

He would wind his legs around the bowsprit or tuck his feet under the lines, tugging with both hands at the jib hanks that always insisted on fouling. He rode the bowsprit like a seal, taking a deep breath as Wind Song *nosed into the wave ahead, shaking the water from himself as she headed up over the wave into the next one.*

Patrick would drag the soaking sail back into the cockpit as Bob scrambled up the deck to join us to discuss the next maneuver.

Already it was time to get the mainsail down so we tackled that next, lowering the boom clear down onto the cabin top, resting it on a cushion, and securing it with a heavy mooring line to the two big brass winches in the cockpit. Then we put an extra lashing, made from another mooring line, on the mainsail itself so that it could not come loose and beat itself to death in the wind. After which we climbed back into the cockpit and huddled in a row with our backs to the rising storm.

With just the staysail and mizzen left up, we were still going quite fast. But the seas were building and the barometer, which had been going steadily down, now started to drop sharply. The sky was darkening with the approach of night and obviously the weather was going to get a great deal worse before it got better. The time had come to lie to and wait it out.

Lowering the mizzen was easy. It was right there in the cockpit beside us. Clambering around on the foredeck, getting in the wet, flogging staysail was another matter. The bow was going up and down so fast I felt like the pilot in a yo-yo. But Bob had once been a tumbler in a circus and seemed quite at home, cheerfully tugging and tying until we got the job done.

As soon as we had both sails firmly secured, I put the tiller hard over and lashed it about two inches from the end of its travel, so that it could not bang against its end stop. *Wind Song* came up into the wind a little, stopped, fell back down and finally found a comfortable angle where she lay remarkably steady, moving through the water at maybe half a knot.

During the afternoon the moan of the wind in the rigging had risen to a steady whine and now its pressure on the masts alone was enough to stop her from rolling much. She would go from the vertical to an angle of maybe 15 degrees and back again, quite slowly, as the seas swept under her. Beam on to them, her keel was acting as a sea anchor, preventing her from moving too fast through the water and she was going up and down without taking any harm.

In a seaway, the main body of the water does not move forward with the waves; it only seems to. In fact, each drop of water goes up and down in its turn and the wave effect is similar to that which you can create by shaking the end of a rope. But the energy of the motion breaks lumps of water off the tops of the waves and flings them forward. And those you have to beware of, since water is remarkably heavy: a six-foot cube of it weighs over six tons. So being hit by a fair-sized chunk of it, moving at the speed of the waves, is not unlike being charged by an elephant.

But it was not yet that rough. The seas were still quite modest, no more than 12 feet high, and their breaking crests were still most-ly loose water with no real weight to them. So while they looked impressive enough, they were not dangerous.

As soon as everything had been checked and rechecked, we set anchor watches. One person would stay in the cockpit, with a life line around his waist, keeping an eye on things outside while the other two would go below and close the hatch.

Going below in those conditions is a strange experience. For as soon as you close the hatch, you shut out the storm. Gone are the wind and the spray. Gone are all the wild noises. Gone are the seas, the lowering, scudding clouds and the darkening sky. The cabin looks much the same as it always does: warm and cosy, with var-nished woodwork and colored cushions, a light over your bunk and books in the rack beside it. There is nothing more to be done for the time being so you undress, put on your pajamas and go to bed.

The pajamas might surprise some people but they perform a very useful function: They make you feel civilized. The same is true of shaving every day, for a man. We always did it, not because we had to at sea but because it made us feel good, and reminded us that we had the situation well in hand.

As soon as you get into your bunk, you fall asleep. And almost immediately a wet and clammy hand shakes you awake.

It is your watch. Dressing, you put on your foul weather gear. Of course it is soaking wet. Can you imagine getting up at midnight and putting on a wet bathing suit? Life is less than pleasant. You scramble out of the hatch, straight into another world.

Outside it is pitch dark. For a while, the only thing you can see is the compass, glowing red beside you. You feel, rather than see the other man push past you, go down the hatch and close it behind him. You are alone.

The noise is appalling. The high whine of the wind in the rigging rises and falls like the note of a siren as the boat heaves and rolls in the seas. Other things, which you can not see and barely imagine, bang and flap furiously in the darkness. There is a rushing sound that starts far away and rapidly comes closer, ending with a thump. The boat takes a jolt and you are hit by the remnants of a breaker. You feel like a bug trapped in a steam whistle.

But you are on duty, in charge of the situation. You check your life line, take a firm grip with both hands on the mizzen, stand up and look all around the horizon. By now you can see the waves quite well because they glow in the dark. As each one breaks, it shines brightly with phosphorescence. And in between, the surface of the water is streaked with glowing foam and bubbles, the remains of previous breakers.

Most of the time, you are in a trough and can only see the sides of the two nearest seas, high above you. So you glance at the one that is coming toward you and wait a few seconds. As it comes closer, it rises up, seeming to hang almost overhead. Then up you go to meet it as it sweeps under, over and around you in a smother of foam. Now is your chance.

For an instant you can see out across the ragged, white tops of the seas and in that time you can usually scan about a quarter of the horizon, if you are lucky. If not, you get the top of the wave in the face, filling your eyes and ears with stinging salt water and sit down, sliding across the cockpit on the wet surface of the deck until you come to a jolting stop in the corner. In which case you scramble back into a more comfortable position, wipe your eyes with the backs of your hands, shake out your ears and start again.

It will probably take you half a dozen attempts to complete the job of checking the horizon all around you. Then you give the bilge pump a few strokes, to make sure that there is no water down there. You note the direction of the wind and try to guess its strength, though that is not easy. Above, the sky is dark with low clouds that blot out every star, so there is nothing else to observe up there. In the cockpit, you tidy up any loose lines you find, securing them so that they can not wash around, and check that the flashlight is working in case you need it.

By that time you feel you have things pretty well in hand, as you snug back into the most sheltered corner and think of more pleasant things, like calm, sunny afternoons in grassy meadows, for 10 minutes or so. Then you start the whole routine again.

Time behaves in a strange way in a watch like that. At first it hangs back, then it goes quite fast for a couple of hours, until you begin to think your watch will soon be over. Then it hangs back again, so much that you feel it will never end. Then suddenly it has. You nip below, shake the next person awake, go back on deck and wait with pleasant anticipation to be relieved.

Next morning the wind veered into the northeast and the sky cleared. By noon there was not a cloud in sight. But the wind did not ease off. If anything, it got stronger. And the sky was not a soft blue but a hard, China blue. We were in a "blue nor'easter."

After the wind shift, the old sea was still running out of the southwest but now it was going against the wind, while the smaller surface waves soon built up in the opposite direction, which left us batting around like a birdie in a badminton game. But not for long. By mid-afternoon the seas and the waves were going the same way, the great seas sweeping majestically along while the waves ran up and down their backs.

A gale like that on a clear day is a truly impressive sight. The seas may be close to 30 feet high (though they look much higher) and perhaps 300 yards from crest to crest. They are probably moving at 15 to 20 miles an hour, so that it takes you half a minute to go from the top of one to the top of the next.

For a second or so you can see far out to the distant horizon, lumpy and irregular with piled-up seas, the space between you and it carpeted white with foam and spray. Then down you go, dropping swiftly into the trough, looking up at the great hills of water on either side, until the next one begins to loom above you. You stare at it with a kind of detached interest, for there is little you can do about it. Then comes the moment when its crest seems about to fall on you and the boat makes a sudden rush to the top, getting there just in time to avoid the disaster that was obviously bound to happen. And so it goes on.

A few hours later, your watch comes to an end and you go back to your bunk, anxious to go to sleep and get away from it all.

Being at sea for the first time and not at all aware of the righting characteristics of a heavy displacement hull, I found riding down the sides of the waves a bit disconcerting. Wind Song *seemed to be exactly the length of each wave. Her bowsprit would be in the water, I would be lying flat against the cabin side, hanging on to the tiller which appeared to be above my head. Just when I had resigned myself to the inevitable pitchpole, the world would fall away beneath her keel and suddenly we would be climbing up a wave, her bowsprit in the air and me braced tightly in the far corner of the cockpit. Hour after hour the same scene would be replayed, until I was numb from the sensations.*

Most of the time, in spite of being hove-to, we stood our routine watches. There was nothing to do but hang on and watch out for trouble.

All through that night the gale went on. But you get used to anything in time and with the stars to look at, it did not seem as bad as it had the night before. And by the next morning it was certainly beginning to ease off, for *Wind Song* was rolling more.

As a storm builds up, the wind on the mast is usually enough to keep a boat from rolling much. But there is a lag between the time when the wind begins to ease off and when the seas follow suit. And then she will start to roll. So you watch the mast and as soon as you see it go past the vertical to windward, you know it is time to set sail again.

That is a bad moment, for by then you have become accustomed to the easy motion and light duties of lying-to. You really do not feel like going up on the foredeck and struggling to get the staysail up. You know that as soon as you start making headway through the rough water it will be a wet, jumpy ride. So you tend to put setting sail off, rationalizing that the gale may get stronger again before it finally blows itself out.

But by midday there was no longer any doubt about the need for sail, so we brewed up a strong pot of coffee, then assembled on deck to get on with it. And as always, it was not as bad as we expected. Soon we had the staysail and mizzen set and we were bouncing along, rather wet but glad to be under way again.

Once the gales started we were never on deck without a life line. I kept mine fairly short. I didn't fancy falling overboard and being towed along like an irate dinghy.

Sitting alone, holding the tiller and trying to keep Wind Song *vaguely on her heading in the confused sea, it came time for the every-fifteen-minute scan of the horizon. I chose a poor time to stand up, for the boat gave a sudden lurch as a wave hit her and she fell down on her side into the sea, in a moment to right herself and lurch in the opposite direction. But time enough for me to be thrown toward the water, only to be caught by the short line tied around my waist to a cockpit winch.*

We were going northwest and the storm was moving east, so that we parted with it quite rapidly. Before dark we were able to set the double-reefed mainsail and soon after dawn the next day we shook out the reefs and set the jib. We were back under all plain sail, heading toward the Gulf Stream.

When you approach New York from the southeast, the Gulf Stream lies across your track and at that point it is about a hundred miles wide, moving to the northeast at a couple of knots. Its far side forms a boundary between its hot, tropical water and the much cooler water beyond. Like all such boundaries, it tends to upset the weather. And since the weather systems move from west to east in those latitudes, you can expect to find unreliable weather all the way across it.

But that was still two days ahead. Meanwhile the wind continued to ease off, the seas died down and we sailed peacefully along, our wet clothes hung out to dry, cleaning up the mess below and eating large meals to make up for those we had missed.

It is amazing how quickly you recover from a storm. You may not forget it for 20 years, but as soon as it is over, it becomes academic: an interesting thing to discuss but no more. Already you are busy with the problems of daily living, like what to have for dinner. Soon you are rested, relaxed and well fed, the boat is clean and tidy, you have taken a couple of sights and know exactly where you are. Everything is back to normal.

By the time that we entered the Gulf Stream, the wind had gone back into the southeast and fallen light, so that we needed all our plain sail to keep moving. You do have to watch out for squalls in that area. Like the ones that you find in the tropics, they pass over quickly but can be quite violent while they last. Which means that the crew has to keep a sharp lookout, see them coming in good time and get all the sails down before they arrive. But we had been at sea for two weeks and had plenty of practice. It was a nice evening and I went to bed, confident that all would be well.

Soon I was awakened by a great fuss: there were footsteps overhead, bangings and flappings, shouts. I fell out of my bunk, slipped on some clothes and was on deck within seconds.

A large, black squall was bearing rapidly down on us. June was standing in the cockpit, the tiller between her legs, furling the mizzen and steering the boat. Bob was on the foredeck, lashing down the jib. But the full mainsail was still up and that had better come down before the squall hit. I called to Bob to start lowering it, took over the tiller and sent June to help him.

As soon as it was halfway down, I put the tiller over and ran *Wind Song* off before the wind. Just in time. The squall struck hard, sending her scudding forward over the water, blotting out everything with driving rain. But with just the staysail up, she was riding nicely, rolling gently as she hissed along in the darkness.

Then June went by. She was sitting astride the main boom, trying to lash down the sail. But the main sheet still had some slack in it and the boom was swinging to and fro in great arcs, coming to a jolting stop at each end. June was clinging to it like a monkey, to avoid being thrown off into the darkness. So I hauled in the sheet, reducing the travel of the boom to a few inches each way and before long she and Bob were back in the cockpit, with every-thing secure up forward.

A few minutes later the squall went off ahead of us, leaving us rolling and dripping until we got the sails back up and *Wind Song* on her proper course. Then we sat on deck for a while, drinking coffee and relaxing before going to bed.

And listening to an irate skipper repeat for the hundredth time just when not to leave a sail up and when not to take chances and when not to think we had all the answers, etcetera, etcetera, et-cetera.

All the next day and night we sailed on, watching out for more squalls, but though we sighted three or four, none of them hit us. And the next morning, when June leaned over the side to get a pan full of water for the galley, it was cold. The sea temperature had gone from the 80's down to the 60's. We were across the Stream.

With only a couple of days to go, you begin to think about what you will do when you get ashore. You can spend a happy night watch making a mental list of things that you will eat and other luxuries you will have, like a shower and a drink and a warm, dry, soft bed that does not lurch or rock. But first you have to get there.

Soon after we left the Stream the sky clouded over, the wind picked up and backed into the southeast, dead astern. That is a deceptive condition, for your forward motion makes the wind seem less strong than it really is. The boat rides easily and feels all right, but if you are not careful, you can let the wind build up to the point where you may have trouble getting the sails down. So you read the barometer every hour, write down what it says and keep a sharp eye on the sky behind you.

Slowly the barometer went down and the wind came up. Over-head, the clouds became more dense. Below, the seas got longer and higher, with occasional breaking crests. We were making good progress but the time had come for the storm trysail.

Taking our time and working in daylight, we had no trouble getting the mainsail down, lowering its boom to the deck and lash-ing both securely in place. Then we dragged out the heavy trysail and set that instead. Quickly we picked up speed until we were going almost as fast as before but in far greater safety.

The trysail is smaller and stronger than the mainsail, so that you can leave it up in almost any weather. But its greatest advantage is that is does not need any boom.

Running dead before the wind with the mainsail up, you can only turn one way, away from the side that the mainsail is on. If you start to turn the other way, as little as 10 degrees, the wind will get behind the sail and the boom will come rushing across in an uncontrolled jibe, which can be dramatic in heavy weather. For if the boom does not hit you on the head as it goes by, the sheet will take a shot at garrotting you and if that fails there is a decent chance that something important will break when the boom comes to a stop. Like the mast for instance.

But with the trysail set, you can go all over the ocean as if you owned it. When you turn, the sail merely flops placidly across from one side to the other, doing no harm at all. Of course as long as you have the mizzen up, you have to jibe that. But it is quite small by comparison with the mainsail and conveniently located where you can control it. So steering the boat is far less exacting. You can take the time to look around for ships and you can dodge them if you have to.

On the open ocean you meet very few ships. We had not seen one in two weeks. But as you approach a major port like New York, shipping lanes from all over the world come together and the chances of seeing a ship at any moment are quite high. And in that kind of weather, they certainly would not be looking out for little boats like ours. In fact they would have trouble seeing her at all.

For the wind was still rising and the seas were increasing all the time. The barometer was falling, so it would get worse before it got better. We took down the mizzen and were rushing along with nothing but the storm trysail and the staysail set: a small white boat with two tiny white sails amid the white foam and spray.

By late afternoon the color of the water had changed from blue to green. That meant we were over the Continental Shelf, where the bottom rises sharply from around 12,000 feet to less than 600 feet below the surface of the sea.

We had not been able to see the sun or the stars for two days and we had no electronic equipment aboard, so we were relying on my dead reckoning to take us safely into the harbor. If we missed the sea buoy, we would go charging up to the low, sandy coast with a rising gale behind us: not an attractive prospect.

All through the night we went on, looking anxiously ahead but seeing nothing new at all. No ships. No lights. Just the dark sky and the breaking seas and an occasional rain squall.

Soon after dawn, June took over the watch while I went below to fix breakfast. A few minutes later, she called me to come on deck. I stuck my head out of the hatchway, looking aft to where she was sitting.

"What is that?" she asked, pointing ahead of us.

I turned around. No more than a hundred yards away, gray in the driving rain, was a large, black sea buoy. I had forgotten that June had never seen that type of buoy before.

We called Bob up to see it, the first man-made thing we had seen for 17 days, and swept close by it to check its identity. Sure enough it was buoy "B", about 20 miles southeast of the Ambrose lightship. We had a solid fix and were on our way into New York Harbor.

Soon we began to see ships. They would materialize out of the rain, already quite close, so that you had to look up to find them, instead of down on the horizon. First you would see a few smudges of black and white in the gray rain. Then you would make out the shape of the ship. Then you would start figuring what her course must be, so as to avoid her.

As soon as you had sorted that one out, you had to start looking for the next one, for they came at closer intervals all the time. And among them we found the Ambrose lightship, anchored out in the storm, leaping like a fish so that she sometimes showed half her keel out of the water. It was hard to imagine that *Wind Song* was scarcely any bigger than the boats on her deck.

Sailing up the Ambrose Channel, we expected the sea to get worse, as the waves piled up on the shallow sand bars on either side, but in fact it got steadily better. Probably it is the friction between the waves and the bottom that absorbs all that energy. For a while, the rain eased off and we could see a little more. Over to starboard, we could make out the dark gray outline of Coney Island and ahead we could see the two high headlands of The Narrows.

There it started to rain again, cutting down the visibility so that we had to lay a compass course across New York Harbor, dodging the occasional ship or ferry as we went, barely catching a glimpse of the city as the current swept us up the East River, through Hell Gate and out beyond to City Island.

Kretzer's yard is sheltered from the southeast, and the rain had stopped again, so that it was calm and peaceful as we motored up to the dock, to be greeted by a bossy woman who insisted on telling us exactly how to moor our boat.

Three days out of St. Thomas, Bob and I were feeling fine, but June was seasick the whole way to New York. For 17 days she hardly ate a thing. She was able to do her work and was one of the best deckhands I ever had aboard but she could not keep any food down. Many people are that way. Lord Nelson is said to have been seasick most of the time and half the ocean-racing people that I know have the same problem.

But the moment she stepped ashore, it went away and she was hungry. So we found an Italian restaurant and sat down to dinner. I forget what Bob and I ate, but June, who weighed 115 pounds, ate three orders of ravioli, a whole loaf of bread and two desserts, at least. Possibly more. Then she felt better.

The worst time for seasickness was always during the blistering hot calms. The boat would heave and roll on the glassy sea and I would heave along with it. A good gale generally gave me a few hours of rest. The boat would lurch and jerk in a gale— a very different motion. And I would be quite cheerful about the whole thing. But under ordinary sailing conditions life was just miserable.

I would marvel at the crew adjusting to the life aboard, a few days out, while I returned to normal only when land was within walking distance.

We tried all the imaginable remedies. No red meat or wine for three days before sailing. All the latest drug store remedies. All useless. It ceased to be a challenge and became a way of life.

But I could steer a good course and the cockpit was a convenient place to be. And I could keep the head halfway clean, another convenient location. And when the boat was in port, the crew was well fed. So we would weigh the plus against the minus and I'd pack my bag and do it again.

3   EARLY DAYS

Things were not easy in the early days. For weeks on end we would go without any jobs, June working as a waitress to feed us while I sat anxiously by the telephone, waiting for an order. And when we did get one, the boat was not always in the best of condition. But we made some interesting passages and learned a great deal. *Orana* and *Hi Ho* would be good examples.

David Putnam of Fort Pierce, Florida, bought the 60-foot ketch *Orana* from someone in Annapolis, Maryland, and gave him the 40-foot Chris Craft *Hi Ho* as part of the deal. The exchange was to take place in Charleston, South Carolina, and our job was to take *Orana* to Charleston, hand her over to Dave and bring *Hi Ho* back to Annapolis. The route was down Chesapeake Bay to Norfolk, Virginia, and thence via the Intracoastal Waterway to Charleston. That meant we would be in sheltered waters all the way, so that June and I could take *Orana* without any help. And *Hi Ho* would be a breeze, since a twin-engined motor boat is much easier to handle than a large sailboat.

Annapolis is an old colonial city on the western shore of the Chesapeake, not far south of Baltimore, and there at Trumpy's yard we found *Orana*. She was quite large, weighing around 50 tons, with good sails and a three cylinder diesel engine. So making her go would not be a problem but stopping her might. And she had a centerboard that we could raise, reducing her draft to about five feet, but she would go sideways in a cross wind with that up.

It takes half a day to get from New York to Annapolis and the other half to check a boat out, put fuel and water aboard her, shop for food and get her ready to sail. So that evening we stayed in port and at dawn the next day we got under way.

Motoring across the harbor, we stopped to check the compass by comparing its readings with some that I had figured from the chart. The compass was close enough but we found out that the gearshift was tricky. It had a single lever that controlled both the throttle and the shift but the shift took a few seconds to go from ahead to astern. So if you were to come up to a dock and move the lever smartly from the "slow ahead" position to the "full astern" one, it would give you full speed ahead. Which could be exciting.

It was a cool, clear morning with a light northwesterly breeze as we rounded Thomas Point Shoal lighthouse, just outside the harbor, and set our course down the bay. With the staysail and mizzen set and the engine running, we were making about seven knots and riding comfortably. There was no sea but a light chop on our starboard quarter. The visibility was very good and we could see the western shore stretching away into the far distance on our starboard bow, dark gray but clearly defined on the horizon. Leaving June at the wheel, I went below to check the bilges.

Every sailboat has a hatch that you can lift up, usually at the bottom of the ladder down into the cabin, that reveals a deep, dark hole where the bilge water collects, to be pumped out when necessary. Usually there is a little water down there, because the pump does not get it all out. But this time there was a lot.

I had pumped her dry when we first stepped aboard and checked it just before we sailed, so I knew that she had not leaked in the night. Which meant that we had picked up a ton or more of water, in a calm sea, in about an hour. Obviously I could not hope to pump fast enough to keep ahead of it, so I went to the chart, selected the nearest cove that would be sheltered in that wind and figured our course to it. Then I gave the new course to June, explained the problem to her and took down the sails, which were flapping uselessly on the new, westerly heading.

As June took *Orana* inshore, I climbed around down below, peering into every hole and corner that I could, looking for the source of the leak. But there was so much water sloshing around down there that I could not tell where it was coming from. Meanwhile, June was having trouble picking up the cove, which was tucked away behind a headland, so I took a couple of cross bearings to get a solid fix and gave her a more precise course that brought us right up to it.

No wonder she could not find it. It was hardly big enough to get *Orana* into. But it was ideal for our purpose, being flat calm inside and so shallow that we could not have gone down more than a foot or so before we touched the smooth, sandy bottom.

It did not take us long to set the anchor and stop the engine but already there was a small fishing boat alongside, her owner asking if we needed any help. We told him that we had a leak and he lent us a gasoline pump that took the water out of her in no time. Then we set about finding the leak.

For at least two hours we searched but could not find it anywhere. Then we marked the height of the water, checked it 10 minutes later and found that it was the same. The leak had stopped. It was mysterious. But we had a clue. The boat had only leaked while the engine was running. Not before. Not after. I started the engine and watched closely. Sure enough there was a steady stream of water, coming from somewhere aft.

Tracing it was still not easy, since it led away behind the engine into an area where the bottom of the boat was covered with loose pieces of iron ballast, but finally we found it. The drain cock on the water-cooled muffler had been left open. I shut the cock and ran the engine for half an hour. The leak had gone.

On an occasion like that, you first clean up all the mess that you have made. Then you have lunch. Then you get under way again, for a new start, with everything neat and tidy.

Orana had a pleasant feeling about her. She was an old boat and had had quite a bit of use, and she felt homey. Her decks were wide and clear: plenty of room to spread out a cushion and lie in the sun. Below, the feeling of space was unusual. Her centerboard permitted a huge saloon, full of dark wood and bright-colored cabin decorations.

As we left the cove, we set the staysail and mizzen before heading south. The breeze had eased off but it still gave us a little extra speed, while the engine did most of the work. For this was a different kind of passage from an offshore one. Now we had plenty of fuel aboard and plenty of places to get more, so there would have been no sense in drifting slowly along under sail alone, when we could be taking advantage of the fair weather to make good time down the bay.

Chesapeake Bay is about 200 miles long and varies in width from five to 20 miles, generally getting wider as you go south. It is shallow at the edges but quite deep in the middle and always interesting, with great ships steaming up to Baltimore, tugs struggling along with strange-looking tows, fishing boats going purposefully about their business, and on a fine day the white sails of yachts dotting the horizon.

Nearly all the shallow areas are reserved for fish traps. Each trap consists of a row of wooden poles, about six inches in diameter and 20 feet apart, sticking maybe 10 feet out of water. For as much as a mile they run straight across the bay, then at the deeper end they make a series of turns to form a maze. And in between all the poles are vertical nets.

The idea is that the fish run into the long, straight net and start swimming toward the deeper end to get around it, which leads them into the pound on the end, where they get lost until the fishermen come along and take them out.

But the traps are a mild hazard to small boats, especially in fog or at night. I have been in one. It was in 1952 and I was sailing with a Coast Guard officer in his 30-foot sloop. We were bound south, running before a good breeze, and around midnight we ran straight into a fish trap. It was all very dramatic. Suddenly the poles loomed out of the darkness ahead of us, far too late for us to do anything about it and the boat came to a stop, all tangled up in the netting like a gigantic butterfly.

Fortunately she had an engine and after we got the sails down we were able to untangle her and back her out of the net with no more harm than a few scratches on her paint. But it is better to stay out of the fish trap areas altogether, and they are marked by tall, thin spar buoys to help you do that.

Out in the middle of the bay, you find large black or red buoys that mark the ship channels. Those are generally quite far apart and it may take you a couple of hours at seven knots to go from one to the next. You pass close by one, set your course for the next one and relax for a while. On a clear day you can see the shore but most of the time it is too far away for you to make out any details on it. So you watch a ship or a fish boat go by in the other direction, admire it at your leisure and turn your attention to the next one ahead. And in due course you come to a lighthouse.

Bound south out of Annapolis, the first lighthouse that you come to is on Cove Point, about 35 miles from Thomas Point Shoal, and it was early evening when we brought it abeam, half a mile distant to starboard. The wind had fallen lighter and the sea was almost calm, dark blue under the pale blue sky. Green trees along the shore ran down to a low, sandy headland on which stood the lighthouse, glistening white in the sunlight. And *Orana* mumbled by, her engine and propeller making contented noises, her masts swaying gently as she rolled slightly in the last of the chop.

Just beyond Cove Point is the Patuxent River where we could have put in for the night, but in that kind of weather you do not waste time in port and we set our next course, down past Point No Point toward the mouth of the Potomac River.

Staying awake through the night was never easy. At sea, it was nearly impossible for me. Thank heaven Patrick set up a routine that required the helmsman to stand up every 15 minutes and look all around the horizon. We always had a clock tucked away in an odd corner so that the time could be checked frequently. Somehow it helped to keep you on your toes. And forcing yourself to stand up and look out over the ocean broke the hypnotic effect of staring at the compass.

Near the shore or in the busy waterways it was so much easier to stay awake. There always seemed to be something fairly important going on, a lighthouse in the distance flashing its signal or a tug with a long tow coming up the channel ahead of you.

As the sun went down, we did our routine evening check, making sure that the bilges were dry and the engine was happy, seeing that our running lights were burning and so on. The sails were hanging limp in the dead air, so we took those down and furled them to give us better visibility. And soon it was dark.

A night run in tidal waters keeps you busy, for you can see so much more than you can by day. A lighthouse that you might pick up in daylight at three to five miles now shines out bright and clear at 10 to 15 miles. A ship that you would hardly have noticed before looks like a block of apartments about to run you down. And no longer can you tell her course and speed at a glance. Instead, you have to examine her through binoculars and make out her runing lights from all the others, figuring her course from their relationship and estimating her speed from her changes in position over a period of time.

Towboats can be very interesting to interpret, for they may be pushing something short or pulling something long. Or perhaps towing a series of barges with long cables in between them. And while the lights on the towboat itself are usually good and bright, those on the barges are often miserable little glims, barely visible from 50 feet away.

The smaller navigation buoys that are unlit vanish into the darkness, becoming dangers to be avoided (you might as well try ramming a ship as run into one). The larger, lit ones shine out so far that you often see too many of them at once and have to spend time sorting them out. While keeping a sharp eye out for poorly lit sailboats and steering by the compass.

But on a clear, calm night with a good moon it is one of the most satisfying experiences that I know. For once you get the whole picture clear in your mind; it all makes sense. You can see where the coast must lie, where the channels are, what vessels are in your part of the bay and where they are going. You know exactly where you are and when you will arrive at your next mark.

After dinner we both sat around in the cockpit for a while, enjoying the night and watching Point No Point lighthouse slide by the starboard; then we started taking turns to go below for a nap between marks. They were not regular watches but usually lasted for about three hours. And between them, for 10 or 15 minutes, we would both be on deck as we cleared the mark and set our course for the next one.

Just before midnight we passed close by Smith Point lighthouse, south of the Potomac River, the powerful white light sweeping over our heads and the smaller lights of the crew's quarters shining out of the squat, black tower. About four in the morning we passed Wolf Trap lighthouse, taking it farther off to avoid the un-lit buoys near it, and by dawn we were some 10 miles beyond it. There, the bay was much wider, the morning mist reduced the visibility to a mile or so and we began to feel our way across the flats toward Old Point Comfort. That means going through a fish trap area and you would not try it at night, but by day it saves you some time, compared with the deep-water route around Thimble Shoal.

Over the flats, the water is about 12 feet deep, quite enough for a yacht, but the fish traps are close together. A line of poles will come out of the mist ahead of you and as you turn to go around them, more keep appearing. Finally you come to the pound at the end and rounding that, you get back on your course just in time to see the next trap ahead of you. But they do not last for long and after you clear them, you can angle in toward the headland.

Old Point Comfort lies at the entrance to Hampton Roads, which is in effect the outer harbor of Norfolk. There you have finished with Chesapeake Bay and enter the Intracoastal Waterway that stretches for 900 nautical miles, clear down to Miami.

Going through Norfolk on a calm, misty morning, you have to keep a sharp eye out for traffic. While you are watching one great ship back out of her berth across the river ahead of you, another one will come silently up behind you and give you a short blast on her whistle. You look around and she is towering over you, so you scurry out of her way like a startled rabbit, dodging between tugs and barges as you go. But when you have time to look around, there is plenty to see. All kinds of naval vessels, from aircraft carriers to submarines, lie moored in clusters along the banks. Railroad cars full of coal run to and fro on great black frames like roller coasters, dumping their loads into the ships below. Rows of navigation buoys stand on a dock being painted, some of them as big as a city bus stood on end. And then you come to the bridges.

The first two lift straight up, the whole center span rising slowly between tall towers. They are close together and one carries a rail-road, while the other has a highway on it. In a boat like *Orana* you have to open both, since neither is high enough to clear her main-mast when in the down position. You can depend on the high-way bridge to open fairly soon after you signal with three blasts of your horn that you want to go through. But the railroad bridge may not be able to, for there may be a train coming. In fact, the operators of the railroad bridges usually leave them open whenever they can, so that if you find one closed there is a good chance that you will have to wait a while before he will be able to open it for you.

Lift bridges make me nervous. Few of them have height indicators on them, so that in most cases you have no idea how high the thing is. The operator opens it as high as he chooses, then turns on his green light to invite you through. Often there is highway traffic held up and he seems to be in a hurry to get you out of the way and close it again. So you have to assume that he knows what he is doing and go through. And should it be not quite high enough, it will be a mess. Fortunately, there are not many of those along the way.

Most of them are swing or bascule types. Swing bridges are the best from the mariner's point of view for when they are open, they give you unlimited clearance overhead. But more common are bascule bridges, either single or double. A single bascule bridge opens on one side only, the span tilting upwards, but it rarely goes vertical, so that with a large sailboat you have to hang over to one side as you go through it, to keep your masts clear of the projecting girders. The double bascule is better, since it opens in two halves from both sides at once, leaving you a clear shot through the middle.

There is one place in Norfolk where they have a single bascule railroad bridge within a few feet of a double bascule highway one on a sharp hairpin turn with a cross current underneath it, and that thing can give you the willies on a windy day, when the boat is blowing around sideways in the gusts between the buildings. But on a calm day you can take it slowly and it is not so bad.

Soon after passing through that one, you leave the city behind you and come to a fork in the river. One branch leads ahead toward the Virginia Cut while the other goes off to starboard, to the Dismal Swamp Canal. Either route will take you through to Albermarle Sound and both are about the same length, but in those days the Dismal Swamp route was more convenient for sailboats, so we took that. And quite soon we arrived at Deep Creek lock.

Gently we rose the few feet from the tidal waters behind us to the still water of the canal ahead. Then the operator asked us for details of the vessel, so we went to his office. And there we found fine, large glass jars of honey for sale. It was excellent honey, so we bought two jars of it, keeping one for ourselves and mailing the other to friends. But that was not a good idea, for we got a polite note back, thanking us for whatever-it-was. Evidently the jar had broken in the mail and arrived as an unidentifiable, sticky mess. We spent some time wondering how the mailman delivered it.

The Dismal Swamp Canal runs straight ahead as far as you can see, quite narrow, with tall trees rising up out of the dark brown water on either side. After you leave the lock, there is no sign of life for maybe 15 miles. Somewhere in the middle, *Orana*'s engine quit.

There was an eerie silence as we coasted to a stop but that was an ideal place for it to fail, if it had to, since there was no wind, no current and no traffic. There was no need to secure the boat because she would not go anywhere. She just lay there, silent and still, waiting for us to do something.

Quite often, when a boat is not used for some time, dirt collects in the bottom of her fuel tank. Then the first time she goes to sea, it finds its way to the filter and blocks it. So I took off the filter and sure enough it was all clogged up with dirt. You can not clean that type of filter; you have to replace the cartridge. But I had put one aboard in Annapolis, so I installed that and soon we were under way again.

The Dismal Swamp Canal will always be a favorite spot. When Orana *gave us trouble there, we drifted quietly toward the bank. Suddenly, instead of the constant beat of the engine and the smell of the fumes, we were surrounded by miles of honeysuckle blooming along the banks. The fragrance engulfed us. And through the still woodlands beyond the banks, you could hear the tips of birds' wings touching the leaves as they flew lazily from here to there.*

It was late afternoon when we cleared the other lock at South Mills and went winding down the river toward Elizabeth City, but we thought we would make it in daylight until we found that the railroad bridge was closed. That was an old one and the operator had to open it by hand. The whole job was done with a tool about six feet long, like a huge crowbar. First he put it in a hole in the deck of the bridge and started walking around in circles with it. And slowly the wedges that take the weight of the draw span at the ends drew back. Then he put it in another hole and seemed to be straining hard but hardly moving, as though pushing something very heavy. He was. The whole span, that must have weighed well over 100 tons, began to swing open, so slowly at first that you could hardly see it, but it gathered speed until he was able to relax and let it go on swinging. He did not open it all the way but neither would I have. It was still calm, so we sneaked *Orana* through and went on to arrive at the Riverside Boat Works in the pitch dark.

Gliding quietly across the smooth, black water toward the lights of the town, we drifted to a gentle stop alongside the dock and within ten minutes we were in bed.

In the morning there was a strong northwesterly wind as we sailed down the beautiful river and across Albermarle Sound but it was not as rough as we had expected, though the water is only 15 to 20 feet deep. With her staysail and mizzen set, *Orana* was soon romping up the Alligator River and just after dark we arrived at Belhaven. But this time it was not calm, it was stormy.

The only available dock was about 40 feet long and lay across the end of a narrow channel with the wind blowing off it but we needed fuel so I took her in fast, made a slight turn to port, then spun the wheel to starboard and backed her down hard. Her bow came around fast until I stopped it with left rudder and a touch of power ahead and her momentum carried her sideways up to the dock. Meanwhile June had the fenders out and leaped onto the dock with the bow line, while I cut the engine and jumped across with the stern one. Two seconds later, both lines were fast to the dock and *Orana* was tugging at them, trying to get away as another gust of wind caught her.

Pat claims there is no need to shout if the docking is properly done. Each does exactly what is supposed to be done, exactly when it should be done. Why shout?

And there have been times when all has gone according to schedule but more often there is some small thing that doesn't happen to go quite right. A six-inch nail sticking out from a piling, for example, or a friendly dockmaster pulling hard in on the bow line, upsetting the whole maneuver.

Patrick never shouts. He just paces back and forth ranting in the low, well-modulated voice of a true Shakespearean actor.

With her bowsprit sticking out at one end and her mizzen boom at the other, she overhung the dock by 30 feet and it took us half an hour to moor her for the night, with doubled bow and stern lines, spring lines and chafing gear. But the next morning we got our fuel and went on our way.

Ordinarily we would not use a technique like that, but it is good to have it up your sleeve when you need it, for you have to weigh the risks: the chance of running out of fuel in a narrow spot against the chance of making a tricky dock in a storm, the chance of doing it in the dark against the chance that the weather may be worse in the morning. In fact, much of my time was spent figuring odds, deciding how we could make the best time with the least risk. For the risk of minor damage is far greater in narrow waters than it is on the open ocean and even minor damage can be serious when you are handling a boat worth as much as ten new Cadillacs.

Leaving Belhaven, you sail south into Pamlico Sound. That is a great place for boating, with vast areas of relatively calm water surrounded by an attractive shoreline of tall pine trees, but it is remarkably little used. A few inshore fishermen work its waters and the migrating power boats rush across it on their annual pilgrimage to Florida but otherwise it is usually empty, one of the last remaining places where you can find peace and quiet.

There is no tide in that area, since it is cut off from the sea by Cape Hatteras, but as you go down the canal to Morehead City, you are back in tidal waters. Morehead is a fishing port, and passing through it, you come to a long, narrow sound that runs parallel with the Atlantic Ocean, with the mainland on one side of it and sand dunes on the other. At first sight it appears to be about a mile wide but the deep channel is only about 200 feet across and all the rest is very shallow, so that you have to stay exactly in the channel all the way.

To help you, they provide day markers every couple of hundred yards and beacons at the corners. A day marker is just a pile sticking out of the water with a sign on it, while a beacon is more elaborate and has a light on it. They are about 15 feet high and nearly every one has a bird on it who takes off as you get there, does a lazy circle in the air and lands back on it behind you.

At modest speeds, that goes on with minor variations for a couple of days, until you come to a long canal that strikes inland and brings you out near the top of the Waccamaw River.

We would anchor in the last light of the day and by the time we were sure the hook was holding and had carried the chart below, along with the pencils, binoculars and the beanbag ashtray that kept the chart from blowing overboard, darkness would surround the boat.

A white anchor light would be tied to the forestay and sometimes if we felt the anchorage a bit vulnerable, we would leave a mast light on.

Then below to the cabin and galley for dinner. The cabin would feel hot and smell of the hot engine that had been running since early morning. And after having sat all day in the open cockpit, our faces would sting and our skin would crack and peel. Our noses would be blistering red and there would be great white rings around our eyes where our sunglasses had been.

Dinner would be fast and simple. A bit of fresh meat, some salad and vegetables and something sticky sweet for dessert. While things cooked, we would sit in the cockpit or around the table, Patrick plotting the courses on tomorrow's charts, while we sipped beer or a glass of wine if luck had taken us near a good supply.

We'd try to stop every three or four days for provisions. Canned food was only for ocean trips. We never considered the waterway trips anything that should change our living pattern. So whenever we did tie up to a dock to fuel, I would dash ashore to replenish our supply for a few more days.

Orana had settled down by then and was purring along nicely as we followed the looping curves of the river, first between high trees and later through more open countryside. And there we saw our first eagle's nest. It was made of sticks and perched on the very top of a bare, dead tree. An eagle was sitting on it as we passed and looked as though she were hatching some eggs.

Then we got a whiff of Georgetown, still several miles ahead.

There is a paper mill there and when the wind is right, you can smell it long before you can see it. But fortunately we had a fair tide down the river that swept us mercifully past the mill, into the clean, fresh air beyond it.

On the Waccamaw, as at other points along the Intracoastal Waterway, you will see signs pointing to spots a bit off the main channel, down a spur of the river. A sign like "Conway — 8 miles."

The river branches off to the side, calm, yellow-green from the cypress trees along its banks, inviting you to Conway. What could there be in Conway? Stately old Southern mansions set in smooth green lawns, guarding the banks of the river. Charming nineteenth-century villages, all stone and magnolias. All just around the bend in the river, just eight miles off our track.

Some day, we promise ourselves, we will take time to visit Conway. Perhaps it is better to keep the dream than the promise.

As you leave the Waccamaw River to enter the next canal section, you come to an old cable ferry. There is a flat, rectangular barge, big enough to hold two cars, that pulls itself across the canal with a steel cable. When not in use, the cable lies on the bottom of the canal but when the operator is ready to make a trip, he tightens it with a winch and it leaps out of the water, to hang dripping about three feet above the surface. (Which is all very well unless you happen to be approaching it too fast.) Then he starts up an old engine and the whole contraption goes clanking across the canal to the other side, comes to a wheezing halt and drops its cable.

All through that part of the waterway you meet towboats, each pushing two or three great barges laden with pulpwood for the paper mills. The barges are square across the bow, curving up out of the water, and would undoubtedly run right over you if they hit you. So you move over to the side of the canal, as far as you can without going aground, and keep close control of your boat to prevent her from taking a sudden sheer when the surge of water in front of the barge catches her. But the towboat captains are very good and give you more room than you really need. It just does not look that way.

However, it would never pay to anchor for the night in the waterway, for the towboats come through at all hours. They have large, powerful searchlights that make it possible for them to run by night but they might not be able to stop in time to avoid you. So you have to plan each day's run to bring you to a dock or a safe anchorage off the channel, out of their way.

South of Georgetown, you have to watch out for the ranges. Those are markers on the shore that look rather like archery targets. They come in pairs and the idea is to keep them in line with each other, so that you stay in the center of the channel, but they are often hard to find against the background of trees.

All that afternoon the weather was hot and sticky, the clouds building up until thunderstorms began to form here and there. For a while we watched with interest as they went by on either side of us, full of lightning and fury. Then one of them hit us fair and square.

As it approached we put on our foul weather gear and closed the hatches. I brought *Orana* to a stop beside a marker and turned her bow into the rising wind, using just enough power to keep her steady. And soon the rain swept over us, reducing the visibility to about 100 feet, while the wind increased until I was using 40 or 50 horsepower to keep her from being pushed backward. For several minutes we lay there, across the canal, peering at the marker and trying to stay within view of it, while the lightning crashed down and the teeming rain drummed on the deck. Then it was over. The rain stopped and the wind subsided. The cloud overhead moved away and the sun came out. Soon we were motoring peacefully down the waterway again, to put into McClellanville for the night.

Just before dawn we got under way and by mid-morning we were approaching Charleston, across the wide harbor. On our port hand lay Fort Sumter. To starboard the buildings and spires of the old city gleamed in the bright morning sunshine. And ahead lay the yacht basin, where we were to meet Dave.

We had been cleaning *Orana* as we went along and it did not take us long after we docked to finish the job. But we were hardly through when he appeared, anxious to be aboard his new yacht. So we transferred our gear to *Hi Ho* and started getting her ready for the trip back to Annapolis.

Hi Ho was another kettle of fish, which is not a bad description, though possibly unkind. She was an old 40-foot Chris Craft, built on the general lines of a house trailer, completely boxed in with almost nowhere to sit outside except the steering position perched on the roof. She had a double cabin at each end and between them a saloon, under which we found two rusty gasoline engines and sundry pieces of archaic equipment. But she would be safe enough on the waterway, so we checked her out as best we could, filled her tanks and went ashore to buy food.

Under way, she made a steady 10 knots with a motion much like that of an elephant, a sort of gentle jiggling and swaying. There was nowhere to put the chart, of course, and less shelter from the weather than you get in a sailboat, but you could always tell where you had been by the pall of black smoke on the water.

The first day's trip was uneventful. Once plugged in to a dock for the night, we had all kinds of electric conveniences like hot water, a cooking stove and lights. But on the second night we anchored, for docks were not as plentiful in those days, and having made sure that the anchor was holding, we went below.

Nothing worked. There was no light. We could not cook. We could not even get cold water. The whole thing depended on shore power and without it she was dead. Mildly amused, we sat in the dark eating cold beans out of a can by flashlight.

But the steering worked and she did not leak much and the engines kept going. Until we reached the Fear River.

The tide in the Fear was running against the wind, kicking up a moderate chop in the wide river. *Hi Ho* was bucking and splashing along, moving quite slowly through the water but making good time because the current was going our way. And we were both on deck when there was a change in the sound of the engines.

Immediately June went below, opened up the hatch in the saloon and found flames about two feet long coming out of the starboard engine, with a great roar like a gigantic blowtorch.

Closing the hatch, she opened the side door and called up to me to shut down the starboard engine. And as soon as I did, the flames stopped. Then she took over the steering while I checked things out below. It turned out that a piece of the exhaust manifold had rusted through and fallen off. But fortunately the flames had not had time to set fire to anything before we stopped them.

We became very sensitive to sounds. The slightest change in the steady beat of a boat under power meant something.

Perhaps the channel led over a sudden patch of sand, perhaps you were headed off the channel onto a shoal, perhaps the wind had shifted. Or the water cooling intake was clogged or the boat was on fire. You had to find out.

So one of us would check below while the other went over our position on the chart.

By the time I got back on deck, June was taking *Hi Ho* into the canal that connects the Fear River with the relatively calm sound beyond, so I eased back the port throttle to reduce the load on that engine and we carried on at about six knots toward Wrightsville, some 15 miles ahead, where there was a marina.

When both engines are working, a twin-engined motor boat of that size is so easy to handle that it is dull. You can go right up to a bridge, even with the current behind you, back her down and stop while it opens. And docking is a breeze. All you have to do is to set the throttles in the idle position, leave the wheel centered and drive the thing like a bulldozer with the two gearshift levers. But with one engine dead the boat handles rather poorly, for the remaining one is way off center, so that the boat wants to turn one way when going ahead and the other way going astern. But in this case it was easy, for the dock was on our starboard hand and the current was behind us. The port engine took her around to face the current and the wind, which was quite light under the trees, took her gently up to the dock.

There we were lucky to find a helpful mechanic, for it was a job to fix the engine. The bolts were all rusted solid and had to be cut off. Then he had to locate a new manifold; that was not easy, since the engine was so old. And finally he had to drill out the old bolts and fit new ones. But he kept at it and several days later we were on our way again.

Crossing Albemarle Sound, we met a blimp, which was based near Elizabeth City in those days and patrolled the area regularly. Looking for smugglers, I suppose. They were fascinating things and I often wondered how they got that name, until one day I was reading my father's manual on air combat, dated 1916. And there was the answer. Aircraft were divided into two classes: 1–Lighter than air, and 2–Heavier than air. Within class 1 there were two categories: A–Rigid and B–Limp.

As we passed through Norfolk, there was a strong wind blowing out of the north and while *Hi Ho* had been running steadily since leaving Wrightsville, we did not want to take any chances with her and put into Hampton Creek to wait for it to ease before going out into Chesapeake Bay. But the next morning it was calm and we left early for the 14-hour trip to Annapolis.

For several hours we ran in fog, up past Wolf Trap lighthouse toward Smith Point, following the line of buoys that marked the edge of the fish trap areas. They were mostly spar buoys in those days: tall, thin wooden poles painted black and white that would appear out of the mist a couple of hundred yards away. They were hard to see but very handy, since by following them we could stay clear of the fish traps on one side of us and the ships on the other.

Later on, as the fog lifted, a southwesterly breeze came up and with it a slight sea that made *Hi Ho* roll and wallow her way past Cove Point. And just after dark we arrived in Annapolis, to spend the next day cleaning her before going home to do our laundry and wait for the next job.

4   SIX TO PARIS

That winter there were no jobs for us in New York, so we went to England to visit my relatives, and within a few days of arriving in London, we had a job. We were in the Royal Ocean Racing Club when John Illingworth, the Commodore, walked in. He was an old friend of mine and when he asked what we were doing, I told him about our new venture.

"You know," he said, "there's someone I think you should meet. A chap called LeRoux is getting together some English boats for charter in Paris. He might need some help."

It turned out that he already had two boats waiting to leave the south coast of England for Paris and was glad to turn the job of moving them over to us. We needed some crew but John found a couple of people while we found two more, and soon I was on my way down to the tiny port of Emsworth, just east of the Isle of Wight.

The boats were called *Isla* and *Pelican*. *Isla* was an elderly motor yacht, 60 feet long, with a single diesel engine. *Pelican* was a converted ship's lifeboat, 30 feet long, with a small gasoline engine. Neither was in very good shape but both looked as though they would probably make the trip, with luck.

You have to be careful of the weather in the English Channel in mid-winter. In fact you can only expect to get a few days a month when it is suitable for boats like that. But we were in luck: The forecast for that night was excellent. Hurriedly we put aboard fuel and prepared to leave. I would sail as skipper of *Isla*, with John's two friends as my crew, while Joe Cunningham and a midshipman would take *Pelican*. June could not go but would join us in a couple of days, when Joe and the mid had to leave.

The estuary of the Seine River is tricky, with twisting channels and offlying shoals, but there is a canal for small craft that starts from Le Havre, joining the Seine a little higher up and we decided to take that, sailing in company across the Channel.

Neither boat had any radio or other equipment except a compass so we agreed on flashlight signals. There were two kinds. If all was well, we would wave the light straight up and down. But if anything went wrong, we would wave it around in circles. In which case the other one would steam over to within hailing distance.

It was late afternoon when we sailed and soon the lights of the English coast dropped away behind us, leaving the two boats alone in the darkness of the winter night, steaming along a quarter of a mile apart. *Pelican* could only make six knots, so I kept *Isla*'s speed down to stay within sight of her. Every now and then her flashlight would shine out across the water, going up and down to signal that all was well. Then we would go out on deck, make the same signal to her and nip back into the shelter of the pilot house.

The Channel is about 100 miles across at that point and we were more than halfway, in the early hours of the morning, when my lookout reported distress signals from *Pelican*. I went out on deck and sure enough there was Joe's flashlight, going round and round, fading rapidly into the distance behind us.

Putting *Isla* about, we went back and came close alongside *Pelican* to find out what the trouble was. Her engine had quit. If we hung around while Joe tried to fix it, the weather would probably turn sour. But for the moment it was flat calm. So we passed him a line and took him in tow.

At dawn a light breeze came up, freshening steadily. Our spell of calm weather was coming to an end. Soon the Channel would be back to its normal winter condition: far too rough for us to tow *Pelican* any longer.

But *Isla*'s engine kept running steadily and soon we sighted the French coast, gray in the distance. Slowly it got higher and we began to make out details, comparing them with the chart. We were right on our track, headed straight into Le Havre. Before noon we steamed into the harbor, to spend the afternoon dealing with the customs and immigration people.

It took us half a day to get *Pelican*'s engine going, and it ran long enough to make the trip through the canal to the Seine River. But it was tricky to operate, being a converted automobile engine with all kinds of home-made levers and knobs that you had to fiddle with, so I decided to tow her for the rest of the way.

Early next morning, June arrived in the overnight ferry from England. She did not speak any French, so I went to meet her and take her aboard *Pelican*, where she replaced the mid as Joe's deckhand. Then we took them in tow behind *Isla* and set off up the Seine toward Paris.

For the night Channel crossing I had taken a cabin on the ferry and was sound asleep in an upper berth when we docked in the morning.

I awoke to the chattering of two people right beside my head. The woman was one of the ship's French maids, the man, a rather shoddily dressed Frenchman in a blue denim jacket, the usual beret and one of those stinking French cigarettes bobbing dangerously between his lips as the chatter became more intense.

It was my first visit to the Continent but after all the stories I'd heard, I was not surprised that the French would allow a strange man into my cabin while I was still in bed. But did all Frenchmen smell like that?

The man glared at me, continuing to jabber. I couldn't understand a word of it, so I simply glared back. Then he said: "For Heaven's sake will you tell this woman I'm your husband? She doesn't believe me." It was Patrick. His years with the British secret service in France had not been forgotten. He melted into the surroundings like a native.

Where the canal meets it, the Seine is still wide, curving between low banks, but the deep channel is narrow and that morning it was full of ships, steaming fast up river, one behind the other. We had to tow *Pelican* with a long line so that she could ride over their wakes and she had to be steered all the time, to prevent her from swinging wildly from side to side. It was bitterly cold and *Pelican* had an open cockpit so the crew took turns coming aboard *Isla* to have breakfast and warm up. Joe came first and I stopped *Isla* while the towline was hauled in, taking her back up to cruising speed as soon as he was safely aboard. Then everyone went below to eat, leaving June alone aboard *Pelican* and myself alone in *Isla*'s pilot house.

A short while later I took a routine look astern and saw that *Pelican* was adrift, far behind *Isla*, lying across the channel in the path of an oncoming ship.

There was no time to mess around. The ship could not possibly stop or even change course in time to miss *Pelican*. I put *Isla*'s rudder hard over to port, pushed the throttle wide open and shouted to the crew below to get on deck. Racing back down the river, it was obvious that we would not have time to stop and take her in tow, or even get June off her, before the ship reached her. There was only one chance. I kept *Isla* going at full speed, aiming wide to starboard, then slammed the rudder hard over to port, throwing *Isla* into a tight turn that took most of the speed off her for a moment as her stern swung close by *Pelican*'s bow, with her engine still going full speed ahead.

Meanwhile June was busy. The towline had come adrift at our end and she climbed up onto *Pelican*'s ice-covered foredeck to get it aboard and coil it down. Then she turned the coil over, so that the line would run clear off the top and held the end out.

Joe took it from her, gathered some in and took a couple of turns around a bollard. Then as the strain came on, he let it slip a little to ease the shock as we snatched *Pelican* out of the way and the ship went hissing by.

Realizing that Pelican *was no longer attached to* Isla, *I started jumping up and down, waving and shouting. I could see Patrick standing at the wheel inside the deckhouse, wearing his huge old Navy duffel coat. Of course he couldn't hear me.*

Pelican *still had a bit of way. Perhaps I could coax her to the nearest bank. That freighter coming steadily toward us didn't give me much time.* Pelican *soon lost all way. For some reason I thought if I waggled the rudder, something might happen. Nothing did.*

I could try to swim to the bank, leaving Pelican *to her fate. But the river was full of chunks of broken ice, and I'm no swimmer.*

Might as well stay dry for a little longer. The ship wasn't on top of us yet.

Then Isla began a turn. They had missed us. The towline was still attached to Pelican's bow. I'd better get that out of the water. If it were to catch in Isla's propeller, none of us would have a chance.

The foredeck of the converted lifeboat had a slight camber, with a thick layer of cream enamel and then a thin layer of ice. The boat bobbed gently in the icy, still morning air as I slid on all fours to the bow. Bracing a foot against a cleat on each side, I pulled the wet line aboard.

Joe was standing on Isla's stern with a line ready but dropped it when he saw mine. Thank goodness a pro was going to handle things now. Patrick brought Isla's stern so close that it was not difficult to toss the rope from my sitting position. Joe picked it up first shot, taking a hitch around a cleat while I braced myself for the shock when the line became taut.

Isla rushed to the right and then straightened her heading down the channel, causing Pelican to arc out from under the freighter's bows, and I slid back into the safety of the cockpit.

Looking up at the ship, I could see no one the least bit interested in our plight. Perhaps they hadn't noticed or perhaps they preferred not to. You can't blame them. There was really nothing they could do.

Investigating later, I found that the towline had been handled by a young man aboard *Isla* who had taken a few turns around a bollard but not enough to hold for long. Then he had announced with great confidence that he had secured it, with the result that nobody else had checked it. Of such things are disasters made.

That evening we arrived at Rouen, where Joe had to leave. It is an interesting old city with a Street of the Fat Clock that does indeed have a truly fat clock right across it and a fine dockside store called *Au Marin Chic* where they sell clothing for seamen, most of which you can put on either way. The shoes will go on either foot and the smocks will go on frontwards or backwards. So when you get out of your bunk in a hurry to go on deck, you can put them on without stopping to think about them. It is all very practical.

Above Rouen you see no more ships. The Seine meanders along through pleasant countryside, little affected by commerce of any kind, with locks every now and then to control it. Going up, we would first come alongside the training wall and let off two crew members with long lines, then steam slowly into the lock while they walked along the wall beside us, climbed a steep flight of stone steps and continued along the higher wall of the lock. This was all very well except for the fact that the steps and walls were covered with great patches of ice.

Another problem was that the mooring lines would freeze solid in the night, so that you had to pry them off the bollards in the morning. And when you got one off, it would retain its shape, standing like a coiled spring on the dock and refusing to be bent any other way.

Even in deep winter the approach to Paris is impressive. You pass through a couple of locks, under some fine bridges, and begin to see large buildings. It is never ugly and suddenly you are there, tying up to a quay in the middle of the city.

In Paris we met Monsieur LeRoux who asked us to bring him some more boats, so after a day off we flew back to England and started searching along the Thames River west of London for suitable ones.

It took several weeks but eventually we found six boats whose owners wanted to put them into the Paris charter fleet. They were a mixed bag: an old 60-foot motor yacht called *Spitfire*, four smaller boats and a truly odd one called *Ventura III* that looked like a houseboat but was built on the hull of a 50-foot crash boat and still had the original 600-horsepower gasoline engine in her.

Next we had to gather them together, for they were scattered over a wide area. One converted lifeboat was in the Grand Junction Canal just outside London and when we went to get her, we got lost in the middle of the city.

My sister Rosalind joined June and me on that trip and we found the boat in the narrow, calm canal in one of those sprawling London suburbs where everything looks the same in all directions. It was raining lightly so that we could not see the sun and the boat had no compass. We had no map that showed the canal and no way of telling which way was north. So we got the engine going, picked the most likely looking direction and started out.

On average, that canal has a lock every mile and you work them yourself. When you get your permit to go through, they give you an iron handle that opens and shuts the paddles in the gates, to let the water in and out, while the gates themselves are attached to wooden beams, about a foot square and 20 feet long, against which you put your backside to push them open. It is very good exercise.

Let us say that you arrive at a lock that goes down to the next level and it happens to be empty. First you bring the boat along-side the training wall and make her fast. Then you walk down to the far end of the lock and crank those two paddles shut. Then you walk back to the near end, open those two paddles and wait for the lock to fill. Next you open the gates, move the boat into the lock and close the gates. Then you close the upper paddles, open the lower ones and wait for the lock to empty, letting out the boat's lines as she goes down. After which you open the lower gates, move the boat out and make her fast to the lower training wall. Then you go back, shut the gates and close the lower paddles. And that is one lock done.

Since the Captain never leaves his ship, guess who got to open the locks?

The locks are built to take a barge 12 feet wide and when our boat was in one, she left a strip of water maybe two feet wide along one side. The only water for miles around and Rosalind fell into it. She was so bundled up in winter clothing that we thought she would sink like a stone but she came back up and we dragged her out, soaked to the skin, to dry off as best she could in the un-heated cabin.

Then the engine broke down and for several miles I towed the boat by walking along the bank, heaving on the anchor line, while the girls steered her. And all the time the buildings got higher and closer together, until we came to a dead end. We had taken the wrong way at the start and were in the middle of London. We tied the nasty thing up and took the subway home. The next day we went back, fixed the engine and took her down to the Thames.

I had no idea of the suitable garb for an English winter. So when Rosalind and I divided my clothing, there was little to go around.

One of us got the underwear, the other the slacks. One took the duffel coat, the other the sweater. It was a long, cold subway ride home that night.

By early February, four of the boats were ready to leave but two were not, so we left those behind to go later and took *Spitfire*, *Ventura* and the two smaller ones down the Thames to Rochester. On the way, *Ventura*'s engine quit and we had to tow her. But she had a fine, deep bow so that she could not be towed forward without sheering all over the river. To avoid this, we decided to tow her backward and arrived in rather grand style, with one small boat in front as a scout, then *Spitfire* (going forward) towing *Ventura* (going backward) towing the other small one (going forward) to keep *Ventura* straight.

From Rochester, our route lay down the Thames estuary and across the English Channel to Calais, after which we planned to take the French canals to the Oise River, sail down it to the Seine and up that to Paris. But first we held up for several days, waiting for the weather to moderate, while the wind howled and snow flurries swept across the icy water and we huddled over smelly little kerosene stoves in our various cabins, trying to keep warm. There were 10 of us altogether in the four boats: *Spitfire*'s owner, June, another girl, myself and six young men whose enthusiasm for the adventure of the trip was rapidly waning in the cold.

One day it eased off and we ran down the estuary to Ramsgate before it shut us in again. Then more days in port, listening to the marine radio forecast on a portable radio every few hours, waiting for another spell of relatively calm weather. But it was worth the wait, for one night the wind fell light and by the next morning the sea was almost calm. Our chance had come.

Everything was ready and we sailed immediately. I took *Ventura* since she was tricky to handle, while June sailed aboard *Spitfire*, and soon we were out of the harbor, steaming down the English coast. It was calm enough out there but it felt somehow pent up, as though it would not stay that way for long. The sky was an ominous leaden gray and the sea slopped vaguely around as though waiting impatiently to get rough again. It was raw and cold and bleak. We saw no ships or other boats. The only sign of life was the gray smudge of shoreline to starboard. But we kept moving steadily along and before noon we were off the South Foreland.

Taking our departure for France, we headed out into the Channel and rapidly the coast of England disappeared in the murk behind us, leaving us alone in a gray, bleak world. But ships would keep materializing out of the haze, to rumble and splash past us and dissolve into the haze on the other side, coming and going in all directions, so that we never knew where to look for the next one.

Perhaps an hour later *Spitfire*'s engine quit. We were steaming along close together, taking care to keep each other in sight, when suddenly she slowed down and stopped, falling rapidly astern until we went back to see what was wrong. They were not sure but they thought it was fuel trouble. They were working on it.

We waited, rolling and wallowing in the gray sea, watching out for ships that might run us down before they realized that some nuts were out in small boats in the Channel in February. We kept an anxious eye on the sky for signs of any change in the weather. It seemed like several hours but probably it was more like 40 minutes before there was waving and shouting from *Spitfire*'s decks. They had cleared the blockage. We could get under way again.

Moving once more, we began to think about the fine dinner in a warm restaurant that we would have as soon as we arrived in France. And then we looked across at *Spitfire*. She was stopping again.

From what we could gather, it was the same problem: dirt in the fuel. And again we lay rolling beside her while they worked on it. But the current runs strongly through the Straits of Dover, so that we were in fact moving sideways quite fast. Carefully I figured our new position and corrected our course for that.

By the time *Spitfire* started moving again, it was getting dark and we were somewhere in the Channel, with nothing in sight. But as soon as it got really black, we could see everything: the lights of the French coast and dead ahead, the port of Calais, little more than an hour's steaming away.

As the shore lights appeared out of the darkness, Spitfire's *skipper announced that Patrick, in the lead boat, was heading for the wrong harbor. He didn't know what the lights were that Patrick was aiming toward but obviously the lights about 20 degrees to port were Calais, and that was where he was going.*

In spite of our recent adventures in London, I still felt that of all things, Patrick Ellam could read a chart. Perhaps, with night coming on, it was best for the boats to stay together, even if we were headed the wrong way? Besides, why not catch up to Ventura and tell her we thought the heading was wrong? Well, all right. He reluctantly turned to pursue the wayward Ventura. We were close enough to make contact as she began to steam into the harbor. Calais. No more was said. But I was determined never to sail again with just any skipper.

Next morning, as we were clearing through customs, the weather was back to its normal winter self, howling and raging down the Channel. But we no longer cared, for ahead of us lay miles of canals, with quite a different set of problems.

Leaving the tide lock, we set off along the calm waterway and promptly came to a bridge that would have to open to let us through. But when we signalled with our horns, nothing happened. We tried again. Still nothing. So we made fast to the bank and went ashore to investigate. The operator's hut was empty. Going down the street, we inquired at the first house and were directed to another one. There we found his wife, who took up the search, finally locating him in a bar. And in due course, he came and opened the bridge for us.

But the French locks were far more modern than any that we had seen in America. They were built in pairs, side by side, and operated by one man in a control tower. He could push a button and either lock would go through its cycle automatically, while he could talk with the barge masters through loudspeakers on poles, half a mile down the canal in each direction.

The barge masters also had loudspeakers with which to answer and we soon found out that it was possible to get caught in the middle, between two angry Frenchmen arguing through loudspeakers. But you do not do that twice.

The barges were very large, almost filling the locks, and were worked by two men. The captain lived with his wife and children in the stern, while the mate and his family lived in the bow, with the cargo space between them. Each family had a living room, bedroom, kitchen and bathroom, always warm and cozy, clean and well kept, with much shining brass. And along the canals there were schools for the children to attend as they came and went.

The barge engines were very small and while they could push the barges along at four or five knots once they got going, they would not stop them. That was done by hand. The captain would bring the barge alongside a dock or wall and the mate would toss a wire hawser over a bollard, take a few turns and surge the barge, which must have weighed hundreds of tons, to a gentle stop.

At night, they would tie up wherever they happened to be, but often the canal would be shallow at the side, so that the barge went aground, leaving several feet of water between it and the grassy bank. Then they would go ashore by leaning across a long steel pole hinged at one end and pushing off with their feet, the way you would swing on a gate. Usually we would tie our boats alongside a barge for the night and soon we got into the habit of going ashore that way, coming back with armfuls of groceries and bottles of wine by the same route.

One of the small pleasures of travelling like a snail with your house on your back is coping with the routine things always in a different place. Even so mundane an errand as buying a quart of milk becomes something of an adventure.

I remember standing knee-deep in mud and manure in a French farmyard, trying in my non-existent French to explain that I would like to purchase fresh milk. Café au lait flashed through my mind but somehow when I spoke, it sounded like "Olé." The good lady of the house understood and the purchase was completed.

After a couple of days of slow running, *Ventura's* engine gave up and the engineer set about cleaning its spark plugs by dunking them in a saucepan full of gasoline. Suddenly there was a shout and I looked down the hatch to see a mass of flames, so I started down the help him. But at that moment he ran toward the ladder with his pan of gas and set my pants on fire.

There is something embarrassing about having your pants on fire, so I went back out and rolled in the snow while he followed, setting his beard on fire on the way out. At which point June came out of the galley, hit him in the mush with a wet dishcloth, took a fire extinguisher and put all the various flames out.

But after that, we decided to have the engine fixed properly and spent several days helping a French mechanic take the thing apart, fix it and put it back together. Then her performance was impressive. Her absolute minimum speed was far in excess of the legal limit and there was no telling what her maximum might be.

Eventually I had to find out. Rationalizing that the engine needed clearing, I gave her full throttle down a quiet reach in the lowering dusk. There was a thundering roar and behind us I saw a gigantic stern wave that was going over both banks of the canal and off across the countryside. Relenting, I shut the throttle and the engine promptly died. At that moment, a man on a bicycle came along the bank toward us and we shot past him in total silence, trailing a wake like a destroyer. But he lifted his feet to keep them dry and did not even look back.

The winter rains had caused some flooding on the Oise River and the barges were backed up halfway to Calais, creating a monumental traffic jam. We would come to a lock and find a line of barges literally stretching for miles, waiting to go through. At one lock we waited four days for our turn, moving forward a few feet every half hour, so as not to lose our places in the line. But after that, things improved and the lines got shorter.

Then we came to a dead end. Ahead we could see a tall structure of steel girders but beyond it was a hill, rising steeply up. There was no lock that we could see, and no more water in sight.

As we got closer, we saw a training wall at the base of the steel tower so we made for that, tied up the boats and went to investigate. It was a vertical lift lock, built in the nineteenth century and still in fine working order. There were two huge tanks, each as big as a conventional lock and full of water, balanced so that one went up while the other came down. And high above us was an aqueduct leading to the top of the hill.

The operator raised a vertical gate in front of the lower tank and we sailed into it. Then he dropped that gate back into place and let a little more water into the upper tank, so that its weight carried it down and us up, high into the air, peering over the sides of our boats, down into the valley below. Then he lifted the gate in front of us and we sailed on, down the aqueduct into the next canal. But the most impressive thing was that none of the gates leaked. They had been in daily use for more than 100 years, yet they dropped easily into place and held back hundreds of tons of water, so well that the concrete pits beneath the tanks were almost dry.

Another impressive thing was a tunnel that took us all night to go through. They do not allow engines to run inside it but there is an electric towboat that hauls itself along a chain which lies on the bottom of the canal, taking a string of barges through at a time.

The barges line up along the bank, each with a cable to the one ahead, and wait. There were 62 of them that evening, plus our small boats at the very end. Important-looking people went along the towpath, writing things on pieces of paper. Then there was a distant clanking, as the towboat took up the strain. For a long time, nothing happened at our end. But eventually, almost imperceptibly, we began to move toward the black, unlit tunnel.

Inside, we got out our flashlights to see what was around us. The low roof curved overhead, dripping with damp, and dropped into the still, black water on our right. But on our left it came down to a narrow towpath and here and there, along the wall behind the path, were crosses marking the graves of men who had died building the tunnel. And so we went to bed that night, moving slowly and silently through a dark, damp graveyard.

There were actually two tunnels. The first one was very long and we didn't emerge from it until well after sunrise. Then the boats came to a gentle stop along the left bank. Time enough for some of us to leap ashore and learn that the tunnel ahead was quite short. In fact, if we were quick about it, we could walk over the hills and meet the boats on the other side.

Not relishing two or three more hours of darkness, we left a crew aboard each boat and the rest of us hiked over the hills, to arrive ahead of the towboat.

By breakfast time we were out of it, using our greater speed to get ahead of the barges, and soon we were locking down toward the Oise River.

There the water level was still high and the dams were open. In the flood season, they open all the sluices and let her rip. So you come sweeping around a curve, the current strong behind you and find a row of arches across the river, with a lock at one end. Ignoring the lock, you pick an arch and head for it, lining the boat up carefully as she rushes toward it. Her bow will dip a little as it drops maybe a foot underneath the arch and with a kind of slither and wiggle you are through. It is quite exhilarating.

The Oise leads into the Seine, which is more sedate, and going up that, we were joined one night by an elderly French lady who had come to take an inventory of the boat's equipment. We were ashore when she arrived and had left a tarpaulin on *Spitfire*'s deck, covering a large hole where a hatch should have been. We had also left a plank from the deck to the shore. So she walked up the plank and fell down the hatchway, about seven feet, into the cabin below. Then she did a press-up out of the hatchway and when we came back she was sitting on deck, waiting for us, the feather in her hat bobbing in the night breeze.

The next morning we steamed into Paris, past the Eiffel Tower, to tie up near the other yachts at a quay on the Left Bank, within sight of the Louvre. There we stayed for a couple of days, living aboard the boats and enjoying the city, before flying back to England. In the spring we went home to New York.

5   MARIBEL

Early in June we got our first major order that year. Gosta Ahlen of Stockholm had sailed his 52-foot yawl *Maribel* from Sweden to Barbados but had to fly back home from there. Now he wanted her taken to New York, so he called Bob Garland who called us. And the next day June and I went down, with Kent Paxson as deckhand, while Joe Pelich flew in from Texas to sail as mate.

It took all day to get from New York to Barbados, so we stayed ashore that night. And when we found *Maribel* in the morning, she was a mess. She was lying at anchor in the care of a watchman who had been doing just that. Watching her rust. Nothing worked. Neither the main nor the auxiliary engine could even be turned over, let alone started. The anchor windlass was rusted solid. She needed a lot of work before she would be ready for an ocean passage.

She was anchored off the old Aquatic Club so we checked in there for a few days. It was a wooden structure with balconies all around the second floor and a tiny elevator on the ocean side. There was just room in the elevator for two of us and a suitcase. To operate it, you pulled on a rope leading through the wood and wire cage, and lifted yourself to the second floor.

Our room was simple. A bed and a dresser. There was some sort of closet and a bath with tepid water. Over the bed was draped netting, hung from the ceiling and reaching to the floor. Just like the movies — with a huge four-bladed fan over the center of the room.

*The balcony overlooked the long, empty beach to the right and the
dining room, open to the elements, to the left. There we breakfasted
on flying fish, while a one-legged black bird begged for crumbs from
one table to the next.*

That was a long, hot, tiresome job. Working on the engine of a
sailboat, tucked away in the tight space beneath the cockpit, is
always difficult. But *Maribel* was rolling constantly. And working
aboard a rolling boat in the tropics is that much worse.

It had its lighter moments, however, for there were all kinds of
supplies aboard, carefully packed and labelled. In Swedish. We
would pick something, read the label and wonder what it was.
Grease, perhaps? Or maybe glue? Sometimes we guessed right. And
then again sometimes we did not.

Working in Barbados was interesting. It is different from the
other Caribbean islands, being low and sandy, and *Maribel* was
anchored in a beautiful, sweeping bay. To get ashore, we had to
row our dinghy to the steel pier at the Aquatic Club. There was a ladder down its side, but there was always a heavy swell there and if
you stepped onto the ladder from the bottom of a wave, the next
one would catch you before you could reach the top. So we would
wait until we were on the crest of a wave, then take a flying leap
for the ladder. After which, we would take the open-sided bus along
the shore to Bridgetown and search for the parts that we needed,
often finding them in unmarked buildings in back streets that you
would not think were shops at all.

*The motion of the boat at her anchor was violent enough to make
me sick. How the men were able to work on the engine, I'll never
know. My time, therefore, was spent running errands. There seemed
to be endless needs as each part of the boat was inspected and repairs were made, only to uncover more problems and make more
repairs. Within days we knew the entire stock of most of the hardware and ship's stores in Bridgetown and the local bus schedules.
It was hot and sticky and we always seemed laden with heavy purchases. I envied the tall, stately Barbados women who strolled calm-
ly through the crowds with huge crocks of cold fruit drinks on their
heads. They would reach into an apron pocket, locate a tiny paper
cup and without turning their eyes, press the spigot above their
foreheads. Out would pour the cool liquid — just the right amount.*

They would exchange the drink for the money, never looking at the coins. Change was made from another pocket, again without a glance at the results.

But basically *Maribel* was a fine yacht and eventually we had everything working. Then we got our clearances and sailed. It was a beautiful night with a gentle trade wind as the lights of the island fell astern, and when the dawn came up we were surprised to see that the forestay was coming apart.

Strands of the steel wire had broken in several places and were standing out in great loops. The stay was still holding but it might let go at any moment. Carefully we ran the boat off before the wind, taking most of the strain off the forestay and heading her toward the island of St. Lucia, about 100 miles away.

All through the day we sailed on, rolling before the wind, anxiously watching the stay. Every now and then, a strand would break in another place. We never saw one go but we would look up and there would be another loop. Still it held and soon after dark we picked up the lighthouse on St. Lucia. But we were not in yet. There are no ports on the bleak east coast of the island. We had to sail around to the other side and it was already daylight when we lowered our sails and motored into Castries Harbor.

St. Lucia is a high, mountainous island covered with dense jungle, and the port of Castries lies at the end of a deep, narrow inlet near its northern end. But just before Castries, in a small creek on the left, was Ganter's boat yard. There we tied up and after relaxing over a leisurely breakfast, took down the forestay. There was no way that it could be repaired. We would have to replace it. But soon we found out that there was no wire even close to the size that we needed on the island.

A feeling of hostility overwhelmed us in Castries. St. Lucia was less touristed than Barbados at that time. There were few white faces on the streets and the black faces seemed to show suspicion and dislike. Bridgetown was a busy port with many people going about their business. Castries seemed quiet and unhappy. There was little activity in the port and the streets were half empty. Entering the market with its long rows of fresh produce and dozens of tense, unfriendly stares, I quickly made a few purchases and left.

There was no chance of communication in the short time we spent in St. Lucia. I often wonder if things are better for the people on the island today.

After a day of fruitless searching, I asked Joe to have a go. He has a knack for these things. And before long he was back with a piece of steel cable. Cautiously I asked him where he found it.

"Oh, I hit up a freighter for a barrel lashing," he remarked cheerfully, laying it out on the dock.

It was long enough but far heavier than we needed. Still it was better than nothing and we set about making eye splices in it. That took some time, for there was no rigging vise available and neither Joe nor I had spliced a wire for years. But when it was done we had a forestay. It hung in a majestic curve and swung from side to side as the boat rolled but it was not about to let go.

The time had come to celebrate, so we sailed out of Castries Harbor and up the coast to tiny Pigeon Island. There, in the calm lagoon, the water was so clear that we could see every detail on the bottom. Palm trees lined the white sand beach and dense jungle rose steeply up behind it. And on the beach was a thatched hut where Josset Leigh ran a restaurant for passing yachtsmen.

She and her mother had come out 20 years before bringing with them clothes of that period, and it was not uncommon to find the older lady sipping tea in a long afternoon dress and a big, floppy hat. Then a rat would scurry along a beam overhead and quite casually she would reach for her .38 and take a shot at it.

There we anchored and took a whole day off, doing nothing but swim and eat and roam the island, climbing up to the lookout point where Admiral Rodney used to watch for the French fleet and back down to the hut on the beach for a dinner of freshly caught fish. Late into the evening we sat talking by lamplight, of other times and distant places. And I remember watching a small, brown mouse climb into my coffee cup, eat the sugar that I had left in the bottom of it, climb out and wander contentedly off.

But such moments can not last and the next morning we left, drifting out of the calm lagoon, picking up speed as our sails caught the morning breeze and heeling to the trade wind as we cleared the island, bound away north.

Josset was considered a strange one by the people of Castries. There was talk of asking her to leave Pigeon Island. She was a squatter after all. She had no real claim to the land.

But when she had first arrived, with her trunks of dresses and her silver tea set and stories of her days on the London stage with the d'Oyly Carte opera company, to set up a tiny restaurant on the uninhabited island, the local government had taken her quite seriously.

Things went well at first. People moved out to share the island with her, giving her labor to build her restaurant and bringing ashore the fish and shellfish for her to serve. A husband, known as Mr. Snowball, appeared and installed a lighting plant; for a while there were dim bulbs dangling from a wire hooked under the roof beams. But he left and with him went the dynamo, we're told. Josset said he was the only one who could ever make the thing run, so she returned to the old oil lamps and candles.

She had a small fleet of goats and a squadron of ducks. They would all march through the open ramada that served as her dining room, day and night. The ducks provided the eggs for breakfast and, according to Josset, boats from nearby Martinique would land in the night and carry off her goats. Pigeon Island goat became a Martinique specialty.

But now she had a theory that, of all things, submarines were using Pigeon Island as a refuelling stop. Old men had told her that the island covered huge, half-submerged caves; that there had been supplies carried through a tunnel into the caves during the years of wars between the British and French and Spanish. She said that from time to time she would hear engines running. Huge, massive engines. The island would tremble. But always at night, after everyone had left her, for the local people would no longer stay on the island through the night. Perhaps because they believed her stories, perhaps because they didn't.

We hiked through the hills that afternoon, climbing to the rocky top to gaze down at the other side of the island. All cliffs, falling straight down into the sea. There might be a landing spot you could not see. Or perhaps there was a pipe, led from underground fuel supplies to a calm patch near the cliffs. But certainly Josset believed it.

That evening, after our dinner of sea eggs and grouper, we sat under the oil lamps, sipping our coffee and watching the mice at play.

I heard a noise — or perhaps felt a vibration is a better description. It made me jump. Josset was looking at me. "You felt it too, didn't you?" she said. I had to agree. We listened but now we could hear nothing. It was as if an engine had started but so far away that you hear the sound for just an instant, then the throbbing blends into the sounds of the night. The others heard nothing.

Josset gave me a soursop as a parting present. It was a new fruit to me then and I can't remember seeing it since. I was told to wait until it was very soft and ripe, peel and mash it, and add a little sugar and canned milk. It was supposed to taste something like a sweet, soft sherbet.

I tucked it away in the galley and planned on serving it when the other fresh supplies had run out, as a sort of surprise treat. Unfortunately, seasickness overcame me, as usual. And good old Joe, my friend in need, took over the galley. He found a disgusting looking overripe fruit which he hurriedly tossed overboard.

Standing clear of the Leeward Islands, we carried a fair wind across the Caribbean Sea. By day *Maribel* would churn along at her best speed, the sun would glint off the breaking seas and great schools of flying fish would go by, five or 10 feet above the water. But at night the wind would ease a little, the motion of the boat would be more comfortable and we would sail serenely over the moonlit swells. In those conditions one person would be alone on watch, clad only in a swim suit, enjoying the cool night. And suddenly he would be hit by a flying fish.

You are sitting there, full of dinner and contentment, idly contemplating life as you steer by a convenient star, when you are hit in the back by a wet fish. Then there is a great banging and flapping as it tries to flip itself off the deck, back into the sea. The first time it happens, it is quite unnerving. But in the morning you may find three or four of them on the deck. They are about the size of a herring with long, fragile-looking wings like a dragonfly's. And fried, they make an excellent breakfast.

Not to be outdone, *Maribel* herself gave us a scare one night. She had an auxiliary engine for making electricity, tucked away in a lazarette just behind the cockpit. Once a day we would throw a switch and with a sputtering roar it would spring to life and do its duty. But otherwise it lay silent and inert in its locker. Until the great night.

Kent was on watch in the early hours of the morning, the sea had calmed down and we were creaking peacefully along when without the slightest warning, the engine cranked up. Kent went up several feet in a sitting position and by the time he recovered the rest of us were on deck, staring incredulously at the lazarette. Tentatively we tried the "Stop" button and sure enough it stopped. Then we peered around inside its locker with flashlights but we could not find anything wrong with it. For quite a while we sat around in the cockpit, expecting it to go off at any moment but it did not and one by one we went back to sleep.

Most of the actual work seemed to be done in port before we left and after we arrived. The time at sea was spent on endless watches, steering by the compass or the stars to a point clearly fixed in the navigator's imagination.

We were never out to win a race, just to arrive in good condition, in good time, with as little breakage as possible. So the tacks were long, the sail changes few.

Your world from the deck was completely circular. You felt like a Blue Plate Special, a bit undersized for the enormous circular plate surrounding you. You were essentially alone, small and insignificant. And most of us liked our time alone on watch. A ship charging across your plate of sea or a crew member playing a radio seemed to interfere and grate. It was a time to think and to wonder, a time of quiet.

Soon we passed the Dutch island of Saba and came up to the Anegada Passage that leads out of the Caribbean Sea, back into the Atlantic Ocean. Mr. Ahlen had asked us to stop at Bermuda and give *Maribel* a refit before going on to New York, so we took our departure from Sombrero lighthouse and laid our course toward Gibbs Hill lighthouse, about 900 miles ahead.

While sailing with Patrick I saw all sorts of places, from afar. He would point out some puffy clouds in the distance and say: "See those? They're the land clouds over Antigua. Now you've seen it."

For the next couple of days we were in the trade wind, churning along at a good speed, *Maribel's* bow wave wide and white on the deep blue water. Quite often a small school of porpoises would come over to play in that, so close to the boat that we could lean over and scratch their backs with a scrub brush, which they thought was great. Then we ran out of the steady wind, into the uncertain area of the Sargasso Sea.

But this time the wind did not leave us completely. Instead, it died down to a light breeze that kept us sailing steadily along, rising and dipping over the gentle swells. Then we were able to rig an awning over the cockpit to ward off the noonday sun and cruise along in the shade, peering out from under the canvas at the slowly undulating horizon. There was far less weed in the Sargasso than we had seen before, with large patches of clear blue water between islands of yellow weed, and one day when the wind was very light we decided to run the main engine for a while.

Being a diesel, it was economical of fuel and *Maribel* had good tankage, so that we could afford to use a little fuel to speed our progress across the Sargasso, but it did not work out that way.

For as the wind had fallen lighter, we had rigged more sails and exhausting the conventional ones, we had improvised. Wherever there was room to hang a piece of canvas, we hung one. There were spare jibs beneath the booms as watersails. The dinghy's tiny sail was flying from the mizzen head as a Chinese topsail. And everywhere you looked there were lines: sheets, guys and braces jury-rigged in all directions. So naturally the moment we started the engine, we picked up a line in the propeller.

That was stupid. We should have checked more carefully. But like actresses, such things will happen once in a while in the best families. Joe volunteered to go overside and clear it but the thin line was wound around the shaft several times, so tightly that our sharpest knife would not cut through it. Besides which, *Maribel* had a long, overhanging counter stern that kept banging down on the water as she pitched in the swells and threatened to crush his head if it caught him on the surface. So he came back aboard. And five minutes later we saw the sharks.

There must have been a dozen of them, searching around beneath the boat, gray and silent and deadly. Sharks have poor eyesight but a fantastic sense of smell that guides them toward food miles away. Evidently they picked up Joe's scent so far away that it took them several minutes to reach us. After watching them glide in and out of the shadow underneath the boat, we decided to sail on to Bermuda without the engine.

Joe and Kent would insist on swimming now and then. We trailed a line behind us, for the boat, in spite of the lack of wind, moved steadily ahead. You had to be a strong swimmer to stay near the hull. The sea would look calm but there was always the swell that carried the swimmers off. I usually stood watch for sharks. And sooner or later a fin would appear and all hands would return to the deck.

In fact it worked out all right, for the breeze soon picked up again and stayed with us, day after day. Until one night, just before dawn, we saw Gibbs Hill lighthouse dead ahead.

That is the perfect time to make a landfall. In the darkness of the night you can see the light 20 miles away and by the code of its flashes you can identify it. You know exactly where you are and can head straight for the harbor. Then you relax, waiting for the sun to come up, when there will be trees to look at and houses and beaches. Birds will range out from the shore. And as you get closer, there will be the half-forgotten smells of earth and grass. Perhaps a whiff of wood smoke. But this time we had an interruption. As we closed the island, a whale came clear out of the water ahead of us.

He was about 60 feet long and doubtless weighed more than our boat. When he breached, he went straight up into the air until his whole wide tail was clear of the water. For a second he hung there, then he fell back into the sea, sending up a column of water like a depth charge. He must have been nearly half a mile away but still it was an impressive sight. Then he did it again, perhaps a quarter of a mile away. And that was even more impressive. He was between us and the sea buoy, so we changed course to give him a wide berth. And the next day we were told he had gone mad and attacked a fish boat, the remains of which were for sale cheap.

Just past the sea buoy we took the channel into St. George's Harbor, losing our wind in the narrow cut but picking it up on the other side, and prepared to dock *Maribel* under sail.

The yacht space was on the inside of a long dock, close to the shore, that had a low fixed bridge from its far end to the bank. There was no room to turn around. We had to sail along, between the dock and the shore, find a space and stop. The wind was abeam, so first we stowed everything but the mainsail, then lowered that by degrees as we ran in, keeping just enough speed to control the boat. But there was no room for us, except at the far end, just before the bridge. Just beyond a speedboat that was moored alongside a fish boat.

Lowering the last of the mainsail, we drifted in. Kent got the fenders ready, Joe stood by with a line forward and June coiled a long one down on the deck aft, with its bitter end made fast. As I swung *Maribel* into position, Joe leaped off the bow to the dock while June jumped onto the speedboat, scrambled across the fish boat and took three turns of her line around the muzzle of a convenient cannon. And as she and Joe took up the strain, *Maribel* came to a stop, with several inches to spare between her bow and the bridge.

That afternoon Joe dove under the boat to clear the propeller while we waited for the customs and immigration people to come by and in the evening we went to the yacht club for a shower. But it was for men only. No women were allowed on the premises, let alone in the showers. So we stood guard at the bathroom door while June climbed in through the window, took her shower and climbed out again.

Motoring around the island the next morning inside the reef, we picked up a mooring off Darrell's boat yard, launched our dinghy and pushed off toward the shore. But we had forgotten the oars and it took us quite a while to get back to *Maribel* against the wind, paddling with our hands.

That sort of thing is quite common at the end of a long passage, though. For days and weeks on end you are slightly keyed up, watching over the boat and keeping her out of harm, constantly trying to forestall any possible dangers. Then you arrive, get her safely moored and relax. And you do curious things. I have seen someone come out of a boat's hatch at night, turn the wrong way and carefully step over the side into the water. But nobody seems to get hurt and it provides entertainment for one's friends.

The job of refitting *Maribel*, getting her back into first class shape, took three weeks. First of all, she had to be hauled out of the water, so that we could work on her bottom and topsides. But the only available marine railway was at Bert Darrell's yard and he had never slipped a boat quite that big before. In fact there was some doubt as to whether it could be done. But his calculations showed that if we went in at the very top of the tide, she would go on the cradle with two inches to spare, so we gave it a try.

As we eased into position, Bert ran into the water and disappeared underneath the boat. Then he surfaced, shouted something to his men and disappeared again. And so it went on for quite a while, with Bert diving like a duck all around us, as inch by inch they slid her into position. Then they started the winch and so slowly that you could hardly perceive it, *Maribel* rose up the steep track, to fetch up high out of the water, her bow almost over the road ahead.

And there she stayed while we helped Bert's men overhaul her, fixing and cleaning and painting until she was like new. We had to move ashore during that time and stayed at a guest house on the harbor nearby, commuting to work on the pedal-assisted motorcycles that they rent in Bermuda. All day we would work in the yard and in the evening we would ride around the beautiful island on the bikes or take the ferry boat that ran from Salt Kettle across the harbor to Hamilton.

Bert was a great man to work with and taught us many things. How to prepare wood for painting and how to cut a line. How to check a shaft and how to caulk a seam. But he had trouble finding men to work to his exacting standards. And he was often excited. One day we found him standing by the boat looking exasperated and asked him what was wrong. "You can't find a good man these days," he complained in a loud voice. "There was only one good man and they crucified Him."

Joe Cunningham was at Bert's yard, fixing up his 25-foot sailboat, on his way from England to Canada. During World War II he was a doctor in the British army and was in Scapa Flow when the German submarine fleet surrendered and put in there. For several days the ships were still under the command of their own officers and during that time, fire broke out aboard one of them. So Joe organized a rescue party, saving several lives, and the German commander pinned an Iron Cross on his chest. Which looked very fine on his British lieutenant's uniform until they took it away from him and gave him a British medal for it.

Joe Pelich, who was sailing with us, was also an ocean voyager, having sailed his 33-foot sloop *Festina* across the Atlantic Ocean from Denmark to Texas, and Bert Darrell was the champion sailor in Bermuda, so the company was good and the work went fast. Soon we had *Maribel* back in the water, looking like a brand new boat. And soon we were under way again, sailing down the long channel past the pink and white houses, around the island and out to sea.

We've sailed hundreds of miles with Joe Pelich. Whenever we were faced with an ocean passage, we would try to get Joe to join us. He grins and grumbles and plows ahead. No matter that it is 110 in the shade. If the generator has to be torn apart, there is no time like the present to do it and get it over with.

At sea he is exactly the same. When there is trouble, he is the first on deck. When the call goes out for help and he is in his bunk, there's no thought of shoes or foul weather gear. It's best to stand back and let Joe through the hatch, he's going to beat you there anyway.

And he never once complained about sailing with me and my sea-sickness. Whatever had to be done, he willingly did his share and more. For that kindness, I will always be grateful.

Bound away northwest for New York, you sail around the edge of the offlying reef and can see the breakers on it close beside you, long after the land has dropped out of sight astern. But as darkness fell, Gibbs Hill lighthouse started flashing away, bright and clear behind us and from it we took our departure as we settled down for the night.

The wind was light when we left but piped up steadily through the night. In the morning we took a reef in the mainsail and by that afternoon we were banging and bouncing along in a strong northeasterly wind under a clear blue sky. But *Maribel* was a powerful boat and we made good time for a couple of days until the wind veered into the southwest and fell light, leaving us rolling and slatting at the edge of the Gulf Stream.

The sky clouded over and stayed that way for days. The sea calmed down but the wind was fitful and irregular. We jogged along, trimming our sails to each new wind shift, clear across the Stream and out on the other side. And then we saw the lights.

Joe picked them up just after dark. Dozens of white lights, in no particular pattern, spread across the horizon ahead of us. Just like the shore lights of a village. But we were still at least a hundred miles from the nearest land. Or were we? As we sailed toward them, there were mutterings from the crew in the cockpit. About navigators who did not know where they were. But as we drew closer, the lights began to move, swaying and bobbing over the water. And finally we realized what they were: a large fleet of fishing boats, spread out over several square miles, working their gear with the aid of powerful lights.

Sailing through the fleet was interesting, for each boat was going around in its own complex pattern, unrelated to the others as far as we could see. We would steer for a gap between two boats and before we got there it would close up. But another gap would open beside it. And so it went on. With a great deal of second guessing, we wove our way through them and eventually they thinned out ahead of us until we were in the clear again.

But looking back, we were almost sad to see them drift away behind us. For five days we had seen no people, no life beyond our boat. Then for a few minutes there had been people all around us. We could see them working on the decks, moving around. Their engines rumbled and their gear splashed in the water. It had been like being in the middle of a community. But we had passed through and now we were on our own again. Alone on the dark sea.

Later that night we ran into fog and before dawn it was thick. Sailing along over the gentle swells, we first noticed the red and green of our running lights reflected in the mist. Turning on our lantern, we shone it ahead. The beam went out maybe 50 yards and came to a stop, as though cut off with a knife. Overhead it was the same. Perhaps thicker. We had a problem, for a wooden boat gives a very poor signal on a ship's radar. One that she might well fail to notice. And that close to New York, we could expect to meet a ship at any time. We got our fog horn ready and waited, listening.

Far in the distance there was a faint hissing noise. A watery noise, coming steadily closer. A noise just like the bow wave of an approaching ship. But there was no sound of her engines. We let off our horn and listened again. The hissing noise was still there, louder and closer. But still no engines. We tried again. Still no response and the noise getting closer. Much closer. With a rush it came right up to us and a huge school of porpoises, there must .have been hundreds of them, went bounding by us on either side.

As they left, the sound went with them and we relaxed a little. But it was not until well after daylight that the fog lifted and we could see the horizon again, maybe three miles away. And by then we were approaching our landfall.

The sky had been overcast for the past four days, so that I had not been able to get any sights. There were no electronic aids aboard. Our only means of knowing our position was my dead reckoning, which had been computed every four hours since before we had entered the Gulf Stream. The crew all sat around in the cockpit, as crews will when a landfall is due, making snide remarks. And showing proper confidence, the navigator retired to his bunk.

I was fairly sure that we were not more than a mile or two from my calculated position, so I did some figuring. The visibility was improving and was probably seven or eight miles. The coast just south of New York Harbor, which I had selected for the landfall, is low and sandy. From the deck, they would see it at three or four miles. But from higher up, they would see it much farther away. Glancing at my watch, I turned over in my bunk and called up the hatch: "If anyone cares to go up the mast, he will see New Jersey on the port bow."

There was a scrambling and rattling on deck. Various cries and shouts. Then loud mumblings in the cockpit. Some crews are never happy. But we had our landfall.

Closing the coast, we tried to start the main engine but the starter was stuck. So we sailed around behind Sandy Hook and anchored while we worked on it, staying there for the night and taking the fair tide through New York Harbor in the morning.

It was a fine, clear day as we passed through The Narrows, dodged the ferry boats beyond them and headed for Governor's Island. On our right rose the high, brick apartments of Brooklyn.

To our left, the older buildings of Staten Island stood out between the green trees on the rolling hills. Ahead was the Statue of Liberty and to her right were the tall buildings of downtown Manhattan. Ships lay at anchor, waiting for berths. Tugs fussed everywhere, some straining slowly along with great loads, others running free, pulling huge wakes. And in the water were logs and trash of all sizes. Railroad ties, barn doors, you name it and in a moment you will come to one. Joe climbed up and stood on the main boom to spot them as we threaded our way through them.

At Governor's Island we took the Buttermilk Channel to avoid the ferries at Battery Point that come bounding out of their holes like jackrabbits and go rushing off to Staten Island every few minutes. Then up the East River past the United Nations building.

We do not wear any flags at sea, since there is nobody to see them and they wear out quite fast in the wind. But going up the river we hoisted *Maribel*'s Swedish ensign. It must have been made for a fair-sized ship, judging by its size, and it caused quite a stir. A blonde girl started waving wildly from an apartment window and a large tug came thumping over. Close beside us, her captain leaned out of his pilot house and shouted "Fucking squarehead" at Joe. We really felt welcome in our old home town.

Leaving the city behind, we came to the Whitestone Bridge, which was being painted. Half a dozen men were standing on planks, high overhead, wielding brushes full of silver paint. And as we passed underneath them, they waved at us. With their brushes.

Down came the paint in a fine rain, catching *Maribel* from bow to stern, spotting everything, sails, decks, cabin top, with silver. Frantically we all rushed around with pieces of cloth, wiping it up. Then again with paint thinner. And by the time we got the last drop off, we were entering Glen Cove on Long Island, to dock at Fyffe's yacht yard.

Taking advantage of the fine weather, we dragged the bedding and sails ashore to dry while we cleaned and tidied everything below. Then we put the gear back aboard, scrubbed our way off the decks and stepped ashore, to go our separate ways home: Joe to Texas, Kent to Larchmont, June and I to New York. And waiting for the train, I finished writing up the log book, drawing a line across it and underneath that putting: Delivery Completed.

6   LY KOU

Later that summer, Henry Meneely called us from Annapolis. He
had just sold the 40-foot ketch *Ly Kou* to a client in Michigan
City, Indiana, and wanted her delivered out there. That meant
sailing the lengths of Lakes Erie, Huron and Michigan, clear into
the midwest of America, so June and I left the same afternoon.

*Patrick only seems to remember packing the bags for another
trip. He has forgotten that usually the brokers would put us on
standby. If they made a sale, if the owner wanted it, would we be
available and about when? Wish I had a record of all the jobs we
didn't do.*

Ly Kou had been built in Saigon and sailed from there to America. She was all teak, very heavily built but rather crude in her
finish. She had the basic sails (jib, staysail, mainsail and mizzen)
and a small diesel engine that gave her great range but not much
speed. In the flat calm water of Annapolis Harbor, she got up to
five knots, but going up Chesapeake Bay, with a smart breeze from
dead ahead, she slowed right down. Still it would not pay to sail
that boat to windward in narrow waters, so we stayed in the deep
channel while the tide was running our way and moved over
onto the flats, where the current is less strong, when it turned
against us.

The upper reaches of the Chesapeake are beautiful in the summer.
Well-kept farms lie amid tall trees on rolling hills that come to
a sudden stop at the water's edge, with a high bluff that drops

down to the sandy beach below. Fleets of white boats cruise slowly along, dragging for clams. Steadily the bay gets narrower until
you come to the Chesapeake & Delaware Canal.

That is an artificial cut some 15 miles long, a wide strip of
calm water with riprap along its edges. And behind that on each
side there is a steep bank, maybe 80 feet high, of brown earth.
Motoring along the canal, there is not much to look at. Until a
ship comes around the bend ahead of you.

Probably she is an ordinary freighter bound for Baltimore but
there in the canal, moving rapidly toward you, she looks very large
indeed. You scooch over to the bank to let her by, staying on the
inside of the curve in case her stern should swing out and her huge
propeller swat you like a bug. As she comes alongside, all that you
can see of her is a black steel wall, rising straight up out of the
water. Normally you never get that close to a ship, certainly not
to one under way, and you watch with fascination as she hisses
by, every weld in her plates clearly visible. Then if she is light, her
propeller comes chomping past you and you are left swirling in
her wake, back in the center of the canal.

*The channel through the canal is wide, so it pays to watch the
tree tops ahead of you. Often your first warning of a ship coming
around the bend is a glimpse of her upper decks and masts above
the trees.*

*Patrick thought the bridge tender was being too mean with the
electricity at the lift bridge. The current was swift and behind us,
so if Ly Kou's mast should touch, we could never stop in time to
save it. So he turned her around.*

*Now we went under the span backwards. But we were headed
forward through the water, against the current. So if our mast
should hit, we could go full ahead and stop. Of course, it didn't.
We had feet and feet of clearance. But looking at that massive span
of iron, you're sure you could reach up and touch it.*

But soon we were out of it and running down Delaware Bay,
a wide, desolate place with marshy banks, a line of buoys down
the channel and not much else. However, the wind was fair, so
we set the mizzen and staysail and made good time down to Cape
May Harbor, where we stopped for the night before running the
Jersey coast.

Leaving Cape May, the coast runs for about 120 miles, first northeast and then north to New York. It is low and sandy all the way, with only two good ports: Atlantic City and Manasquan Inlet. Running along the shore a couple of miles off the beach, there is little to do except count the water tanks of the resort towns, so we sailed through the night, taking turns napping below, and arrived off Sandy Hook the next morning.

Going through New York Harbor we took the North River, past the berths where the passenger liners lie, past the skyscrapers of Manhattan to starboard and the smoky commercial area to port, under the George Washington Bridge and off up the Hudson. With the three knot current in the river, we were making eight knots over the ground, while it was going our way, but when it turned against us, our speed fell to two knots. And so we went on, sometimes sweeping along in fine style, sometimes hardly moving, all the way to Troy.

The banks of the Hudson, from its wide mouth emptying into New York Harbor to its less majestic junction near Albany with the Mohawk River, are dotted with the remains of its nineteenth-century industrial greatness. Many of the old factories have been abandoned but some are still in use, looking very little different from the empty ones except for an occasional open window showing a face or two.

It was very hot and still the day we motored through Troy in Ly Kou. *Her forward motion gave us a slight reviving breeze as the channel led us close along the right bank with its endless rows of red brick factories backing to the water's edge. Passing one, we could hear the grinding machinery above* Ly Kou's *diesel. All of the old four-by-eight windows that would open were open and on the second floor a number of women appeared, waving as we passed under them.*

I returned their waves as one woman leaned over the sill and shouted: "Honey, you don't know how lucky you are."

The tide was high when we reached the Federal Lock and we only had to go up a few feet to the calm water of the canal beyond. But ahead, for the next 300 miles, were fixed bridges 15 feet above the water, so we pulled on to the commercial boat yard on the west bank to take out *Ly Kou's* masts.

Docking under the old steam crane, we undid the rigging while the yard's people made wooden horses and put them on deck. Then they lifted out the masts and laid them on the horses, with the heel of the mainmast forward and several feet of the mast sticking out at each end of the boat, over the water. After which, we filled 12 burlap bags with hay and hung them around the boat, to protect her as she went through the 36 locks ahead.

Locking up in a motor boat is quite easy but with a sailboat like *Ly Kou* it is another matter, for as the water comes into the lock, the strong currents catch her deep keel, pushing her hard this way and that. So you stand well apart, controlling her as she goes up by pulling on your lines and pushing with your feet, sometimes getting your backside against the cabin trunk and pushing with both feet to keep her out of trouble.

By the time we got through the first flight of five locks, we had really had enough exercise for the day. But *Ly Kou* was fine and off we went up the Mohawk River, relaxing on deck and enjoying the peace and quiet as we puttered slowly along through the pleasant farm country of upper New York State.

There were very few marinas of any kind on the Barge Canal in those days but plenty of terminals, long concrete walls with mooring bollards along them, built as unloading places for barges but hardly used any more. And there we tied up each night, walking ashore to a village when we were near one for groceries and newspapers.

We picked up a pigeon along the way. A messy guest he turned out to be and we finally had to ask him to leave but we couldn't just let him drown.

We were going under one of those old-fashioned arched bridges and on one wall was the pigeon, trying to fly up. He didn't seem to understand that arches curve and each time he attempted to go up, he would find himself flying backward and fall into the water.

Our wake was the last straw. By the time it passed over him, he was soaked and there was no hope of his being able to fly out. The current swept him gently down the river.

Patrick turned the boat back; we passed through the arch again. I could still see the pigeon's head. We swung around and came slowly up to it. Patrick held my ankles while I slipped head first over the rail and grasped the thing. And again we passed through the arch. This time to continue toward Buffalo.

Our guest showed no signs of life but we wrapped him in a towel and held him; soon he blinked and then he started twitching. The spasms lasted several hours but by nightfall his breathing was regular, so we gave him a warm corner and left the hatch open in case he wanted to fly home.

He didn't. He preferred to sit on a shelf and watch the world go by through a porthole.

We would put him ashore at night. Only to find him right where we'd left him in the morning. We pointed at other birds, we flapped our arms. He took no notice.

But it was quite clear by that time he was a perfectly normal pigeon. So stopping at a lock one sunny morning, we found a convenient tree near the quay and put him on a branch.

He just sat there, looking at us. And as we passed through the lock and out the other side he sat. Then quite suddenly he flapped his wings and flew away, back down the river.

Before dawn we would be under way again, gliding over the smooth, still water through patches of damp mist until the sun came up and dried things out, then taking it in turns to eat a leisurely breakfast in the cabin while the other steered. Soon we crossed beautiful Oneida Lake and came to Three River Point where the canal divides, one branch going down to Lake Ontario while the other, which we took, going past Rochester. And there the engine gave up.

It was cooled by sea water and had accumulated salt within its system that came loose in the fresh water of the canal, blocking it up. And it was a foreign diesel, so that it was hard to get anyone even to look at it. But eventually we got it fixed and continued on, past Lockport and down Tonowanda Creek into the Niagara River.

Chugging slowly up the river, with no sails to fall back on and lousy holding ground for the anchor, I fell to wondering what would happen if the engine quit again. We were barely making headway against the current and behind us, not far away, the water was thundering over Niagara Falls. But it kept going and at Buffalo we went to a ship yard to have *Ly Kou*'s masts put back in.

There June excelled herself. There was a Great Lakes steamer in the dock next to us with a badly bent rudder and she asked a man standing nearby how it happened. Patiently he explained to her that in turning around, the ship had backed into a stone wall.

"I wonder if they fired the captain for that little goof?" she asked with a bright smile.

"Madam, I am the captain," he replied stonily, "and I do not recall the company bringing any such matter to my attention."

At which point we sort of stood around on one foot until we could excuse ourselves and get out of there.

She has a knack for that sort of thing, though. The next day we were tidying up *Ly Kou* at the Buffalo Yacht Club when a man proudly asked her how she liked his new racing yacht. She took one look at it and said: "There's a cotter pin missing from your headstay." Which was quite true but rather slowed down the conversation, for there was a myth in those days that only men could understand the mysteries of boats.

Leaving Buffalo we sailed out onto Lake Erie, heading southwest toward Erie, Pennsylvania, about 90 miles away. It was calm but misty that day and the land soon fell away behind us, leaving us alone on the lake, motoring along with the sails hanging limp over our heads. It was a new experience for us to be on a lake as big as a small sea and it took a little getting used to. For we were out of sight of land, yet there was no swell and the water in those days was pure enough to drink. I dipped a cup over the side and tried it. It tasted fine. And the charts were different. The distances were in statute miles and there were references to curious items such as "cribs," that turned out to be square, docklike structures sticking a few feet out of the water that were used for various commercial purposes.

Navigation was simple because there were few offlying shoals or rocks, no rise and fall of tide and virtually no currents. And while it was calm, the lake was quite smooth. But obviously a body of water that size would build up a sea once the wind got up, and in those latitudes the weather would most likely change suddenly. So we had better keep an eye on the barometer.

During the afternoon several Great Lakes steamers came past us. They are quite unlike other ships, having blunt ends and parallel sides of a barge, and their deck layout is odd. The pilot house is right in the bow, so far that they have a sprit sticking out forward to show the helmsman which way he is going. Then there is an enormous hold, hundreds of feet long, and all the way aft are the engine room and the crew's quarters. There must be great numbers of them for as soon as it got dark we could see their lights, going along one after another, stretching as far as we could see in both directions. We counted 16 of them in sight at one time.

In the morning we were off Erie and were thinking of going on down the lake but the barometer was falling and the sky was dark in the west, so we decided to put into port. And as we motored across the wide harbor, a cold front moved in.

For a moment we remained in the sunlight under the clear blue sky, watching a line of dark gray clouds move toward us. Then there was a puff of cold wind, a pause and rapidly it rose to gale force. A wall of driving rain swept across the water and within minutes it was so dark that we could hardly see. Going around behind McAllister's boat yard we found a snug berth, sheltered by high buildings on all sides, and there we lay for two days until it blew over.

Ashore, we learned that the wind was reported to have gusted to 90 miles an hour. A good time to stay in port.

The next few days were fine, mostly calm but foggy in the mornings, and we made the 160 miles to South Bass Island without any trouble. But they have two kinds of fog there: ordinary fog and lake steam, which looks like thick, white fog but lies so low on the water that you can see over it if you climb up the mast.

The effect is weird. You are motoring along over flat calm water in fog so thick that you can barely see the bow of your boat. Then you start climbing and 10 or 12 feet up, you stick your head out into clear blue sky. The shore is plainly visible and a passing steamer glides by on a cloud of steam.

Approaching South Bass Island, we were baffled for a while by a tall lighthouse that did not seem to be on the chart. But going over the fine print, we found it: the Perry Monument, well over 100 feet high but not officially an Aid to Navigation. However the island itself was fun. Its only industry was making wine but they did not export much since they drank most of it. So they catered to the tourists who came from the mainland on a scheduled airline equipped with Ford Trimotors that came winging across the lake, low over the water, like giant pelicans.

The western end of Lake Erie, past the islands, is shallower than the rest of it and the next morning the water there was as calm as a millpond, stretching clear to the far horizon, mirroring the tiny wooded islets along the way to the Detroit River. But as we approached it, the steamer lanes fanned in on either side and before long we went running up the narrow river in heavy traffic.

We were told that the Detroit River carried more tonnage in the half year that it was open than the Panama and Suez canals combined did in a full year and it was certainly believable, for the big steamers were moving fast up and down the river, one close behind the next in each direction. And dotted over the water were hundreds of small outboard-engined pleasure boats, their owners placidly fishing. They did not seem to have the faintest inkling of what was going on around them, that a fast-moving ship simply could not turn or stop quickly enough to avoid them. Slowly they would troll across the channel, from one side to the other. Then, whenever the fancy took them, they would change course and go the other way. We asked if they ever got run over by ships and the answer was: "Yes, all the time."

This particular problem plagued us as the numbers of small boats increased in American waters. Few boatmen seemed to realize what a marked channel was for. Or perhaps they were unaware of the existence of a channel in the first place. Taking a deep-keeled boat through a narrow passage is nerve-wracking enough without the added danger of local day fishermen staking claims to the middle of the channel. They had some chance of survival with us but none with a good-sized ship.

Passing through Detroit, you cross shallow Lake St. Clair and continue up the St. Clair River. That is an interesting river with wooded banks and old houses along both sides but it was slow going for us, making a bare two knots against the swift current, and we were glad to get out of it, into Lake Huron.

Leaving Port Huron bound north, you pass one of the few black lightships in American waters. Nearly always they are red with white trim that gives them a jolly, Christmas-like air but in black they look somehow dowdy and even slightly ominous, which seems a pity. However, the lake itself is beautiful, with high bluffs along its western shore, and it was a pleasant run to the tiny port of Harbor Beach. But there our good weather ran out. Another cold front came through and we had to wait a day for it to pass over.

Most of the small ports on the Great Lakes are artificial and look like scaled down versions of big ones, complete with harbor walls and lighthouses and stone jetties, almost like gigantic toys. Such a port is Harbor Beach, but continuing up the lake we came to Presque Isle, which is quite different. There the coast line is low and rocky as you enter the narrow inlet that leads to a sheltered natural harbor surrounded by tall pine trees, with just a couple of houses on the shore and an old wharf on a sandy beach where you tie up. It was clear and cool as we took our stroll that night along a country lane lit by the stars, the only sounds those of the forest. But the next day, as we rounded into the Straits of Mackinaw, it turned cold and windy.

Day after day the wind blew at 30 to 40 miles an hour out of the west, sending a sea rolling through the straits that kept the ferry in port, and a steady current ran from Lake Michigan, eastward into Lake Huron. Nothing was going our way.

After a day of waiting in Cheboygan, we decided to have a go at getting through the straits. Motoring out of the harbor, we set the mizzen and staysail, sheeted them hard in, gave the engine full throttle and headed *Ly Kou* close into the wind. Heeling until her lee rail was under water, she went banging and bouncing along, drenching us in cold spray. But after tacking across to the other side and back, we found that our net gain was very little and it took us all day to make good 12 miles of westing.

There is a high bridge across the Straits of Mackinaw and we saw it for three days as we beat our way through. Gradually the wind eased and veered into the northwest, sending us scurrying down Lake Michigan toward Sturgeon Bay. And as it eased, it got even colder.

Coming on watch at midnight, I found June standing inside the hatch facing aft, looking rather fat for a 110 pounder. She was wearing two sweaters, her foul weather gear and my heavy duffel coat and had rigged lines from the tiller around the winches, with which she was steering from inside by reading the compass backward. But she had a point, for it was truly cold outside and even in daylight it was not a great deal better. But as we entered the harbor, the temperature rose sharply and ashore we found it warm and pleasant.

It was unbearably hot and sticky. After nearly freezing to death the night before, the shore heat was too much. We headed out on the lake as soon as possible.

The next day, the wind backed into the southwest as we had expected it to and gave us a good slant down the lake to Holland, Michigan, where *Ly Kou*'s new owners, Harry and Dora Panos, came aboard. It was a nice evening, so we went straight back out onto the lake and headed south along the eastern shore, showing them what we had learned about their new boat as we sailed along.

I grew up along Lake Michigan but had never, unless you count the excursion boat out of Silver Beach, sailed on it. But I knew the towns along the shore and it was fun to sail into the little harbors.

A town is so different when you arrive by sea. No endless highways, countless gas stations and hamburger stands, motels and discount houses. The water leads into a river or harbor, with green banks coming down to its edge. And you tie up to an old dock, close to the main street, where you can stroll in the evening, looking in the shop windows.

Ly Kou was the Panos's first large boat. We stayed with them for a day after we arrived in Michigan City, going over the routines for handling her in different situations, with Harry taking over my part while Dora took over June's. After which we went to June's home town of Benton Harbor, a few miles back up the lake, to see her folks before flying back to New York, with the Barge Canal and three of the Great Lakes added to the waters that we had sailed. We were beginning to know our business.

7   GOLDEN EYE

Next spring, I was making a routine delivery passage in a sailboat when we put into Manasquan Inlet and first saw *Golden Eye*. She was a 46 foot Consolidated motor boat with twin gasoline engines and had just been bought by a man from Bermuda who wanted to take her back under her own power. But his insurance company would not cover her for the trip and I entirely agreed with them.

For while the run to Bermuda at the proper time of the year is a routine one for an offshore sailboat, it is far beyond the capability of the average motor boat in the 40- to 60-foot class. They are simply not designed or built for that kind of service. They give their owners what they want: comfort and speed. But to achieve those ends, they sacrifice seaworthiness and range. They should not be expected to survive a storm at sea and even if they did, they would never get to Bermuda, which is about 750 nautical miles straight out to sea, wherever you start from.

If you look at the map, you can see why. The American coast from Cape Hatteras to Cape Cod closely follows an arc of a circle, with Bermuda at its center. So there is no way of beating the odds. You have a long passage to make across open water.

Which being so, I told him to put the thing on a ship and went on my way, feeling that I had done him a service. But a couple of weeks later I was in Manasquan with another boat and he was still there. His insurance company had said that if I would take her, they would cover her. Which was flattering, to be sure, but again

I told him to forget it. It was far too dangerous to make any sense. But foolishly I gave him my telephone number and he began calling quite frequently. The cost of loading her onto a ship, taking her to Bermuda and unloading her would be very high. There was also a duty of 15 percent payable if she arrived by ship but not if she came in on her own bottom. All of which added up to far more than he had expected to have to pay when he bought her, so I agreed to inspect her and see what could be done.

I urged Pat to try Golden Eye. *The passage revolved around weather and detail — two of his consuming interests. And I did think I would be permitted to sail with them. But it turned out that the owner had too many crew at the start and kept adding more daily.*

She was an elderly vessel but better built and with a more seaworthy type of hull than most current ones. Intended for sport fishing, she had a large cockpit aft that was a hazard, since a wave falling into it would dump tons of water into her, but that could be covered over. She would need a steadying sail, but again that would not be hard to rig and an old sail could be cut down to fit. She had two steering positions. The one in the saloon would be useless at sea but the flying bridge would be all right if we could stay on it when she started rolling.

For navigation she had virtually nothing that would be of any use at sea. Her radiotelephone would not reach the shore nor her depth sounder reach the bottom after the first few hours. The compass on the flying bridge, which we would have to steer by, was a tiny, unstable thing, scarcely any bigger or better than the kind that you see in automobiles, faded brown and hardly readable from long exposure to the sun.

Her engines were fairly new and seemed to be in good shape but her tanks only held enough fuel for 300 miles and how to carry more was the biggest problem. For as you add fuel, you add weight. Which slows you down, which increases your fuel consumption. And so on. But figuring carefully, I decided that we could get by with full tanks plus 1,000 gallons of extra gasoline. Next came the problem of where to stow it. Certainly it could not go in the cockpit, since that would make her squat down by the stern, which would slow her down, increase her fuel consumption and make her a sitting duck for a wave from astern. Nor could it go too far forward, for similar reasons. It would have to go amidships. But not too high up, for that would make her unstable. Which left only one place: the cabin.

So what would we carry it in? Not drums because they are liable to roll around, are awkward to stow and concentrate the weight too much. It would have to be in cans. But with gasoline we could not afford to have any leaks that would fill the boat with explosive vapor. So I specified the light, flimsy cans that came in cardboard outers. That way we could spot a leaker by the mark on the outer before we even stowed it in the boat.

Apart from the major items, we would need a decent set of tools to fix the engines with, a hand-operated bilge pump to back up the electric one and it would be nice to have a portable radio direction finder with which to locate Bermuda if the sky should cloud over and foil my sextant. And so it came to pass that all those things were obtained as I suggested, the insurance company gave its blessing and the owner got his crew together: a friend who was good at fixing engines and two native Bermudians, one of them a harbor pilot. *Golden Eye* was as ready to sail as she would ever be.

By then it was late June. The perfect time to make the passage was fast approaching, for the winter gales were over and the hurricane season had not yet started. Daily for almost two weeks I checked the weather map in the *New York Times* until I saw what I was waiting for: a large high pressure system drifting slowly across America from west to east. Alerting the owner, I gathered up my navigation gear (sextant, chronometer, tables, almanac, patent log and charts) and rushed down to the boat to help with the fuelling. Standing on the dock was a huge pile of brand new, empty cans. One by one we took them out of their cardboard outers, filled them with gas and put them back. Then we left them to stand on the dock overnight. And sure enough, in the morning there were the leakers, clearly labelled by the dark brown patches on the cardboard. There were only a few of them, so we discarded those and stowed the rest aboard *Golden Eye*, filling the cabin space about halfway up and putting the mattresses on top of the level pile of cans.

He's forgotten one item of navigation gear: his ditty bag. Where

Patrick went, so went his ditty bag. It contained everything you might possibly have forgotten. Broken pencils, safety pins, can openers, jack knives, bits of tarred twine, rubber bands and matches, aspirin, dividers, 3-in-1 oil, etcetera, etcetera. He couldn't spend a day at sea without rummaging through the ditty bag, let alone navigate to Bermuda.

Now we had a floating bomb on our hands, for in the confined, watertight space of a boat, gasoline vapor does not disperse or blow away as it does elsewhere. Instead it collects silently in remote corners and if you are careless it will blow up. So I threw all the matches that I could find overboard and told each member of the crew not to bring any aboard. There would be neither cooking nor smoking on this trip.

While we were working, a policeman came by. He had some time off due to him and his aunt lived in Bermuda. Maybe he could ride over with us and see her? The owner said yes and he was back within minutes in slacks and a sports shirt. Now we were six.

At noon I put in a last minute telephone call to the duty officer at the weather bureau, who confirmed that the leading edge of our high had arrived and should bring us two or three days of calm weather. Then we cranked up the engines and with a great deal of shouting and goodbyes to total strangers on the dock we pulled away, spun around and headed out to sea.

Outside the harbor we threaded our way through the crowd of small boats that were wallowing around trolling for fish, then eased the throttles open as the engines came up to their proper operating temperature and synchronized them carefully to spread the load evenly between them. After which I took a rough speed check. We were making less than 11 knots, as compared with the 16 knots that *Golden Eye* would normally have done at those revolutions. Still I was not surprised, with all that weight of fuel aboard. In fact, I expected her speed to increase steadily, throughout the passage, as the fuel was used up, which would make the navigation that much more interesting.

Meanwhile the low, sandy coast of New Jersey turned gray and faded into the misty horizon, leaving us alone on the ocean. It was a beautiful day but the sea had not been calm for long and there was still a gentle swell, over which we slowly pitched and rolled. On the flying bridge, the motion was more noticeable and felt as though you were riding a camel over an endless, rolling plain. But from below came the steady drone of the engines and for the time being, all was well. Except that there was nothing for the crew to do.

It is a common mistake of new owners to take too many people along on a passage and the snag is that in a motor boat there is no work to do. So they sit around, staring vacantly into space and getting in the way. Conditioned to driving a car, they all wanted to steer the boat but only a couple of them could hold a decent course and the best by far was the policeman. Hour after hour he would sit up there, large and placid, holding her as straight as you could wish. Until finally I asked him where he had learned to do it. I should have guessed. He had spent five years as a quartermaster in a destroyer. He just had not mentioned it before.

We had always sailed with a short crew and found it much more pleasant for all. It gave each of us plenty to do, so we were seldom bored. Pat taught me that if you weren't on watch or some other duty, you were to stay in your bunk, out of the way. Each person had a right to do his job in peace without spare people always underfoot, interrupting the routine. So our social calls on the helmsman, for example, were kept to a regulated minimum and became an event in the long hours. We would have pleasant chats and then be off about our business, leading separate lives in a space 40 by 8 by 7 feet.

He was also good at spotting logs in the water, which was a great help, since even at 11 knots, the impact of striking anything would be four times as great as it would be in a sailboat at half that speed and a sharp blow at the bow of a wooden boat like that could cause one or more planks to spring away from the stem, a condition that might be hard to fix before she sank. And well out to sea, there were great hunks of timber floating around, often nearly submerged and quite hard to find, even in broad daylight. I wondered how we were going to spot them in the dark.

But we were lucky. By the time the sun went down, our high had moved more overhead and it was flat calm. The smooth sea shone like dark metal in the starlight and the logs stood out as dead, black patches that were not hard to see after all. And so we went on, motoring straight away from the land, toward the distant island.

It was an unusual experience to be making that passage in a motor boat and I reviewed the hazards, trying to decide the best way of coping with each one, should it arise.

The key factor was the weather. According to my calculations, we were moving southeast at about 250 miles a day, while our high pressure system should be moving east at about 450 miles a day, which would give us three or possibly four days of calm weather. After that, conditions could easily arise that *Golden Eye* might be unable to cope with. So both those engines had better keep running steadily all the way, for any failure could cost us more time than our high would give us.

For the same reason, my navigation had better be exact. There would be no time to waste searching around for the island. Or fuel, for that matter. The fuel calculations were complicated by the constantly changing weight and speed, but in any case we would not have much to spare when we arrived off Bermuda and if the engines should go out of tune along the way, there might not be any.

Already they were burning around 16 gallons an hour and every four hours we were refuelling, taking cans of gas from the cabin, pouring it into the tanks and throwing the empty cans overboard. Which made a bit more space below and gave the crew something to do but spread sickly sweet fumes throughout the boat, for the air currents inside a boat at sea go from the stern toward the bow, carrying any fumes from the cockpit forward into the cabin space. And there are eddies that will take whiffs of gasoline vapor up to the flying bridge, to swirl around beneath the helmsman's feet a couple of times before blowing away. So it was a shock when I found a can of cigarette butts up there.

Some stupid idiot had been risking all our lives by smoking, for if his match had ignited those fumes, *Golden Eye* would have gone up in a pillar of flames within seconds, leaving nothing but a few charred remains of boat and men floating on the water.

For the better part of an hour, I made myself highly unpleasant and thereafter I found no more butts. However I would not have bet that he would not try it again, for the stubbornness of the truly stupid is beyond belief. So I did what I could to scare him by searching ostentatiously all around the boat every few hours for the rest of the trip, hoping to make him wait until he got ashore.

The second night was as calm as the first and we continued to make good progress but the next day there was a light breeze that kicked up a little chop, so that we started banging and rattling along like a streetcar and throwing up a little spray. Immediately the less experienced members of the crew began to show signs of nervousness and before long the owner started trying to call the Coast Guard on the radiotelephone. But he did not have the faintest hope of raising them or anyone else with that equipment from where we were, so I said nothing and after a while he gave up.

We were well past our point of no return and no longer had enough fuel to get back to America, so that there was nothing to be done but keep her going straight toward Bermuda. Already her speed had risen to 14 knots and I figured that if we did not break down or blow up, we should be there in the morning. But it was hard to convince the nervous ones to rely on the facts of meteorology and celestial navigation.

The lack of amenities aboard did not help. With no flames allowed, there could be no hot food to eat and no hot water in which to wash or shave. And after two days at sea, people who are not accustomed to such things begin to look rather second hand, hanging around unshaven, underfed, nervous and bored, obviously suffering from lack of sleep and possibly from constipation. But there is little that one can do for them until they see land ahead, at which moment their fears disappear and the problem is over.

We were too far from Bermuda to take an accurate bearing on the marine radio station with the direction finder but should be close enough to get a rough one on the broadcast station, so I turned it on. But the boat's electrical system was so poorly shielded that it was impossible to hear anything while the engines were running and I was loath to stop them for two reasons. First, one or the other might not start again. And second, it is well known that a high proportion of all engine fires and explosions occur during starting. So I put it away and went back to the old, reliable methods of navigation.

The sky had been clear all the way, so that I had been able to take a series of sights with the sextant that fixed our position, within three to five miles, twice a day. And in between those, there was my patent log whirring away in the cockpit, clocking off our miles run as its spinner went around in the water 70 feet behind us. The fixes confirmed what the log and the compass said and I was confident that I knew where we were. But I was less certain about the weather.

The breeze had been increasing all day and by nightfall there was enough of a sea running to make *Golden Eye* pitch and roll noticeably, while with her increased speed she was beginning to throw up a lot more spray. It was by no means dangerous yet but the barometer had begun to fall and if our high moved out faster than I had figured, we might be in for trouble before we reached Bermuda.

Fuelling that night presented problems, with the wind blowing the stream of gas away from the funnel and the spray threatening to get into it, the bouncing and swaying motion making it hard to hold the can steady or even to stand up in the wide cockpit. But it kept the crew occupied while the policeman and I took turns to steer the boat, careful to keep her exactly on her course.

By one o'clock in the morning we had less than a hundred miles to go and were making better than 15 knots. With the Bermuda pilot aboard, we were heading straight for the island, planning to save time by the highly unusual procedure of going in through a gap in the reef, rather than around by the channel. He assured me that he could do it and I had no doubt that he was right but it would make an exciting landfall after 750 miles, since we would hardly see the distant shore before we hit the reef.

By dawn we were within 40 miles of the island and 30 miles of the reef but the land clouds do not build up until later in the day and there was no sign of anything but endless ocean. The crew were all on deck, staring hopefully forward and sometimes one or the other of them would think that he saw land but it never was.

It was good to have them watching out, but in a case like that I rely on the instruments for the actual landfall. When the log said that we were 10 miles from the reef I began to look out and half an hour later the land appeared, hazy in the distance and slightly to starboard, where it should be. Almost immediately the color and motion of the water changed as we approached the reef, and cutting back the throttles for the first time since we left Manasquan, I handed *Golden Eye* over to the pilot.

He was a quiet, thoughtful man with a lifetime's experience in that harbor and it did not take him long to get his bearings and take us through the gap in the reef. And inside it, the water was calm, so we refuelled once more, throwing the last of the cans overboard as we rushed across the harbor at our full 16 knots to reach the dock at eight in the morning, two days and 19 hours out of America.

Looking back, I would certainly not try a stunt like that again, but it was interesting to have done it once, since few people ever have, and it was good to know it was safely over.

8   RIO PALMAR

I was about to step ashore from *Golden Eye* after our arrival in Bermuda when a man came looking for me. His company had a tugboat that was ready to leave for Miami but needed a navigator.

"Will you handle it for us?" he asked.

"Why not?" I answered and went to pack my gear.

Driving across the island to St. George's Harbor, he explained that the captains who worked around Bermuda did not need celestial navigation, since they never went that far afield and he had not been able to find anyone capable of doing the job. Then he heard on the radio that *Golden Eye* had been seen coming in from America and assumed that she must have a navigator aboard.

But when we got to his office, we found that the tugboat's captain did not want to sail to Miami in her, so he asked me if I would mind sailing as captain. Again I said "Why not?" for it was that sort of a day and he drove me to a lonely commercial dock.

"There she is, the *Rio Palmar*," he said as he drove away.

A large seagoing tugboat occupied the whole front of the dock, blocking out the view of the harbor ahead, and along one side lay a smaller one, maybe 50 feet long. That must be her. Though not much longer than *Golden Eye*, she was a far bigger boat and should make the passage easily. But there was no name on her and no one aboard, so I went over to the other one to enquire about her.

Strolling across the quiet dock in the morning sunshine, I ran my eye over the vessel ahead. Now there was a boat. She was probably less than 90 feet long but wide and high and built like a ship; she must have displaced three or four hundred tons. Even lying at rest, she was an impressive sight. Her main deck ran in a sweeping curve from her high bow to her low, flat stern. Then came a row of doorways through which you could see cooks and engineers and other people going about their business. High above on the boat deck was her pilot house, just forward of her great, black, smoke stack. And neatly painted on her life ring was the name *Rio Palmar*.

Hesitantly I went aboard her, up the steel ladder to the boat deck and forward to the captain's quarters, just abaft the pilot house. But he was expecting me and after showing me around my new home, he took me on a tour of the ship.

The doorways on the main deck led into the galley, dining room, engineers' cabin, crew's quarters, boatswain's store and the engine room, which extended below to take up a large part of the hull. Looking across, we could see the big main engine, a couple of stories high, with a walkway halfway up it. And down below were three smaller diesels for making electricity and compressing air, plus various items of auxiliary equipment. But none of that was any problem of mine, for the chief engineer who had been with her for 12 years was staying on for the passage, so we exchanged polite greetings and I retired from his domain.

The rest of the space in the hull was taken up with tankage and stowage, so we went back to the boat deck to discuss the crew. The two engineers and the cook were good men on whom I could rely but the other five were inexperienced hands that the company had hired for the passage and would have to be looked after. The Chief had taken the best one as his oiler, so I made the next best one the mate in the hope that he might be able to teach the rest something.

Then we went forward into the big, semicircular pilot house to go over the controls. Amidships was a large brass wheel, useful for steering at sea but too slow for maneuvering, so we declutched that and tried out the electric system. There were three control stations, one amidships and one at each side, where there were small levers that controlled the steering motor. When you moved one of them to the left or right, the rudder would go rattling across but the rudder position indicator did not work, so that the only way you could tell where it was, was by keeping track of the nut in the middle of the wheel as it went back and forth, counting the turns each way.

Below each lever were a brass ring and a thing like an umbrella handle. When you pulled the ring up, it fired off a whistle in the engine room, while the other thing did nothing on the up stroke but clanged a huge gong when you let it go. The whistle was for preliminary warnings and speed signals, while the gong was to start or stop the engine.

If the engine was stopped, one gong meant "go ahead." But if it was already going ahead, one gong meant "stop." If it was stopped, two gongs meant "go astern." But if it was going astern, two gongs meant "stop, then go ahead." The warning signal was three short blasts on the whistle, before the gong, and meant "stand by." But after the gong, that would mean "full speed," while two blasts would mean "half speed" and one would mean "slow." But the Chief did not like running his main engine slowly and would give you half speed for that. So if you really did want slow speed, you had to make it a long, drawn-out whistle. Which meant that the signal for "slow ahead" from "stop" was three short whistles, one gong and a long, drawn-out whistle.

The visibility ahead and to the sides was fine but astern you could only see the ship as far as the end of the boat deck, which hid the rest of her. There was a compass and an engine revolution indicator but no other instruments. "And that's about it," the captain said. "I'm going ashore now but I'll be back later to take her out and show you how she handles."

A few minutes later, I was unpacking my gear when I heard a shout. Going on deck, I saw a Coast Guard cutter steaming slowly toward us, while close alongside us was one of her boats, manned by six men in life jackets. We were in her berth and must leave immediately.

Leaning over the rail, I called down to a passing deckhand: "Please ask the Chief to stand by his main engine." Then: "Mr. Mate, take in all your lines, please. Smartly, now. And send me a hand to the pilot house." Then I went inside to center the rudder.

By the time the crew had the lines aboard, the deckhand was back to say that the Chief was ready. I gave the ritual three blasts on the engine room whistle, pulled up the gong handle and let it go. Immediately there was a small explosion, a puff of black smoke from the stack and a loud rumbling noise. *Rio Palmar* surged forward and before I could complete my signal she was going flat out across the harbor.

A tugboat like that has a very large propeller and when she is not towing anything, it hardly slips at all. It only took a few seconds for the engine to get up to its full 320 RPM and in the same time we went from a standing start to nine knots. Again I pulled the handle and let it go. There was silence, for the engine did not have a clutch; when you rang down for "stop," the engineer literally stopped it.

Then I tried again, giving the long, drawn-out plea for slow speed on the engine room whistle and sure enough we went off at a more leisurely pace, looking for a vacant berth.

It did not take long to find one but I was still unsure of the signals, so I took her around to windward of it, stopped the engine and sailed her in on the breeze, bringing her to a gentle stop alongside the dock. Which was unconventional but effective. Then I went and had a chat with the Chief, to return with a large piece of cardboard on which he had written all the signals.

In the pilot house I found the man from the company. He had arranged for *Rio Palmar* to fuel at a dock a few miles down the coast. Her old captain was busy and I should take her over there right away. So off we went, thumping down the channel with a man at the wheel and another on lookout, while I considered the best way to approach the fuel dock. But in fact it was not difficult and once she was secured the Chief took charge, putting sixteen thousand gallons of fuel into her various tanks.

Back in St. George's Harbor, I was able to get the charts that I needed for the passage but not one of Miami Harbor, so I sought out my friend from the company and he said he would arrange for us to have a pilot there. Then he mentioned that after Miami, *Rio Palmar* had to go to Havana, Cuba, to pick up a barge and tow it to Maracaibo, Venezuela. Perhaps I would like to take her all the way?

Of course I would but it occurred to me that I had no license to handle a ship of that size. However, he took care of that, giving me a large bag of assorted flags and an impressive document that turned out to be her Carpenter's Certificate. Meanwhile strange men kept appearing with great cases of food.

It's hard to imagine someone like Patrick ignoring the fact that he held no license to operate a tug. The temptation of skippering a tugboat must have been too much for him to resist.

Late in the afternoon everything was ready and the old captain came aboard to take *Rio Palmar* for a farewell trip around the harbor, gave me some tips on how she handled and brought her to a dead stop with her bow two feet from the concrete wall in front of his house. Stepping ashore, he waved us goodbye, and very carefully I gave the signal for "slow astern." It was right the first time, which was a good thing in the circumstances and the next signal of "full ahead" sent us on our way to Miami.

It was still quite calm as we drew clear of Bermuda and settled down on our southwesterly heading, making a steady nine knots with very little motion. If you watched closely, you could make out a gentle heaving and rolling but it was not obvious. The ship throbbed with the steady beat of her main engine, a wisp of smoke came from her stack and the white foam of her bow wave hissed along her sides, to go trailing out astern.

At sunset I checked the running lights, made sure that everything was secure on the boat deck and took a tour of the ship. In the pilot house, two deckhands were taking turns to steer and keep a lookout. Below, the cook was clattering in his galley, while the men off duty rested in their bunks. And below again, the Chief was fussing with his engines. Back in my cabin, I wrote up the log book and checked our schedule. With about 950 miles to go, we should be in Miami in five days.

That kind of travelling was quite different from making an ocean passage in a small boat, for with all that power to spare, we could expect to maintain our speed in almost any weather. On a passage of that length in a small boat, you could not be sure when you would arrive at your destination, within a day or two, but now I could figure it to within a couple of hours.

Pat kept detailed logs, making entries every four hours under way, more frequently when things weren't going quite right. A wind shift, a course change, the least action caused him to pencil in a few remarks. We seldom referred to them after a passage and within a week or two the notes would be illegible even to us. But while under way, they gave him the weather patterns, the sea changes and all the tiny details that enabled him to call the shots.

By the time I had finished, it was fully dark. In the pilot house, the red glow of the compass was reflected in the helmsman's face and glinted off the windows here and there, while outside you could see far across the starlit sea. But everywhere else in the ship, including the main deck, was so brightly lit that you could hardly see more than a few yards into the darkness. In fact *Rio Palmar* felt more like a power station in a lonely marsh than a vessel at sea.

The next day I was chatting with the Chief and wondered how he had got into his profession. He said that he had always liked working with engines, especially big ones and had thought of getting a job in a power station. But then he decided that it would be more interesting to work in something that moved around, so he had gone into tugboats and spent a lifetime doing what he enjoyed most. A sensible and happy man.

That was a beautiful day, with a light southeasterly wind and small cumulus clouds dotted across the blue sky and it was a new experience to take the noon sight from the gently rolling boat deck, with a clear view and a clean horizon, so I took several and noted that they came out within a mile or two of each other. But when I plotted our position on the chart, it did not agree with my dead reckoning. Something was wrong.

Going over my figures, I could not find any mistakes. The compass must be wrong. On second thought, that was quite possible, since the previous captain hardly had any reason to use it, working around the harbor he knew so well, and the magnetic fields in a steel ship change in the course of time. He said it was correct but he might not have checked it for years.

Anyway we were far from land, with nothing to run into for hundreds of miles, so I gave the helmsman a new course and the next day we were back on our rhumb line. Now I knew how much to allow for the compass's error on that heading. But how would it be on other headings? Probably it would be quite different.

Approaching Miami from the northeast, you have to go around the shoals north of the Bahamas before turning south to run down between the islands themselves and the mainland of Florida. But the shoals are very poorly marked and strong currents sweep onto them with the flood tide, so I took *Rio Palmar* well to the north of them, planning to make a turn at a calculated position in the middle of nowhere and close the coast off Palm Beach, Florida.

Shortly after midnight on the fourth day out of Bermuda, I went forward to the pilot house and prepared to make the turn. But searching in the darkness toward the shoals, I found a red flashing light that was not shown anywhere on the chart.

That is the sort of thing that gives navigators their handsome gray hairs, for you can never be quite sure whether you have somehow drifted off your course and are about to come to a grinding and ignominious halt on a reef, or whether somebody forgot to tell the survey people he had just put up a new lighthouse.

With instruments it would have been easy. If the ship had been equipped with radar, loran, a radio direction finder and an echo sounder, or even with a couple of those items, it would have been a routine job to verify her position. But *Rio Palmar* had none of those luxuries, so I rang down for "stop" and let her drift while the mate sounded with the lead line. However, he found no bottom, and when in doubt it is always safest to trust to your calculations, so I resumed full speed on the new course and soon after dawn we closed the coast, right off the prominent hotels of Palm Beach.

Running down the coast of Florida, we stayed close in to avoid the worst of the foul current and had a good view of the shore as we passed Fort Lauderdale and Miami Beach and brought up off the entrance to Miami Harbor, where our pilot came aboard.

So far, so good. He would take her into the harbor. But it is the Master's job to dock her and I was wondering how to turn her round in the narrow space between the piers when he came over.

"You know," he said, "I ran one of these boats for 20 years. It's good to handle one again. Would you mind if I docked her?"

"Of course not," I replied politely. "Be my guest." And stood by, watching how he did it, which turned out to be quite simple.

You come up to the dock, have the mate toss a line over a bollard and make it fast at the bow. Then you put the rudder hard over and ring down for "slow ahead." Gently her stern will swing around, until she is facing the other way. And so we arrived, exactly on schedule.

For several days we stayed in Miami, equipping *Rio Palmar* for her new job in the offshore oil fields of Lake Maracaibo. Taking aboard a thousand feet of towing cable was easy but the spare propeller and shaft were another matter, for they were so heavy that we had to back her under a crane to load them. June flew down from New York and was aboard when we went out to correct the compass, by which time I was getting used to handling the vessel. In fact it is not difficult, since a tugboat has a huge steel rubbing strake all around her and a fender on her bow. So you can just bang into a dock, watch it go back a few inches and throw a line ashore before she drifts away. But emotionally that is hard to do if you are accustomed to handling fine yachts with expensive, unprotected paint jobs and I was inclined to be more gentle.

However, you can not get too fancy, for each time you go from ahead to astern, or vice versa, the engineer has to stop his main engine and start it up in the other direction, which he does by turning it over with compressed air. But he only has a limited supply of air on hand, so that you could run out of starts.

Miami in August is not my favorite spot. The heat was over-powering. But Pat seemed unaware of the discomforts. He was en-raptured with his tugboat.

Inquiring around the town, I found out about the red flashing light that I had seen north of the Bahamas. Apparently there was a new installation there belonging to the United States government which was a great secret, so they would not allow the Bahamians to put it on their charts. But they did not want anyone to run into it in the night, so they compromised by putting a red light on it that could be seen for 10 miles.

Meanwhile the company's agent sent aboard all kinds of useful things, like two cases of cigarettes for bribes. They were not called that but if you forgot to give each official in some ports his carton of cigarettes, he would remember a regulation under which you had to pay a fine. So you took plenty of cigarettes with you and gave them out to everyone who looked as though he might possibly be some sort of official.

As soon as the last items were stowed aboard, we sailed for Havana, leaving in the evening and arriving in the morning of the second day. The first night was exciting, running down past the Florida Keys, dodging the fast-moving ships that were riding the Gulf Stream in the opposite direction, often three or four abreast. But the next night I got some sleep and was in good shape to cope with the officials when we steamed into Havana.

Our anchor was hardly down when the visits started. One after another, officials by the boatload would come, imperiously demanding to see our papers and rudely poking around the ship, in spite of the fact that we had merely come to pick up the barge and did not even want to dock the tug. With each one, I followed the same routine: the polite greeting, the formal presentation of the Carpenter's Certificate and the discreet transfer of a carton of cigarettes. A few of them tried to read the certificate but it was in English and they soon gave up on that. I forget what flag we were wearing that day, possibly Liberian, but it tended to add to their confusion and it was the cigarettes they were really after. Once they got those, they began beating a honking retreat like ganders in a farm yard and by evening they were all gone.

Havana in those days was a colorful city and armed with visitor's permits provided by the agent, most of the crew went ashore to watch a character billed as Superman perform with two women, while I dropped into the yacht club for dinner. The next morning we picked up the barge.

She was lying to a mooring across the harbor, so we took *Rio Palmar* alongside her and went aboard to inspect her. My first impression was that you could easily have landed a light airplane on her in a decent breeze, for she was about 40 feet wide and very long indeed, with nothing on her flat deck but a couple of towing bollards all the way forward and a few cleats along the sides. She was rectangular in shape, with swim ends (a bow and stern that curve up out of the water), and painted dull red all over, with her name *Monongahela* in white near her bow. But that was hard to pronounce, so we decided to call her The Barge.

We already had a steel bridle prepared, to go from the bollards to the towing cable, and it did not take long to hook those up, cast off the mooring and get under way, using a short length of cable in the harbor but paying it out to 700 feet as we headed east along the north coast of Cuba toward the Old Bahama Channel that runs between Cuba and the Bahamas.

The trade wind blows constantly from the east there, sending quite a heavy sea running up the channel, so we had to keep our speed down; otherwise the barge would pound her great flat bow into the seas and spring a leak. I asked the Chief to run his main engine as slowly as he could and he kept it down to 140 or 150 RPM, which with the barge in tow gave us about three and a half knots through the water, but there was a westerly current of half a knot, so that our speed over the bottom was around four knots.

Day after day we jogged along, *Rio Palmar*'s bow gently rising and dipping, while the barge slithered along behind us, too long and flat to rise over the waves and pushing her way straight through them. With offlying shoals on either side, we stayed well out in the channel and saw little of the coast, but once in a while we would pass a lighthouse, perched on a lonely rock along the way.

There was no one aboard the barge and I kept our big searchlight aimed aft toward her, switching it on every few hours through the night to see how she was doing. But she was a long way back and all I could see was her bow, splashing along behind us, until we were nearly a week out of Havana and approaching the eastern end of Cuba. Then I turned it on as usual and went out onto the boat deck to see the whole length of her side, lying across our wake. For a moment I thought the towing cable had parted but we had been careful to use chafing gear and it was still holding. Then she swung slowly around until I could see the whole of her other side, slithering crabwise through the water. And examining her closely, I could see that she was slightly down by the bow. Evidently she had sprung a leak in her forward compartment.

Obviously we could not tow her across the Caribbean Sea like that, so I decided to take her into port and get a welder to fix the leak. There were no detailed charts of that coast aboard but not far ahead was the Bahia de Nipe and as soon as it was fully daylight we headed in there.

That is a large harbor, maybe 15 miles long by five miles wide, but it has a narrow entrance with a dog-leg in it, so that as you approach, it looks no more than a deep bay. It was calm under the lee of the high bluffs and there I had the mate let go the towing cable to set the barge adrift, while I took *Rio Palmar* around to come alongside her. Then after taking aboard the cable, we set off again, pushing the barge stern first.

The mate was at the wheel but after a few minutes he asked me to take over, since she was hard to steer that way and none of the crew understood how to operate the electric system. I had no chart to look at anyway, so I might as well steer as stand and worry while we ran deep into the narrow bay, looking for the entrance. But just as we were about to run up on the beach ahead, it opened up to starboard and two sharp turns took us into the wide, protected harbor where we found two pilot boats.

Both came alongside and both pilots came aboard, making it clear in Spanish that since we were two vessels, we must hire two pilots. But there are two ports in the bay and the barge's pilot wanted to take us to one, while *Rio Palmar*'s pilot preferred the other, so I gave each of them two cartons of cigarettes and they agreed that, provided we paid for two pilots, we need only go one way. And so we steamed down to Antilla, where we pushed the barge's bow gently up onto a sandy beach.

But the job of repairing her turned out to be more difficult than we had anticipated, since she was very old and had sprung a series of leaks in different places. Clearly it would be several days before she was ready. And that evening, Fidel Castro's men came down out of the hills. The Revolution had started.

Immediately the whole crew left and as soon as I noticed that they were gone, I went looking for them. Antilla was more like a small farm town than a port and walking down the main street, I could hear rifle fire in the distance but otherwise things were quiet. The dust crunched under foot and a few people stood in doorways looking apprehensive. And at the bus station I found the crew, waiting for the next bus to Havana.

Sitting down with them, I ordered coffee and began telling them the best way to avoid bullets in a bus, which seemed to impress them somewhat. Then I mentioned casually that I was going back aboard *Rio Palmar*, whose sides were made of nice, thick iron and quite bullet proof. After which I left, wishing them good luck and hoping that they would survive the trip to Havana. And before long they were all back aboard.

The telephone system was still working, so I called the company to give them the news and they agreed that it would be best to get *Rio Palmar* out of there, in case she should be seized, and leave the barge behind to be picked up when the political situation improved. Without further ado, we left.

Running light, we made good time down the coast past Cape Maisi and soon we were out of Cuban waters, steaming south toward Cape Dame Marie at the western end of Haiti. As the sun came up, the high mountains on the cape appeared ahead of us and at breakfast time we were skirting around them, to head southeastward across the Caribbean Sea. The barometer was falling and the sky did not look too good.

But then it was August. The hurricane season had started. And the early ones frequently form in the Caribbean. The wind was more from the east than the northeast and stronger than the usual trade wind, building a sea that made *Rio Palmar* pitch and roll appreciably. I had the mate close the half doors on the main deck and showed him how to rig life lines between the bitts, to prevent the crew from being washed overboard if it got really rough. Then I went and read the barometer again. When I tapped it, the needle moved back a fraction more.

The winds around a hurricane rotate anticlockwise, viewed from above, so the storm must be making up to the south of us. And they generally move off to the west before turning into the northwest, in which case we would go through its tail. They are highly unpredictable and if this one should decide to move north, we would be in trouble.

A vessel like the *Rio Palmar* has an easy motion in light or moderate weather but in a very rough sea, she may heel to the point where she can no longer right herself. In fact, I was told that one of her sister ships rolled over and sank with all hands in a gale off Bermuda not long before. And we could not get any weather information on the radio, so I would have to estimate the progress of the storm from the changes in the wind's direction and force, from the look of the sky and the state of the sea.

In a case like that, you play the odds. I laid our course for the island of Aruba, which would give us a good landfall by day or by night and take us a little farther to the west of the storm, figuring that by the time we headed southwest for Maracaibo, it would have moved out of the area. And after making sure that everything was secure, I went to get some sleep.

There were no stars that night but you could tell from *Rio Palmar*'s motion that it was getting steadily rougher and by dawn she was plowing into quite a heavy sea, once in a while throwing spray up to the windows of the pilot house. The barometer had gone down farther and the wind had shifted to the south of east, which meant that the center of the storm had moved slightly to the west as it deepened. The sky was overcast and confirmed that estimate, so it would be best to keep her going the way she was, as long as we could, to get around behind the storm.

With the sea on her port bow, she was not likely to turn over but she was rolling enough to throw a man overboard if he was not careful, so I had the mate bring a couple of mattresses up to the pilot house and for the next two days, he and the deckhands slept there between watches, while the Chief and his men stayed down in the engine room. The ladder from the boat deck down to the main deck was close to the galley door, so that we could climb down and take food passed out by the cook, while they lived on cans of soup, heated on the engine manifolds: But we did not hear about that until later, since we had no way of speaking with them.

All through that day and halfway through the night, the barometer went down, while the wind and sea increased until *Rio Palmar* was throwing sheets of spray clear over her pilot house that glistened red and green in her running lights as it went by, and when it was light enough to see again, the world outside was a gray and ugly place, quite unsuitable for people or boats. But the barometer had started up and the wind had gone into the southeast, meaning that the center of the storm was still moving to the west, while we were in no immediate danger of rolling over on our present course. And though the ship looked like a half tide rock, she was not pounding at all and her great propeller was thrusting her steadily to windward.

In the pilot house, one unshaven man braced himself at the wheel, while another clung by a window, peering listlessly ahead and the rest lay wedged in corners on the floor, trying in vain to get some sleep. We had news of the cook from time to time but we had no way of knowing how things were in the engine room, except that the main engine kept running steadily, without ever missing a beat and we had to assume that the Chief had things under control down there. Meanwhile I stood in the pilot house, drawing diagrams in the condensation inside the windows, figuring the progress of the storm.

As always happens, the wind continued to increase after the barometer started rising and it took the sea about five hours to adjust to the wind, so that the sea condition was worse during the afternoon, but the barometer kept going up and by nightfall the weather was showing signs of easing. The storm must be moving out of the area, as I had hoped. Now I could start worrying about our landfall on Aruba.

For the past two days I had been navigating by dead reckoning, which relied upon the accuracy of the ship's compass and of my patent log, of the helmsman's steering and of my estimates of the currents in the Caribbean during the storm. In those conditions, it would be possible to be out by five percent of the distance that we had travelled since our last fix. And by the time that we got to Aruba, that would be over 25 miles.

But just before dawn I saw a few stars and in the morning there were gaps in the clouds through which I was able to take the altitude of the sun. By noon we had a solid fix and with a slight correction in our course we brought the island up out of the sea in the early afternoon, low and sandy, with silver oil tanks among the green trees along its western shore and a white lighthouse at the end of it.

It was calmer under the lee of the land and we had an easy run through the night down the Gulf of Venezuela. The engineers came up on deck, looking tired but happy. Everyone had a good hot meal and went back to his own quarters. And in the morning we picked up a pilot who took us up the long, winding estuary to anchor off Maracaibo.

When the last of the officials got their cigarettes and finally departed, they left behind an armed guard to watch over *Rio Palmar*, while we cleaned her up and went ashore to the airport. And after seeing the crew off to Bermuda, I took the next flight to New York. But I had left America for Bermuda, where I did not need any documents and when I stepped out of the Venezuelan airplane, the immigration officer was doubtful about letting me in. So I showed him the charts, on which I had plotted all our travels and took him outside to show how the sextant worked. And eventually he said: "You're okay. Go on home." It was nice to be back in civilization.

Over dinner that night, June brought me up to date on the business. My next assignment was to take a 16 foot sailboat 25 miles down Long Island Sound the following day. But a job was a job and you took them as they came.

9   PEACE & PLENTY

That winter we set up an office in Mamaroneck, near New York City, and the next summer we had enough jobs to keep two or three teams busy. I still spent most of my time at sea while June ran the office, but occasionally we would leave one of our skippers in charge of it and go on a trip together. So when Hank Meneely had a 54-foot motor boat called *Peace & Plenty* to come up from Miami to Annapolis, we flew down together.

After so much sailing, it was very difficult to stay at home and mind the office. We both realized that one of us had to remain behind if we were ever to build a business out of a skipper and wife team. But time and again, I would revolt and demand a little bit more sea time. It was very hard to stay behind month after month.

She was a comfortable old boat but built of steel and rather heavy, so that her twin diesels only gave her about nine knots through the Intracoastal Waterway and we had plenty of time to look around us. The first part, as far as Fort Lauderdale, was mostly docks even in those days and we had hardly gone two miles when we saw a motor boat catch fire.

Evidently she was fuelling, for she was lying at a gas dock as we approached and we thought that we saw a flash of yellow in her cabin. But we could not be sure in the sunlight and we had almost decided that it was a reflection when there was a dull thud and flames came out of her cabin windows, rapidly spreading into a wide column of fire, fully 60 feet high. However, there were plenty of people around to take care of her, so we continued on our way and lost sight of her around the next bend.

A few miles farther along, we heard a loud noise and came to some hydroplanes that were racing around an oval course beside the waterway. They looked very unstable as they skittered around the corners, barely touching the water and as we passed, one of them went out of control, flipped end over end and disappeared in a cloud of spray. As it cleared, we could see the driver in the water, with two rescue boats moving rapidly toward him, so we left them to handle the situation.

But as we left Fort Lauderdale, two young women came past us in a speedboat, curved across our bow, ran into the concrete wall on the other side of the channel, bounced back and sank right in front of us. So I stopped the boat, cut her engines to make sure that her propellers were not turning, and let her drift between them, while June fished one out on her side and I pulled the other out on mine. The whole thing took no more than two minutes and we put them ashore unharmed at the next dock.

My young lady insisted on rescuing her handbag. I was having great trouble holding on to her over the high sides of Peace & Plenty *and was terrified that I'd lose her or she would somehow get caught and be dragged under the hull. But all that really mattered to her was the handbag.*

For the rest of the afternoon we ran up the narrow channel through the mangrove swamps and just after dark we were steaming up Lake Worth when we saw a dim light, low on the water ahead of us. Slowing right down, we came to a family in an outboard boat that had run out of gas, so we took them in tow and docked for the night at West Palm Beach. It had been a busy day.

In the morning we continued up Lake Worth, with the big hotels to starboard and the nice old houses amid palm trees along the shore to port, then through more mangrove swamps and out at Stuart into the Indian River, which is much like the waterway south of Morehead City, with a narrow channel running up a wide, shallow lagoon. And it has the same beacons but the birds on them are pelicans.

By day they are fun to watch, for they are large birds and they come in to land like airplanes, with their wing feathers spread out like flaps, gliding down in a serious, controlled manner. Then at the last minute they seem to get bored with the whole procedure and fold their wings, to drop several feet into the water and land with a great splash. But by night they are pests, for they like to sit on a beacon with their wings down over the nice, warm light. So you are going along the waterway, trying to stay in the narrow channel, and you come to a light that is not there. If you are lucky, the pelican will yawn and lift up his wing for a moment, in which case you may see one flash but nothing more until you pass close by and see him sitting there, silhouetted against the stars at the top of the dark beacon.

Another small hazard is the dredgers that always seem to be working in that section of the waterway, for they are very large and sit squarely in the channel, surrounded by great lengths of pipe on floats and barges littered with rusty machinery, making what appears to be an impenetrable barrier across it. But when you blow your horn, the operator responds with one blast of his whistle or two, telling you which side to go, and makes just enough room for you to slide carefully by. And though they are often old and dowdy, they have happy names like *Sandpiper*.

There was a tug named Sampson, *too. Passing them on the waterway was like running into an old friend. We'd wave. I doubt if they knew us. We were always in a different boat, but we began to recognize the crewmen.*

North of Fort Pierce, the lagoon gives way to mangrove swamps and so it goes on, lagoons and swamps, past Daytona Beach to the fine old city of St. Augustine, with its Spanish style buildings, its narrow streets and its French pastry shop that we found on that first trip and returned to ever after. And soon you cross the St. John's River, to leave Florida at Fernandina.

The next section, through Georgia and South Carolina as far as Charleston, is quite different. There you travel the natural rivers and estuaries inside the Sea Islands, winding up to the top of one river, going through a short canal and down the next one. Then across a wide sound, past sandy beaches and up another river, day after day. It is a wild, lonely area and when first we crossed it, we were advised to carry a gun with which to defend ourselves against pirates, but we never did and we found it enchanting, with live oaks along the banks of the rivers and its abandoned rice fields full of wild life.

In some places, the rivers are so wide that you need a compass to find your way across them in the misty morning time, while in others they are so narrow that you have to watch where you are going. Once we had to slow down for a family of deer that were swimming across a narrow cut and once a skunk took a shot at us from the bank. Ibis would strut along the shore, sometimes a great blue heron would flap lazily past us, and at night we would anchor in a remote backwater, silent but for the sound of birds.

Sometimes you would pass an old house along the shore that had seen better days. There would now and then appear a fisherman, rowing out silently from a bank, hardly disturbing the wading birds. In a few years that all changed. There aren't a dozen spots any longer where you can only hear the sound of the blue heron in the tall grass. There are houses and bridges and automobiles and outboard motors and airplanes. There is noise all around you.

You needed range to make it in those days, for the docks that sold fuel were far between and it was common to see the smaller boats going along with cans of extra gas on their decks; but we had enough fuel in our tanks to take us to the Isle of Hope, near Savannah, and from there to Charleston, where we were back on the waterways that we already knew.

Travelling the familiar route, it did not seem to take us long to reach Norfolk, where Hank came aboard with Bob Hewes, who was to be *Peace & Plenty*'s new owner, for the passage up Chesapeake Bay. She ran a knot faster in the deeper water and although there was enough wind out of the west to kick up whitecaps all over the bay, she hardly rolled at all and made it in one day. So everyone was pleased and after cleaning her up the next morning, June and I went back to the office in Mamaroneck.

10   AZARA

Early in the following spring, we had a telephone call from Professor Morris Newman, head of the Lightning & Transients Research Institute in Minneapolis. He was having some problems in fitting out their research schooner *Azara* for operations in the Bahamas and would like me to meet him aboard her in Jacksonville to spend a few days as a consultant. And being available, I packed a small bag and flew down to Florida the same day.

Azara was lying alongside a dock at Southern Marine on the St. John's River. She was a graceful former yacht, 110 feet long by 22 feet wide, with a long bowsprit and a counter stern. Built of bronze in 1904, she once had a crew of 14 men who polished her topsides each morning, though now they were painted white. And she had had three masts but the middle one ,had been taken out to make way for a huge deckhouse, behind which was an open bridge, while her decks were piled high with all kinds of equipment.

Going below, you came into her original saloon, with its wood panelling and a piano in one corner. But going through the door on the other side of it was like stepping from the last century into the next, for ahead was the Generator Room.

The cabins had been removed and the deck above had been cut away, to make a room about 20 feet square that extended up into the deckhouse overhead, in the middle of which stood a fear-some-looking electrical device, all black boxes and insulators and glass tubes that glowed in the dim light. It was a million volt generator, the heart of *Azara*'s research capability.

Beyond it were the two remaining cabins, the original dining saloon, the galley and the crew's quarters, while above in the forward end of the deckhouse was the generator control room. And back aft there was another hatch that led down into the engine room, where I found the professor.

Morris Newman was a smallish man of about 50 with gray hair and a rumpled business suit on which he wiped his hands as he explained his problems. The roof of the deckhouse was made to slide open and on top of the high voltage generator was a reel of wire that could be led straight up, through a sheave suspended between the masts, to a helicopter high above. And when the generator was fired, the wire would act as an antenna. Now he needed a new rig and sail plan that would not interfere with his operations.

No conventional rig would do, so I suggested rigging her as two cutters, one behind the other, with each mast stayed separately. That would meet his requirements, while giving *Azara* adequate steadying sail when under power and the ability to carry enough canvas to bring her home if her engine should fail. And after the sails and rigging were ordered, I tackled the other problems.

Basically they came down to a conflict between the needs of the scientists and the requirements of the vessel. She was badly out of trim and needed to lose several tons of weight but the question was what they could do without. They were so busy preparing their equipment that they had not paid much attention to the boat, but if she was to carry them safely there and back, someone would have to set her in order. And when I pointed that out to the professor, he asked me to get on with it. But first we needed a cook, so June came down to take over the galley.

When Morris first called us, Patrick was off on a job but the Azara sounded like just the sort of thing that he would love, so I told Morris we would contact him the minute Patrick returned.

Then Patrick flew to Jacksonville, only to call me a few days later and tell me to join him. He sounded very happy. The boat was a challenge, the people were fun, and if I would come down and cook for a few of the hands for a week or so, I could enjoy it all too.

It was virtually impossible to tell where the old dock, cluttered with rusty barrels, odd lines, boxes of rubbish and piles of scrap ended and the decks of Azara, cluttered with rusty barrels, odd lines, boxes of rubbish and piles of scrap, began. I was shown the engine room first, which Patrick managed to find someplace under the mess. Then the saloon, her beautiful old panelling and walls of bookcases still intact, and then the generator room. A sight beyond belief. I had to find the galley myself. Another sight.

The galley was a long L-shaped passage with a big refrigerator on your left as you entered from the dining saloon, a row of cupboards with a sink along the port side of the ship, a door leading forward, and then a turn to starboard, with a long freezer running athwartships on one side and a huge old electric range and a water heater on the other.

I've forgotten how many people were aboard those first few weeks. They came and went so fast. But feeding them was like cooking for a gigantic vacuum cleaner. You'd put whatever there was on the table and within seconds it was gone.

Morris was great about letting me buy food. We had good food, balanced diets, very little of the macaroni salad sort of thing. But the stove turned out to be a real problem. It took gallons of electricity which wasn't too much of a deal on Azara, but it couldn't be used when the generator was operating. Which was most of the time. Also, when hot enough to boil water, it would produce enough heat to keep Hell at a reasonable temperature for a week. The galley had only a couple of portholes for ventilation, so I turned to a handy two-burner hot plate. And we cooked for up to 25 people on it.

Fitting out any vessel takes longer than you thought but in a research vessel it takes twice as long. Everyone aboard worked until late at night but three weeks later she was still not ready and I had to leave for another job. But Morris wanted me to sail as skipper of *Azara* for the operations in the Bahamas, so we had Joe Pelich fly in and take her as far as Nassau.

Joe finally said: "We're sailing tomorrow morning — ready or not." Then he carried from the deck to the dock about half a ton of assorted electrical gear, piled it neatly and said: "That's staying."

We sailed the next morning. It wasn't a nice day. Too windy for my delicate stomach. But perhaps things would improve as we wound down the St. John's River to the sea.

Azara qutdid herself on that passage. The storm really was quite mild. A chop in the Stream — gray and overcast and windy, but nothing a good sailboat wouldn't handle with ease. But what held Azara together I'll never know.

The noise was deafening. Her bronze hull worked, creating a weird grinding and crashing din. In spite of careful stowing and bolting, banks of equipment managed to work loose and crazily lurch from one side to the other. I had found a narrow spot on the bare floor of the forward control center where I put a single cot mattress. It was much too wide and had to be folded into a long U shape. Trying to get some sleep with the noise of the plates working and the banks of equipment jumping back and forth was impossible. Like trying to sleep through a two-hour train wreck.

Her aft deck was completely awash. Sometimes the water would be up to our knees. The place with the least motion was low in the generator room. But even there the noise was a lot worse than on deck.

Three of the scientists' wives had joined us with an assortment of children, so with their help, I was freed from trying to cook in the seaway. But not many were eating anyway.

Morris loved to steer Azara and on that first passage we were on a compass course, so that we had to steer accurately. He spent some time at the wheel and I came on deck to find him in a heated argument with Joe. Joe claimed that Morris had made a complete 360 degree turn. Morris was certain that he had only been 180 degrees off the proper course and had come back the same way. But an active mind like Morris's couldn't be expected to rest for any length of time on something as dull as a compass course. From then on, one of the less imaginative — like me — was assigned to watch over Morris when he steered.

And much to our surprise, we arrived in Nassau. Azara wasn't leaking, her engine kept running. There was no reason to turn back.

And once we were out of the Stream, things calmed down considerably.

When I stepped aboard in Nassau, Joe had already dealt with the customs and immigration officials. It was a quarter to eight when they arrived and he led them straight through *Azara's* saloon into the generator room. Without further explanation, he said: "That is set to go off at eight o'clock." And within five minutes they were all gone.

The customs and immigration people may have come aboard at Nassau. I was working in the galley, trying to sort things out after the camel ride. If they did board, they never passed the generator room. We could have had 60 people in the forepeak for all they knew.

Joe also had a way with children. There were several aboard and they were all so well-behaved that I wondered why.

"Oh, I used psychology on them, " he said.

"What do you mean?" I asked.

"Well, before we sailed I took each one aside and said the secret words."

"What secret words?"

"Now, when I tell you to do something, you will do it. Because if you do not, I shall hit you behind the right ear."

With which he flew back to Texas. But things were a bit damp aboard *Azara* after the passage from Jacksonville, so we spent a couple of days drying things out before sailing for Rock Sound, on the island of Eleuthera, for the operations.

Joe had dropped the smaller of her two anchors and the electric winch brought it up to the waterline quite easily but it was so heavy that we had to use a chain hoist to get it aboard as we motored down the harbor. Then we set her steadying sails and stood out past the white lighthouse, into the open sea. And as soon as she felt the first wave, she began to roll.

I have never seen a boat that rolled quite like *Azara*. The removal of her third mast and the addition of a great deal of weight low down had given her a quick, springy motion that made her dip her gunwales under and send water swirling across her decks a foot or more deep, even in light weather. The sails helped a lot but only in a strong cross wind could they steady her completely and the rest of the time we just had to put up with it. On the other hand, she had her advantages. She only drew seven feet of water, so that she could go into remote, shallow places, and her bare bronze bottom made a fine electrical ground.

She had two compasses: the original one down at her old steering position right aft and a new one up on the bridge. But you could no longer see forward from the old one and the new one was quite inaccurate, since it was close to the generator. So June stood by the old one and directed me onto our course, then I read the new one and steered by that until we came to the next turning point, which worked well. But just as we were going into a narrow, rockbound cut that led onto the banks, June found the professor making a hole in the binnacle with an electric drill.

Apparently he had in mind to attach something to it and when she pointed out that it might upset our only good compass, he went off somewhere else. But after that we kept an eye on him, for he was totally absorbed in his work and expected us to look after the boat while he got on with it.

On the banks, the water was quite shallow and *Azara* wallowed comfortably along, past Hatchet Bay and down the western shore of Eleuthera, to anchor off the quiet village of Rock Sound. The next day the helicopter, a two-place Bell, flew in from Miami, and when the pilot had rigged a bridle underneath it for us to hook our antenna wire onto, we were ready to start operations.

Early in the morning we moved out to anchor in the clear, pale green water a few miles from the harbor and the roof of the deck-house slowly opened. Standing on the bridge, you could look down inside it as it went forward, revealing the high voltage generator, glistening and clicking to itself in the dark hole, and on top of it, the reel of wire. The crew led the wire through the sheave and hoisted the sheave into position between the tops of the masts. Then we had to hook the wire onto the helicopter.

Climbing into a 13-foot whaler, two of us went around to the starboard side of *Azara*, where we took hold of the end of the wire. And as it was paid out, we backed off about 50 yards to wait, rising and dipping on the little waves, looking over toward Rock Sound.

For several minutes there was nothing, then a faint hum in the distance and we made out a small dot, low over the water, that expanded rapidly until the helicopter came roaring overhead. Then up it went in a wide, sweeping turn, to come back low and slow and fetch up hovering over us, blowing our hair over our eyes with its downwash and dangling its bridle for us to catch.

Reaching up, we clipped our wire onto its bridle and quickly moved out of the way, giving the pilot a wave to say that it was hooked on. Tilting forward, the helicopter dipped a little and began to go slowly ahead, then climbed rapidly, while the wire spun off the reel and screeched through the sheave. And soon it was high above us, heading into the wind up there but stationary over the ship.

Back aboard *Azara* the reel came to a stop, then began going slowly back and forth, a turn or two each way. From the bridge, the professor gave the word to the control room and with a crack like a rifle shot, the generator started firing.

Looking down, you could see the glow of the tubes and hear a humming sound between the shots. Then as it got ready, it would make clicking noises and when it fired, there was the crack again and a flash of fire like a gigantic spark plug.

In effect it was functioning as a very powerful radio transmitter. The biggest conventional radio station that I know of has an output of 100,000 watts, fed into an antenna about 1,000 feet high. But there we had more like 3,000,000,000 watts going into an antenna, 3,000 feet high, which made possible a number of experiments, some of them secret but most of them in the area of basic research. In this one, the signal was being picked up by equipment aboard our small sailboat, which was some distance away.

The helicopter only had enough fuel to stay up for a couple of hours, after which it came slowly down, giving the wire time to wind back onto the reel until it was low over the ship, then dropping the rest into the water and going back to Rock Sound.

There would only be one operation a day, so we would go out in the whaler and gather in the wire, radio the sailboat to come on back, and spend the afternoon helping to get things ready for the next day, when there would usually be some changes in the experiment that meant new gadgets to be rigged up. And in the cool of the evening we would sit around the dinner table, discussing future projects.

Morris Newman and his staff were a pleasure to be with, for they were truly open minded. No idea, however implausible, was rejected without serious consideration. One evening, someone suggested building an electric helicopter to support the antenna and someone else said that it would never fly. So Morris went and dug out an old 12-volt electric fan, placed it in the middle of the table and tilted its head so that its blades were horizontal. Then he reversed its leads and plugged it into a 120-volt DC outlet. And up it went, to hang for a glorious moment in mid-air before crashing on the table amid general applause.

We soon found ourselves picking up their jargon. A thousand dollars became a kilobuck and one day I overheard June saying to someone: "According to my calculations, our requirement of milk for the coming 24-hour period will be on the order of six quarts." But she could have been pulling his leg.

We worked in bathing suits in the galley. The heat was unbelievable — cooking and doing dishes for all those people. Survival meant every 20 minutes climbing the ladder to the deck, jumping overboard, climbing back down and doing another 20 minutes. It worked quite well.

Virtually all of *Azara's* cabin space was taken up with equipment of one kind or another and when the time came to go to bed, you first had to find a spare mattress and then look around for somewhere to put it, preferably out of the weather. June and I tried several places but our favorite one was under the life raft, all the way aft, where we were sheltered from the occasional rain shower, and on most nights we could look out across the calm water toward the distant island.

It takes a while to get used to living aboard a boat with a million volt generator and you tend to be wary of it, until you begin to know its foibles. Sometimes when it started up in the morning, it would zap a lightning bolt out sideways and on one occasion it sent one clear through the professor's cabin, leaving a neat round hole in the bulkhead on each side, but once it warmed up, it was more reliable. Still it paid to be cautious and we were always very much aware of it when it was operating.

A more elementary though less obvious hazard aboard *Azara* was electric drills. They whirred in odd corners all over the ship most of the time, as constant modifications were made. In fact, it was not wise to stand too close to any bulkhead, in case one should come through from the other side of it.

One day, someone misplaced a drill. I think Joe Pelich pointed out that if we would all stand still and be quiet for half a minute, we would probably hear one.

In about 10 days, the high wire operations were completed and we all took a day off to drive around Eleuthera. Rock Sound was so quiet that the only living thing in the main street was a horse and Governor's Harbor was not much busier in those days, but we found a lovely white sand beach and discovered that once you had one coconut, you could get as many more as you wanted by hurling it into a palm tree and knocking them down. And in the morning we sailed back to Nassau.

Coming into the harbor, the town is on your right, with pink and white buildings among palm trees and in front of them dozens of brightly painted sailboats that trade around the out islands, while just beyond lie the big steamers. Then there are houses along that shore, while on your left is Paradise Island, with its casuarina trees leaning in the wind and over there we anchored for a few days of underwater work.

Various experimental devices were lowered into the water and the current from the generator was fired down into them, while the junior member of the scientific staff crouched in the whaler half a mile away with his head under water, listening for the sound of the shots. Whenever he took his head out to breathe, there would be great shouts for him to put it back but he was a dedicated soul and never seemed to mind. In fact he used to listen to the radio time signals from the National Bureau of Standards in Washington for entertainment in the evenings.

With the deckhouse roof open and the two auxiliary engines making electricity for the generator, we caused quite a stir in Nassau and the natives began to complain that we were lousing up their weather but as soon as the tests were finished, we left for America.

After the experience that they had coming down in *Azara*, we were extra careful going back, leaving in the morning so as to cross the Gulf Stream at the best time and setting all her sails as soon as we cleared the harbor. And with the wind out of the east, she was quite steady, but she was making 14 degrees of lee-way until we lowered the centerboard.

That was very large and we seldom used it, since the winch that raised it was in the middle of the generator. But after making sure that everything was grounded, we climbed inside and lowered it, which did not affect her motion but reduced the leeway to a more reasonable figure.

All through the afternoon we sailed northward past the Berry Islands to Great Stirrup Cay, where we turned into the west. By then it was dark and the mate was Dixon Long from our office, who had sailed halfway around the world, so I handed the ship over to him and slept soundly as he took her down toward Great Isaac lighthouse. Shortly after midnight we entered the Gulf Stream, which is at its calmest about then and by breakfast time we were in Fort Lauderdale, having had a very pleasant passage.

That is a convenient place to enter from abroad, since the customs and immigration people come right down there to the dock. As soon as the formalities were completed, everybody went their various ways, leaving two mechanics aboard the ship to help June and me take her north to Washington.

I had chosen to take her through the Intracoastal Waterway to save wear and tear on her equipment, but lying at Pier 66, she did look rather large. Directly ahead of her was the famous brigantine *Yankee*, looking quite small by comparison with *Azara*, and even turning her around in the wide harbor was a maneuver that had to be thought out in advance. For you would have 60 or 70 feet of her hull in the strong current near the middle, while the rest of it was in the slack water at the side of the channel. Beside which, her control system was truly weird.

Her bridge was a simple platform, built in the narrow space between the mainmast and the deckhouse. A steel pipe about 30 feet long went up at an angle from the old steering wheel, through a bracket on the mast to a new wheel that took up most of the space, and the only other control was the throttle for the main engine, which would give you speeds from four to seven knots. But the tachometer was in the engine room so that if you wanted to set her at her cruising speed, you did it by signals from a mechanic who bobbed his head in and out of the hatch until you got it right. And if you wanted to go at less than four knots, you had to get someone to move the gear shift lever down on the deck back and forth, while you adjusted the throttle on the bridge.

North of Fort Lauderdale the waterway is narrow and goes under numerous bridges, which presented a problem, for you just cannot hang around with a vessel like that, waiting for a bridge to open. But she had a fine, loud air horn and we soon learned that if we went up to a bridge at full speed and gave three blasts, the operator would take one frightened look at us, ring bells, flash lights, stop all the cars and open the thing before we wiped it out.

But going around a sharp corner you had to be careful, for she was so long and heavy that once she started turning, it took quite a lot of rudder the other way to stop her. So you would be going around a curve to the right, busily turning the wheel to the left in anticipation of wanting to go straight soon.

It was June's custom to make lunch, then take over the wheel while the rest of us went below to eat it. We had rigged a large, striped umbrella as a shade over the bridge and she would stand underneath it in a blue bathing suit, with the chart in one hand and no one else on deck. *Azara* must have been an impressive sight going through the waterway, and one day as we came on deck, we saw a small Chris Craft close alongside with the owner looking very serious behind the wheel in a captain's hat and his wife digging him in the ribs and pointing up at June. But I had taught her how to stay within a few feet of the deepest part of the channel and she never had any trouble.

However, docking *Azara* was another matter, for she had no rubbing strakes along her sides, which meant that you had to bring her in so that her small fenders stopped exactly in line with the pilings to avoid scratching her paint. And she carried so much way that you had to slow her right down half a mile before the dock and take the engine out of gear a quarter of a mile away. Then she would go on and on, slowly losing speed until you could stop her by going astern. But when you did that, she would turn sharply to starboard, which you had to take into your calculations, along with the effects of wind and current on her hull.

I think Patrick let me dock a boat once. It went quite smoothly. There were no disasters. But the strain on both of us was too great. I never asked to do it again and he never offered it, either.

Whenever possible, we would plan our day's run so that we arrived at a wide place where we could anchor in the evening. But when we did dock, the small crew was just right, for one of the men would look after the gearshift, while the other took the bow line ashore. June handled the stern line and I stayed on the bridge, leaving no spare people to get in the way. And soon we became quite adept at taking her into tight places, until we got fancy and tried our first one in the dark.

It was a calm, still night when we arrived at Georgetown, South Carolina, and spun *Azara* around in the small harbor to slide her sideways into a vacant berth at an old commercial dock. Everything went off well and she came to a gentle stop with her fenders neatly in place but after the lines were secured and the engine was stopped, I noticed a large, rusty piece of equipment on her deck that I did not remember seeing before. And investigating, I found it was an old crane on the dock that someone had left sticking out over the water. It had missed everything and did no harm but we had to move out sideways in the morning to avoid it.

Steaming up the Waccamaw River we came to fish nets, strung clear across it, supported by floats. At one end would be a flag, while at the other would be a man in a small boat and we nearly ran over the first one before we saw what it was. But after that we wove our way through them, often standing over almost to the bank of the deep, wide river to avoid them.

Passing Morehead City, we came to the more open waters of Pamlico Sound and after Norfolk it was pleasant to sail up Chesapeake Bay and take the Potomac River to Washington, where we left *Azara* for a month, right in the middle of the city, while the professor showed various people her equipment. After which, we sailed back down the Potomac with a full crew for high wire operations in the Chesapeake. But first we docked in the small yacht harbor at Solomons Island to get fuel and meet the new helicopter crew.

After filling her water tanks, I went ashore to take a shower on the dock, where you had to put a quarter in a slot to get hot water. And halfway through, when I was all soaped up, there was a loud clonk and the water went off, leaving me hollering for help until someone came by and fetched another quarter for me.

But the next day, I got my own back. I found a small boy on the dock, trying to get a free soda out of one of those boxes where you open the lid and there are rows of sodas of different flavors. So I went over to the ship and got him a bottle opener and a pack of straws, leaving him happily drinking all he could, right in the box.

The helicopter was the same kind as before but it was flown down from Boston by Bill Anderson, a former Marine Corps pilot, with his mechanic following him in a truck. And as soon as they arrived, we started operations in an area prohibited to air or sea traffic off Bloodsworth Island, just across the Chesapeake.

Each day we would anchor a mile or so off the island, open the deckhouse roof and go out in the whaler with the wire. June and I had taken on that job and I would fiddle with the sometimes balky outboard engine, while Bill hovered low overhead and June reached up to hook on the wire. But it was not entirely a safe procedure, for if Bill's engine had ever quit, we would have been dead ducks. And on one occasion, June got her hand caught in the wire as Bill went up. So we began to think there must be a better way of handling the wire pickup.

As soon as Bill got to the proper altitude, the generator would start firing and for the next couple of hours we would keep a sharp eye out for any aircraft that might wander into the area, ready to radio Bill to drop the wire if one came too close. And when he did, we had to go out in the whaler and pick up a mile or more of wire off the bottom of the bay. By the time that we got it aboard, it was too kinked to be used again, but it was not expensive and we solved the problem of what to do with it by leaving it on the shore for the local fishermen to take.

At lunch time, Bill would land on the scrubby little island and I would take him some more gas, stopping to discuss the morning's flight before going back for a second one in the afternoon. And little by little, we began to understand the special problems of that kind of operation.

In the evening, we would move to a more sheltered anchorage off the village of Wingate and lie there for the night, far from the low, marshy shore but in calm, shallow water, with people going to and fro in the whaler and preparations going on aboard for the next day's operations. And then *Azara* felt more like a town than a boat, with a life of her own, independent of the world in the darkness beyond.

It was nice to be so close to shore that we could replenish our food stocks. Wingate had a plant where fresh crab was packed. It has never tasted better. Unfortunately, most of the crew preferred peanut butter sandwiches and macaroni salad but I ignored them.

Wingate was a tiny, remote fishing village and its harbor was very small: just a shallow, narrow cut running straight through the marshes, to end in a square basin full of small fishing boats, with a wharf about 60 feet long across the far end of it. And one day we had to take *Azara* in there.

First Bill took me down the channel in the helicopter, low over the water, to check for shoal spots. Then he dropped me off on a dock and we moved a couple of the smaller boats, to clear a space on each side of the wharf. After which, we went back to the ship and brought her slowly on, with one of our deckhands going ahead in the whaler to mark the edge of the channel.

Letting her drift almost to a stop, I signalled to the man in the whaler to push her bow around to starboard, then to scoot around to the other side and nudge her in, while I brought her stern around with the main engine. And she came gently alongside the wharf.

All the time, there had been a row of fishermen standing along the wharf, silently watching us. They never said a word but when we passed them our lines, they put them on the proper bollards and stepped back. A bunch of amateurs would have been shouting all kinds of inane instructions, grabbing lines and pulling on them so as to spoil the whole operation. But those men were professionals. They knew that we had a lot on our minds and they left us alone.

Lying at the wharf in Wingate, *Azara* was even more impressive than usual. A sailboat always looks bigger than a motor boat of the same size and a big sailboat is impressive anywhere. But in a tiny port, she literally dominates the village. Her masts are the highest things for miles around and wherever you go, you can see them, while her hull seems to fill the whole harbor.

Bill kept the helicopter in a clergyman's garden in Wingate and whenever he landed, all the flowers would lie flat on their sides until the rotor stopped. But it was a safe, convenient spot and between operations, he gave us a ride each. A small helicopter feels more like a balloon than an airplane, with a soft, floating motion, and when you hit a bump, she yaws. So on a warm day, you are constantly correcting her with the rudder pedals. And cruising along in the round plexiglas bubble at 60 miles an hour and 700 feet, you can see every detail on the ground ahead of you.

When June's turn came, Bill first took her down the street, about five feet off the ground, then swooped up into the air, cut the engine and came down in autorotation, which is quite a trick. But never having landed any other way, she rather missed the point and wondered what all the fuss was about.

Some time later, I had another ride. A life ring had fallen off *Azara* and drifted some miles away before Bill spotted it. So he took the doors off the helicopter while I fetched a grapnel and we went after it. With Bill hovering low over the water, I had no trouble snagging it with the grapnel and hauling it up into the cockpit, where I sat nursing the wet line in my lap all the way back, to keep it out of the controls. But that might be a good way to pick up the wire, one day, if the details could be worked out.

Meanwhile, the experiments were proceeding successfully and the operations continued, so Dixon Long came down from our office to take over as skipper of *Azara*, while June and I went back to take over the paper work from him.

11   FAIR   WEATHER

Things were still quiet for us in the winter time and it was a relief
to get a phone call, just as the snow was melting, with a nice
job in a warm climate. The 60-foot schooner *Fair Weather* was
lying in Kingston, Jamaica. Her owner was in Hong Kong and he
wanted her taken to Miami to be sold. She had just been passed
by a Lloyd's surveyor and was ready to sail.

June and I flew down the next day, while Joe Pelich and John
Little came from Texas to sail as mate and engineer. But while we
were airborne, the boat was driven ashore by a storm and damaged. Which was fortunate, in a way, for she was in no condition
to make a sea passage and she looked so bad that no one in America
would have bought her, except as scrap. You could poke your
finger through most of her heavy canvas sails. Her engine would
not start. She had almost no running rigging and her standing
rigging was so rusted that you could break the steel wires into
pieces with your fingers, like chocolate bars. And looking more
closely, I found extensive rot in the wood in way of her chain
plates.

*Words are inadequate to describe the condition of that boat or
our horror when we saw her. Joe and Patrick discussed the pros
and cons in the shade of one of the yard buildings. We could get
on the next plane back to New York or we could give it a try.
There would be a lot of work ahead. And a lot of worry. At one*

*end of the scale, it was just possible that she could be salvaged.
At the other end, it was just possible that we could lose our lives.
Well, let's get busy now and see what can be done. We can always
change our minds tomorrow.*

So first we made color photographs of her and sent them off to
the owner with our suggestions: As she was, she was worthless, but
if we fixed her up and took her to Miami, he might get his money
back, plus a little for the boat. Then we set about listing the things
that needed doing and looking for ways to get them done, so that
when we got the order to go ahead, we were ready to start.

Since she had been in the accident before we got there, some of
the work was covered by insurance, while the owner sent us the
money for the rest, and after ordering her new wire and rope from
Miami, we started work on her hull and machinery. But we could
not live aboard during that time, so June and I moved ashore into
a boarding house, while Joe and John took a room in a small hotel.
And soon it became clear that the hotel was not quite what it
seemed.

The first night they were there, a girl reached through the fan-
light over their bedroom door and threw water on them to attract
their attention, while more girls broke down the door of the next
room to get at some sailors, and John, who was a minister, sat on
his bed, slapping his knee with glee and saying: "You rascals." But
Joe had a knack for handling such things and later, when the hotel
gave a gala ball, he served with distinction as the Master of Cer-
emonies.

Not long before, Texas had been plagued with minor members
of the European nobility and Joe looked rather European, so he
had himself introduced at cocktail parties as the Prince of Fritaly.
When earnest American ladies asked him where Fritaly was, he
would explain that it was a small principality between France and
Italy. And when they looked puzzled, he would add: "It's just
across the border from Anatole France." Whereupon they would
smile brightly, for they had heard of that.

But he could get far more done in a day than most other people.
John was a skilled mechanic, and the four of us worked with the
boat yard's men for nearly a month, getting *Fair Weather*'s hull
and equipment into shape.

She was afloat when first we saw her and she was hopelessly out of trim, so after she was hauled on the slipway for the hull work, we bought tons of scrap iron and spent many a hot day carrying it piece by piece across the yard, up a long ladder and down into her forepeak, where we stowed it under the sole. And at lunch time we would drive to the suburb of Half Way Tree, more for half an hour in the air-conditioned drug store there, than for the sandwiches they served.

That was just across the road from Chang's Emporium, a large dime store with the usual rows of counters, except that one whole row was devoted to fireworks. There were literally hundreds of them on display, from the small table top kind up to really big rockets, and we often wondered what would happen if someone put a match to just one fuse in that lot.

The Jamaicans with whom we worked were nice people who did good work with limited equipment and we got to know them quite well. They told us that few of them could find even intermittent work and those who were lucky enough to do so seldom made more than $350.00 in a year. Yet they managed to support their families, eating mostly fish and rice and vegetables. But in Montego Bay we saw tourists paying that much a week in the fancy hotels and it was obvious that there would have to be a drastic change in the whole economy of the island before long.

When the work on her hull was finished, we had *Fair Weather* launched and took her down to the far end of the harbor, to the old seaplane base, where we anchored her off a stone quay while we worked on her rigging. The rope and the wire had come from Miami but there was no rigging vise on the island, so we borrowed a large ordinary vise from the power station and made a pair of hardwood chocks that, inserted in it, did the job.

We were near the dock for the gypsum ships. A day before a ship was due in, flour sack tents would appear in the bushes just off the company property, outside the fence. The tents would remain as long as the ship was in port, then suddenly they would be gone.

By then we were living aboard and one morning we were sitting around the cabin table, finishing our breakfast while the riggers had already started work aloft. Suddenly there was a crash and a large iron shackle came through the glass skylight, to smash Joe's plate to smithereens. It had fallen about 60 feet and if it had hit anyone, it would have killed him, but it missed everyone and all we had to do was clean up the mess, refinish the table and replace the glass in the skylight.

And fix Joe another plate of ham and eggs.

The workmen had no way of getting from their homes to the boat in her new location, so every day one of us would drive our small rented car down to fetch them. That was often an adventurous trip along the winding shore road, dodging trucks driven by wild men who were paid by the load and went as fast as they could; but driving in Jamaica was always interesting. The first day that we had the car, we left it parked on a main street in Kingston and as we came back to it, we saw two goats fighting beside it. When the one facing the car charged, the other one sidestepped and let him go head on into it, leaving a large dent. Immediately we phoned the rental office, to be greeted by a tired voice that thanked us for reporting the matter but did not seem to think it unusual.

During that time, we worked six days a week, and one Sunday we went to the top of the Blue Mountain on mules. It took a couple of weeks to arrange, starting with a rumor that led to a girl in a bank, who told us to telegraph Malcolm Macdonald at Penlyne Castle, a remote village accessible only by telegraph or mule.

Peter Aylen, whose boat we had moved years before, was in Jamaica with his wife and son, so they joined us for the trip and we asked for eight mules, including one for our gear. Leaving Kingston an hour before dawn, we drove up to the village of Mavis Bank, where the road ended. That was at about 3,000 feet and there were the mules waiting for us, with the four local farmers who owned them. The mules had had two days' rest in preparation for the trip and before the sun came up we got going.

The steep, narrow trail led through dense jungle at first, constantly doubling back on itself so that from the lead animal, I could look down onto the others almost directly below me, and a stone dislodged by my mule would fall on them. The farmers, who knew things that we did not, walked behind every second mule, hanging onto its tail, while the one behind me hurled rocks over his mule to hit the rump of mine and keep it going, somewhat jerkily, up the mountain.

It was raining gently but steadily, making the trail slippery in places, and after a while it went sneaking along the side of a steep mountain, with a sheer wall rising up on our left and a precipice dropping away on our right. The trail was still narrow and without warning my mule stopped, turned to face the precipice and bent down to eat some grass that was growing just below the edge. The view was impressive. Just a gray back, sloping down to the paler gray clouds ahead and below. And the rickety old saddle was tied on with a girth of tired string. If the farmer behind me had hurled a rock about then, we would have been airborne immediately. But he did not and when it had finished eating, the mule shuffled around to face up the trail again.

Farther on we came to a wider section, where we overtook a man plodding up the mountain on foot with a long plank on his head. Evidently there was a house being built up ahead and that was the way they got the lumber up there.

After maybe three hours we came to a fine old wooden house, quite small but well built, that must once have been owned by a coffee planter. Now there was a Jamaican family living in it who were pleased to see any strangers and there we rested for half an hour before continuing up the trail.

We were shown through several rooms of the old place. Wooden floors, bare and clean. Occasionally a straight-backed chair. All old and hand-made. One room held a hand-operated organ, carried up over a hundred years ago, as was everything in the house and most of the material from which the house was made. A stately copper tub with a high back stood in the center of one room. Water must have been heated in the kitchen and carried into the tub room. You would certainly have all the time in the world to bathe.

By then it had stopped raining, or rather we had risen above the clouds, and whenever we came to an open place, we could see far out across the valley, above the clouds, to other mountains that, while green with dense vegetation close up, were blue and smoky in the distance. And here and there, through gaps in the clouds, we could see patches of the famous Blue Mountain coffee growing on the mountainsides below.

Later, the trail dipped down into a valley that was full of cloud and must have been so most of the time, for its vegetation was that of a rain forest, with mosses and fungi on the trees, which were soggy with the permanent damp. It had a primeval feel about it, as though it had been the same for a thousand years and perhaps it had. Certainly it was mysterious and enchanting: the sort of place where you might expect to meet a dragon. But after a while, the trail wound up out of it and we broke through the cloud into the sunlight above.

We had become resigned to plodding along on the mules and it came as a surprise when the vegetation fell away, the trail levelled off and we found ourselves amid the low bushes on the rounded top of the Blue Mountain, about 7,500 feet above sea level.

The view was spectacular. To the northeast we could make out Ocho Rios, over 20 miles away, and from there we could follow the north coast of Jamaica clear along past Port Antonio, while to the southwest we could look down into Kingston Harbor, which seemed almost close enough to pitch a stone into. But though the sky was clear and there was not much wind, it was so cool that we needed our sweaters when we sat down to eat our lunch. And soon we began to realize how sore we were after riding all morning, for none of us had ridden at all in years. So on the way down, we walked much of the way. Which also hurt after a while, but in different places.

About halfway down, June was riding her mule when it ran away and went galloping down the steep, narrow trail. For a moment we all thought she would go over the precipice, but as she went by John, he grabbed the reins and brought her safely to a stop. And before we reached the bottom, it was pitch dark.

At that point we were back on our mules, for it was easier to let them find their way home than to follow the twisting trail on foot. Sitting there, all I could see ahead was my mule's ears and it felt like one of those rides in amusement parks, where you go through a dark tunnel in a car that swings wildly to and fro, while unseen things slide across your shoulders, until the yellowish light from a house came through the jungle close by and we were at the end of the trail.

The next morning we all had huge blisters and it was several days before we could sit down with any comfort but the experience had certainly been worth it. And a week later we ran into a woman who had just applied to Peter for a job. She thought that he was very nice but she could not understand why he conducted the entire interview standing up.

Back aboard *Fair Weather*, the rigging work continued and one morning we took her out to test the engine. On the way back it quit in a flat calm, leaving us about 200 yards from the quay, so I got into her dinghy, took her in tow and started rowing. For quite a while it looked as though her 60 tons would not budge but eventually she began to creep forward and after half an hour's work, I got her close enough to run a line ashore and let the others winch her in.

We all thought he was going to pop a few blood vessels. He rowed steadily, not moving an inch over the bottom but slowly the tiny dinghy sank down into the water. There couldn't have been an inch of freeboard left when old Fair Weather *began to give. Once she moved, the dinghy regained its buoyancy and the battle had been won.*

But from the way she handled, it was evident that she needed more ballast forward. We found a man down the road who made hand-painted cement tiles that were both heavy and cheap. So we loaded half a ton of those aboard, which trimmed her nicely.

As the riggers completed their work, we finished the painting and *Fair Weather* looked like a new boat. Her engine really needed a major overhaul and the old sails that we had patched up were barely good enough to take her to Miami but we did not feel that we could recommend any further expenditure on her, so we had Richard Dixon join us to bring the crew up to five and left. For the first few days, the weather was light and we made good time to the northwest, through the Cayman Islands to Cabo San Antonio at the western end of Cuba. But as we rounded the cape to head northeast, the wind came up hard from dead ahead.

"See the puffy little white clouds over there, low on the horizon? That's Grand Cayman. Now you can say you've seen it."

The Gulf Stream runs toward the northeast at that point and the strong wind blowing against the current kicked up a short, steep sea that stopped *Fair Weather* in her tracks. Her bow would rise up on a wave, to come crashing down, throwing spray all the way aft, and if you watched the foam on the water beside her, you could see that she stopped completely for a moment before gathering headway, to go a few more feet and be stopped again. But worse was the fact that she was going sideways faster than forward, so that in reality she was making little progress at all.

We thought of using the technique we had used in *Ly Kou* going through the Straits of Mackinaw, but when we tried the old engine, it refused to start and we thought it wiser to keep what electricity there was in the batteries for the running lights. Which left us one alternative: to ease her sheets and get her going, plowing through the seas in a smother of foam but at least getting somewhere, if not in the direction that we wanted to go.

When the time came to tack, we found that her bow would not come up into strong wind, while if we had tried to jibe her, all her sails would have blown out. So we had to take them down, secure them, wear the boat around down wind under bare poles, and set all the sails again. That took us the best part of an hour and cost us fully a mile of our hard-won distance but she fetched up on the other tack without taking any harm.

The storm seemed to intensify hourly, but I was assured that it was not really the storm that was so bad but that we were in the Florida Straits where life is always beastly. If the storm wasn't so bad, why weren't the daylight hours brighter than the night? Why were the seas running in seven directions at once? Why did the sails keep splitting? Why did we all keep reminding each other: "At least the hull is good"?

With the aid of the Gulf Stream, one tack took us northward, while on the other we went to the southeast, so that we were gaining a little, each time around. But every second tack took us in toward the Cuban coast and we always seemed to arrive there in the dark. At which time we would check our lights and find that one or the other of them had gone out. Then Joe and John and Richard would go forward to fix it, while I would try to hold *Fair Weather* on a course that would make it less beastly for them, though not with much success, for every now and then the top of a wave would go over them. Once they mentioned that it was rather difficult to work up there and I told them it was all jolly good practice. And thereafter, as each wave swept across the bow, there would be a pause, then a chorus of voices in the darkness shouting: "Jolly practice, fellows" above the noise of the wind.

In those days the Cubans were very sensitive about foreign vessels approaching their coast at night and each time *Fair Weather* came sailing in, her lights going on and off with the vagaries of her electrical system, they would send a gun boat out to investigate us. Whereupon we would go away and come in farther along the coast. And since motor boat operators seldom understand the problems of sailboats, they probably thought we were trying to make a clandestine landing. But we always turned away when we saw them coming and they never tried to chase us beyond their own territorial waters.

Meanwhile we developed a self-reefing staysail. We had taken in the jib and reefed the mainsail when the wind got up but as it increased in strength, the bottom panel of the staysail blew out, followed by the next one half a day later and so on. At that rate there would be nothing left of it in a few more days but we could not take it in and still hope to make any progress to windward.

It was the second night of the storm, as we were bound north, that the forestay let go. Suddenly *Fair Weather*'s motion changed. She developed a violent wiggle in between her normal pitching into the seas that brought Joe and me on deck immediately, for it meant that her heavy foremast was moving around and we both knew that if ever it jumped out of its step, it would go through the bottom of the boat and sink her within minutes.

Leaving June at the wheel, the rest of us scrambled up to the bow, to find the heavy iron tang that attached the stay to the bow of the boat broken. So first we led a halliard forward to take the strain and then we set about rigging a jury fitting. By that time, *Fair Weather* was dipping her whole bow under water every second or third wave, so we had to remember to breathe in when our heads were in the air and out when they were under water, which tended to slow the work down, and it was a couple of hours before we had things under control again.

It was closer to six hours. Things take so long to repair in a seaway. And the motion of Fair Weather *was anything but kindly. She lunged and lurched and the men held on to the rigging and bowsprit, trying to rig a jury, trying to keep the working of the mast in her step to a minimum. Joe, tremendously strong, would hold the stay in place while the others tried to attach its end to something. The wire cutters were in the cockpit near me, in case some rigging should go and the mast go over.*

Also lines and life jackets were within my reach. If someone should go over, I had one chance to get something to him. Better throw a life jacket out first and hopefully someone would be left to help turn the boat around. But just in case, I planned to throw four over.

If I left the wheel, Fair Weather would blow off down wind. There were boom guys rigged to keep her from a major jibe. If I let her go slowly, she might sneak around and I could get near anyone in the water. But could I see them at night? In the storm, the water was black. If I took the sails down, I'd never be able to get them up again. All old-fashioned hoops — no winches that I could even turn.

The Florida Keys were somewhere to the west. I'd best go that way and keep as much northing in her course as possible. Hope to go aground on the sandy keys.

Worry about that later. First things first. Listen to hear a shout above the screeching wind. Watch the water passing on both sides in case you think you see a head. Let the life jackets go — don't hesitate an instant. Get a line over if there is a chance.

Then it was over. The job had somehow been done. The men were exhausted, but we were alive and afloat. All the worry had been for nothing.

Still it was not exactly a permanent job and toward the end of the fourth day, the storm was if anything worse, while the mainsail had a hole in it that you could have driven a bus through and the staysail reefed itself down to a small triangle near the top. So I decided that we really should put into Key West and tidy things up. But since the whole trip was little more than a thousand miles, I had not brought my sextant with me and after days of banging around in the storm, we could not be too sure of exactly where we were.

However, I had brought a chart of the approaches to Key West, in case we might need it, that showed the location of a commercial broadcasting station, inland from the harbor entrance. And we had aboard a small transistor radio with a crack in its black plastic case, where the two halves came together. Also there was a crack between two boards in *Fair Weather*'s chart table that I was fairly sure ran fore and aft. So I tuned in the station, turned the radio around until the signal was weakest and measured the angle between the two cracks with my protractor, from which I was able to calculate our bearing from the station.

All through the night I sat below in the dimly-lit cabin, figuring our position and calling out course corrections, and the next morning we came right up to the sea buoy before we even saw the land, gray in the distance behind it.

Sailing into the harbor, we dropped anchor in the calm water and got the engine fixed, then went to a dock and took the sails ashore to be patched while we rigged the forestay properly. After which we telephoned Miami, to find there was a berth waiting for us in Fort Lauderdale, 20 miles farther north. John had to leave us there but by the time we were ready to sail again, the wind had gone into the northwest and we had a pleasant sail in the shelter of the Florida Keys up to Fort Lauderdale.

Just off the entrance, we were taking the sails down when *Fair Weather*'s heavy main boom came swinging out of the darkness with a rushing sound that I recognized just in time to duck. Still it took off my thin fisherman's cap, so it could not have missed my head by more than a fraction of an inch. I was quite glad to motor into the harbor and anchor for the night.

The next morning we went up the river to our berth at Broward Marine, where we unloaded our tiles and sent them home before giving *Fair Weather*'s decks their final coat of paint. Then we made some pictures of her, all clean and sparkling, to send to her owner and went home: Joe and Richard to Texas, June and I back to the office in Mamaroneck.

12   SKYLARK

During the summers we did many jobs Down East to Maine and beyond, though to be more precise the majority of them were back from that area, since the owners of the boats would cruise down with the prevailing winds behind them and return by air or car, while our people went down to bring their boats back. But typical examples would be two passages that we made in successive years for our friend and neighbor, George Kirstein.

The first was from Northeast Harbor, Maine, to Mamaroneck, New York, in his 40-foot yawl *Skylark*, a comfortable old boat that he had for many years. He let us know before he left that he would want us to bring her back, so I took the opportunity to sail with Brian Loe, a New Zealander who had just joined our firm after sailing around the world in the 26-foot *Marco Polo*. And when the time came, June drove us to Maine, left us there and drove back with George and his wife Jane.

Pat spent many months at sea, checking out and training new people in our way of doing things, while I stayed back in the office. When things were quiet, I would find a part-time job for its entertainment value as well as for money. Sitting and waiting for the telephone to ring didn't please me.

It did not take us long to reassure ourselves that *Skylark* was indeed ready to sail, for George was an experienced yachtsman and kept her in good shape, but the harbor was filled with white fog so dense that you could not see more than 50 yards.

No boats were moving except for a dinghy or two and there was no sound but the cry of an occasional gull, the dipping of the oars of a passing dinghy whose owner was trying to find the shore and the dripping of the damp from the boom onto the cabin top. But it is often that way for days on end in Maine in midsummer and *Skylark* had the basic instruments aboard: an echo sounder, a radio direction finder and a patent log; so we started her engine and motored cautiously out toward the open sea.

That is not a happy coast to navigate in fog, for it had offlying rocks, miles from the shore, and strong currents that sweep through them with the ebb and flow of the tide. In one place we were a few yards to one side of our track until we heard, rather than saw, a cloud of gulls rise up ahead. And changing course, we saw a black rock slide close by us, gray in the fog. But after a couple of hours, we were in open water and laid our course down the coast toward Portland lightship.

There was a light southwesterly wind and with *Skylark*'s mainsail sheeted hard in and her engine running, we made good time into the light sea and I was glad to find that Brian was a highly competent sailor. For with two experienced navigators aboard, the night run through the fog was a piece of cake and by the next afternoon we were approaching the lightship.

Using the direction finder, we took a series of bearings on her but with our engine going, we did not hear her horn until we were almost up to her. Then the noise seemed to come from all around us and she appeared out of the fog, so close ahead that we had to alter course to miss her.

That is a funny feeling. For perhaps 30 hours you have been alone, wrapped in a cocoon of fog, isolated from the world outside and knowing it only as a series of squeaks in a radio. Then you look up and there are faces looking back down at you from the lightship's deck as you pass under her stern. There is no time to think of anything to say, so you stare silently back. And as quickly as they came out of it, they go back into the fog.

By then we needed fuel and taking back bearings on the radio, we found our way to a gap in the rocks that leads into Falmouth Foreside, a small yacht harbor where we filled our tanks and had a night's sleep, hoping that the fog would go away. But it did not and after going back to the lightship the next morning, we headed south toward Cape Ann.

The wind and sea were still light, so we used the same rig as before, and heeling slightly to port, we pitched gently along, the engine muttering to itself and nothing much to do but wait for the blare of the foghorn on the cape to come abeam, early in the evening, so that we could square away for the Cape Cod Canal. Then the horns of a few ships to wonder about as we crossed the approaches to Boston Harbor and nothing more until just before dawn when we approached the canal itself, taking careful bearings on the radio that led us right up to it.

At the entrance, we got a glimpse of the sea wall to our starboard and after that we sort of caromed through the canal, steering compass courses as best we could and altering them a little each time we saw one side or the other go darker than the surrounding fog, so that the first thing we saw clearly was the lift bridge at the far end, low across the water and very close ahead of us.

We were expecting it but still it was an eerie sight, stretching right across our path like some gigantic steel trap, with the water swirling silently underneath it. But when we blew our horn, it opened noisily upward and when it gave us a toot to go ahead, we ran from buoy to buoy down Buzzard's Bay.

The buoys there are not far apart, so it seldom takes more than half an hour to go from one to the next, but even in that time, you can wander off your course by 50 yards and if you are careless, that is all it takes to miss it. So you start your stopwatch as you pass one buoy and steer very carefully until the next one is almost due. Then you both look out, one on each side, to catch the dark shape as it glides by, and estimating how many yards you were to the side of it, you correct your course by a degree or two for the next one.

But they must have been running low on buoys when they got to Buzzard's Bay, for you will be looking for one with a light and a bell on it and instead you will find two, one with a light and the other with a bell, close together. Which can be exciting in a thick fog, for while you are staring at the first one, wondering why it does not agree with the chart, you can easily come to a clanging halt against the other one.

Passing the last of the buoys, you come to a clear stretch of water as far as Point Judith, but even though it was late afternoon when we got there, the fog was so thick that we had to use our instruments to find the entrance to the harbor, where we anchored in the shelter of the low sea wall. All through the night the deep fog horn on the headland blared away, while the high-pitched siren shrieked hysterically on the wall. And in the morning it was the same but with no wind and a calm sea, so off we went under power alone toward Race Rock.

Chuffing quietly along over the calm, gently heaving sea, we heard a powerful horn behind us and responded with a blast on our little one. A minute later it happened again, rather closer and a minute later it was closer still. But after that, it stayed the same for fully an hour. Whoever it was was keeping pace with us, following us through the Race into Long Island Sound at a stately six knots.

Then just as Race Rock lighthouse came abeam, the fog lifted to reveal a nuclear submarine close behind us, a man in a life jacket standing lookout on each of her diving planes and her captain peering down at us from her conning tower. Immediately he put on speed and swept past us, several million dollars worth of electronic wizardry that had evidently been baffled by the echoes it was getting from poor little *Skylark*.

With visibility of nearly a mile, we had an easy run down Long Island Sound, to put into the pleasant harbor of Milford for the night and arrive at *Skylark*'s mooring off Mamaroneck early the following afternoon. That was convenient, since George had a house at the water's edge and we owned the one behind it, so that we only had to leave the dinghy at his dock and carry our duffel bags across his lawn to get home.

Brian Loe was known as Tig, after Tigger in *Winnie the Pooh*. By sailing with him, I had both satisfied myself that he was a really good sailor and shown him how we did things, so he was cleared to sail as skipper for our firm, and after a night at our house, he went off on another job, while I went back to the office.

With a telephone line run from the office to the house, we were able to give pretty good service. Twenty-four hour coverage, in fact. The daytime calls were mostly owners with requests for estimates, arranging deliveries, etcetera. At night the skippers would report in. We expected each to give us a call every few days, when possible, so that we could keep all interested parties well informed, from the owner of the boat to the mother of the deckhand.

By the following year, George had sold *Skylark* and had a new boat built that he called *Shag*. And in her he cruised farther afield, leaving her at Saint John, New Brunswick, up the river beyond the famous Reversing Falls. So when I flew in there with my deckhand, we first went to take a look at the falls. That is a curious situation. There is a narrow cut between high, rocky cliffs that connects the river with the sea. But the river is large enough to stay pretty much at one level, while the sea goes up and down fully 20 feet. So for half the time, there is a waterfall about 10 feet high in the cut going one way, while for the other half, it faces the other way. And only for a few minutes every six hours is the water at the same height on each side, so that you can pass through the cut in a boat.

There is a bridge over the falls and looking down from that, we could see that we would have to be there at exactly the right time and even then it would not be an easy passage, for the cut is on a sharp bend. But the next morning we were under way in good time and 10 minutes before we were due, we were waiting a hundred yards away from it, watching the last of the water swirl toward us. Then we went full ahead for the cut. And so did everyone else.

Every tugboat, fishing boat and pleasure boat that wanted to go through the cut in either direction that morning converged on it at the same moment and for a minute it looked as though they would all wind up in one great collision. But somehow they all missed each other and within five minutes we were safely through, to stand out to sea and head west under a clear blue sky, with a light northwesterly wind and unlimited visibility.

And so it remained for day after day as we sailed along the beautiful rocky coast, with the mountains standing up behind and the white sails of the yachts dotted across the calm, blue sea. *Shag* was about the same length as *Skylark* but she was a more powerful boat, able to stand up to her canvas better, and she had a diesel engine that gave her much greater range, so it was not until we were approaching Cape Ann that we needed fuel. And it being the evening time, we anchored in the sheltered bay just north of the Annisquam Canal.

That is a nice little canal, scarcely a mile long and not very wide, that takes you inside Cape Ann and brings you out in Gloucester Harbor, where we got our fuel the next morning. Still the weather held fair and with a good breeze we stood along the coast past Plymouth to the Cape Cod Canal, which on a clear day looks much like the Chesapeake & Delaware Canal.

Sailing down Buzzard's Bay, we could see the low hills of the mainland over to starboard and the string of rocky islands that separate the bay from Vineyard Sound to port. Off Point Judith, we could clearly see Block Island and going down Long Island Sound, there was the rocky coast of Connecticut on one side and the sandy shore of the island on the other. And so we arrived in Mamaroneck, after a pleasant and trouble-free passage.

But that is the way it is Down East: Either you are socked in or it is as clear as a bell. And for perfectly sound reasons, for the prevailing southwesterly winds carry warm, moist air over the cold sea to cause the fog, while the cool northwesterly winds associated with a frontal system blow it away. So it has always been and so it will always be.

13   HOME WATERS

By then it was the summer of 1960. We had been in the yacht delivery business for nearly five years and we knew the east coast of America from Canada to the Caribbean quite well. But we thought of the section between Marblehead, Massachusetts, and Annapolis, Maryland, as our home waters. And when we were asked if we could move a boat through there for Henry Cabot Lodge, June and I snuck away from the office to do it.

Just before midday we arrived at the dock in Marblehead to find an elderly sport fisherman about 40 feet long, whose owner was tinkering with one of her engines. And looking up, the owner said: "Oh, Mr. Ellam, it's nice to meet you. I've read your book *Sopranino*."

He liked to go fishing but every time he went out, the Coast Guard would come rushing after him with an urgent message to hurry back to the United Nations. So, sadly, he was getting rid of the boat and as he waved goodbye from the dock, we motored out of the harbor, steering from the flying bridge and dodging the lobster pots.

All along that coast there are pots but around Marblehead they are thicker than elsewhere. And they put them right in the narrow channels between the offlying rocks. Dozens of them, so closely spaced that you really have to watch out not to pick one up in either propeller. But as you move away from the shore and head across toward Scituate, they thin out rapidly.

Scituate is a pretty little harbor, with rolling green hills coming down to the water's edge, nice houses along the shore and the town itself farther back. But it is so conveniently located that it is always full of yachts and you have to go through to the marshy pool beyond the main harbor to find a berth for the night. Still it was one of our favorite ports and we used it often, because there really is not another good one for yachts until you get to Onset, at the western end of the Cape Cod Canal.

That is a quiet, pleasant harbor just north of the canal with docks, a boat yard and acres of sheltered anchorage, but whenever we were in there, it was half empty. Perhaps the reason is its location, for most people like to keep their boats where they can get out to sea quickly and down Buzzard's Bay there are plenty of such places, all the way to Point Judith.

There was a strong northwesterly wind that would have kicked up a nasty little sea against the fair current in the Race, so we went inside Fisher's Island that time, following the chart carefully as we swept between the rocks and shoals, with the current making the buoys spin and bob in the swirling water, past Stonington and Mystic, to enter Long Island Sound off New London.

Halfway down the Sound, we were going along at our full nine knots when a powerful motor boat about 30 feet long came rushing up alongside us and a man yelled: "Which way is Mamaroneck?" Keeping my cool rather well, I shouted back: "Third on the right" and with a yelp of thanks he thundered over the horizon ahead.

But Mamaroneck is easy to find, for the ornate tower on the sewage disposal plant is clearly marked on the chart. And if you ever want to find the fancy residential section called Premium Point, just look for Satan's Toe.

In Mamaroneck we picked up my parents who were visiting us and had been left behind when the job came in. We wanted to take them through New York Harbor on the boat. No matter how many times we had made the run down the East River, it still gave us great pleasure. My parents sat on the bridge with Patrick, watching Manhattan go by. There is something very special about New York from the water.

On a fine summer's day, the whole of the Sound from there to City Island is strewn with small sailboats, earnestly racing around in triangles and it is a full-time job to take a larger boat through them without disturbing any of them. But as you pass under the Throgg's Neck Bridge, they thin out and by the time you fetch down between the Brothers, you are clear of them.

The Brothers are two small islands in the East River, with a narrow channel between them. North Brother Island has some buildings on it but the South Brother has nothing but a few scrubby bushes and one fine day a family landed on it from their boat. When they came to leave, their motor would not start, so they shouted and waved at passing boats. And the people in the boats shouted and waved cheerfully back. But it never occurred to anyone that they were in trouble and for three days they stayed there, marooned on a desert island in the middle of New York City, until they were rescued.

Just beyond is Hell Gate, with Gracie Mansion looking over it, and going down the long, narrow channel between Manhattan and Welfare islands with a fair tide, you can often see that you are making far better time than the traffic ashore.

There is a bridge that goes across Welfare Island on its way from Manhattan to Brooklyn and midway along it, there is a turnoff to an elevator that takes cars down onto the small island. Late one night, a couple of us were strolling down that way when a car pulled up beside us.

"Say, how do I get to Welfare Island?" the driver asked.

"Go halfway across the bridge and turn left," we replied.

"Wise guys," he said and drove off looking cross.

Not far down is the United Nations building. One night at dinner I asked Frank Lloyd Wright if he had been inside it and he said: "No, I couldn't bear it. You see, I'm an architect." But it does look jolly around Christmas time, when they put colored cellophane in the windows and light it up like a huge tree. And on the bend of the river is the 23rd Street Yacht Basin.

Run by the city, it is a scruffy little dock but well located, so that you often see a small seaplane land on the East River to drop someone off there. And though there are none of the big old commuter yachts left, you still see an occasional 40-footer leaving

there in the afternoon with half a dozen men in business suits
bound for their homes on Long Island.

The bridges over the East River are so high and wide that they
do not affect a yacht, but they are rather grand to look at and the
grandest of all is the Brooklyn Bridge, with its hundreds of steel
components forming a delicate tracery against the sky as you pass
underneath it. By comparison, the skyscrapers are dull from close
up, though looking back as you go on down toward the Narrows,
the skyline of Manhattan as a whole is impressive.

Most days in the summer, the wind is out of the southwest or
the northwest and in either case you can stay in calm water all
the way to Manasquan Inlet. Leaving The Narrows, you stand down
across the flats west of the Roamer Shoal and bear away for the
low headland of Sandy Hook. There you cut close around the
point, inside False Hook, and close the beach off the Atlantic High-
lands, which drops off so steeply that you can run within 100
yards of it, motoring along in smooth water, admiring the old beach
houses even when the wind is so strong that their flags are standing
straight out from their poles.

From Manasquan to Cape May there is an intracoastal waterway
that is narrower and shallower than the one south of Norfolk. It is
no good for sailboats, because of its fixed bridges, but fine for
motor boats up to 60 feet or so drawing less than four feet of water,
and we used it on that trip.

Arriving in the evening, we went through the narrow cut into
the head of Barnegat Bay and pulling off the channel, we anchored
in a cove for the night. As the sun went down, the breeze died
away, leaving us silent and still on the flat calm water, with the
stars overhead and the lights of the houses along the shore. And
sitting out in the cockpit after dinner, we wondered why so many
people spend their nights at noisome docks, when they could be
anchored in a place like that.

Early next morning we were steaming down the shallow bay,
past men in garveys clamming with rakes in the misty dawn. As
the day warmed up, we passed Barnegat lighthouse and wound our
way across the marshes to Atlantic City. And in the afternoon we
went along behind the small beach towns, with their rickety old
docks and odd little boats, as far as Cape May.

There we put my parents ashore, while we continued with the delivery.

The next day was unusual, for we carried a fair tide up the Delaware, found slack water in the canal and picked up another fair tide going down the Chesapeake. More often, you slug your way up one bay against the ebb tide and arrive at the top just in time to fight the flood tide down the other. But it was nice while it lasted and we got to Annapolis the same evening, to relax aboard over dinner before going home in the morning.

14 KITE FLYING

That winter, Morris Newman was planning a new series of research operations in *Azara*. I had already taken her back to Jacksonville and in March, June and I went down there to help get her ready. Morris had installed a new and more powerful main engine, with instruments and controls on the bridge that would be a great help in close maneuvering. And while he was flush, I asked him for some other luxuries.

One was a loud hailer from the bridge, so that I could speak to the men on the foredeck. Another was a better rig for opening and closing the deckhouse roof. And last was a new boom for loading heavy gear on and off the ship.

The boom was about 35 feet long but the aluminum tubing of which it was made only came in 20-foot lengths, so the foundry that made it had to splice two of them together. However I insisted that they put a collar inside the joint a foot long and when it came aboard, they assured me that they had done so, though I had no way of checking it, since both ends were closed off.

Meanwhile Morris and his people were rebuilding the high voltage generator, so June and I offered to help with that. While the scientists built the timing equipment, the mechanics installed about nine tons of new capacitors on longer insulators and I assembled the brass parts for the spark gaps.

Then one day Morris came up to me and said: "You seem to

understand what's going on now. You can wire it up if you like."
With which he sketched the circuit for me on a shingle and left.

Obviously, droopy wire would wiggle in a ship at sea, while the
wires would have to be spaced accurately, so that the current
would not jump where it should not. And conventional insulation
would be a waste of time at a million volts, so I went to a hardware
store and bought several coils of aluminum clothes line to do
it with. That was fine, for you could bend it anywhere you wanted
it and it would stay there. And while I put in the spark gaps, June
wired it up.

When it was ready, the professor decided to test it. He had it
all charged up and ready to go before I noticed what he was up to
and looked around to see if we were clear of danger. And across
the wooden dock from us, no more than 20 feet away, was a
tanker. You could see that she was light, for she was floating high
on the water. So her tanks were empty. Which meant that they
were full of explosive vapor. Quickly I went to point that out
to him.

Smiling politely, he picked up a pad of yellow paper and started
doing arithmetic. When he got to the bottom of the page, he had
a number and looking at it, he said: "It won't blow up." And
fired the generator.

There was the usual crack like a rifle shot and bright ring of
fire down below. But that was all. The tanker lay there, gently
surging against her mooring lines in the tideway. He was right.

Checking, I found that he had calculated the currents that would
be induced inside the tanker and from those he had figured the
temperatures that would arise, which were well below the flash
point of gasoline. So we were perfectly safe and I went back to
work, while he zapped off a few more shots. At least it had worked
the first time that he tried it.

As we tidied up, we sent for two deckhands from our firm to
round out the crew and sailed down the Intracoastal Waterway for
Fort Pierce. But passing inside Cape Canaveral, we came to a new
set of overhead power cables that were not on the chart. That
was embarrassing, since I could not be sure that our tall aluminum
masts would clear them, so I asked Morris what he thought.

Taking the binoculars, he studied the wires for a moment and said: "That's only thirty thousand volts. Have a go."

It is virtually impossible to tell, from the deck of a sailboat, whether her masts will clear an overhead wire, for even if they will, it always looks as though they cannot possibly do so. But this was a special case. We had an important operation ahead and a schedule to meet. Slowing right down, I took *Azara* up to them, while Morris made impatient noises like a tea kettle about to boil. And just as I was convinced that our masts would plow into them, they slid underneath, one after the other.

The only dock big enough for *Azara* in Fort Pierce was at the marine terminal that had a concrete overhang, about four feet above the water, that would have wiped off her railings if we had gone alongside it. So we got some old tractor tires and made two fenders, about 60 feet apart on the wall. And each time that we docked, we would have to take the ship in so that her own fenders came exactly in line with those.

But there was a fine clear space behind the dock, with a fence around it for privacy and a large shed in which we could stow our spare equipment, while the harbor had a well-lit channel out to the sea that was easy to run in any weather, so that altogether it made an excellent base of operations.

Patrick and I moved ashore for this assignment. We turned up early every morning to get the ship ready for the day's operations. I usually prepared lunch ahead of time so that when we did get offshore, I wouldn't be stuck in the galley while everyone else had all the fun.

By then it was mid-April and Bill Anderson flew down from Boston in the helicopter, following the beach most of the way, with a copilot aboard and his mechanic chasing after them in a truck. And as soon as they were ready, we went out to sea for our first high wire operation of the new series.

The weather was marginal, in my opinion, with a stiff onshore breeze that would certainly kick up a moderate sea in the Gulf Stream. But there were pressures for us to get on with it right away, so out we went with a full crew aboard, plus Bill's new wife and an Air Force lieutenant.

His job was to check two racks full of fancy communications

equipment that had just been installed aboard *Azara*, bringing the total number of antennae sprouting from her masts up to eleven, not counting the long wire one. We also had a large reflector on our foremast, so that a shore station with which we were working could track us with radar, for this series of operations was to be altogether more elaborate than the last ones had been.

Going down the channel, we could see the big sea buoy ahead, wagging from side to side like a windshield wiper. Obviously it was rough out there but I was pretty sure that I could find a smooth patch to turn *Azara* around in, so that as long as we went straight out to windward, we could always get back. Meanwhile we steamed along in the calm water, past the bending casuarina trees, our decks lined with happy, complacent people.

Passing between the breakwaters, we began to pitch into the seas, throwing up a little spray, and the ship gave a couple of lurching rolls before we cleared them, to head directly into the wind. She was good on that heading, for she was long and thin and sliced through the seas with little fuss. But to operate, we would have to turn her beam on to the wind, so as to carry the wire clear of her masts and the plan was to do that six miles out.

About 30 miles south of Fort Pierce, the Gulf Stream begins to angle away from the coast of Florida, leaving a wedge-shaped area of relatively calm water between it and the shore. For the moment we were in that, as you could tell from the color of the water and the shape of the seas, but once we entered the Stream, it would be really rough. So halfway out, I tried a little experiment. Slowing the ship down, I turned her across the wind.

Immediately *Azara* began to roll her damnedest, flapping wildly from side to side, picking up tons of water as she dipped her gunwales under and throwing it across her decks, to shoot up in fountains of spray wherever it hit anything.

A few people kept their cool. Two scientists stood on the deck abaft the bridge, so deep in discussion that they did not seem to notice the water that sometimes came above their knees. But in general, the reaction was to call for help. And suddenly our fine, new communications gear was all in urgent use.

Needless to say, nothing worked. Not a single radio could raise anybody. Meanwhile Bill came overhead in the helicopter and looking down, he was convinced that *Azara* was about to turn right over. With his wife aboard. So he got on the radio and reported the situation to Control, who started frantically trying to reach the ship but equally without result. And in the midst of the confusion, the telephone rang.

It was a mobile phone of the kind that you have in cars, that everyone had forgotten. And the operator had called to ask to whom she should bill a call that had been made the day before.

By that time, everyone was convinced that we could not hope to operate in that weather, so I ran *Azara* off before the wind and she wallowed her way back into the harbor without any real risk. And as we steamed down the calm channel, there were animated discussions going on all over the ship. But my immediate problem was to dock her so that she could get out again, for the strong wind would surely pin her firmly against the concrete wall.

So I worked out a procedure by which two men went ahead in the whaler and one got off on the dock, while the other came back to push *Azara*'s bow around. At the same time, I brought her stern round with the main engine, while another man dropped the anchor and laid out its chain cable on the bottom of the harbor, ready to haul us out the next time. Meanwhile the man on the dock worked with those aboard the ship to set her lines and as she came to a stop, with her fenders exactly in line with those on the dock, the gangplank rattled out, I shut down the main engine and the job was finished.

It looked complex, with nine people doing different things at once but it went off smoothly every time, mainly because there was no shouting. I told the man in the whaler what I wanted by hand signals and the man forward when to drop the anchor with the word "Okay," while the rest went about their jobs in silence.

After that first day, Bill and I would go up in the helicopter each morning, he to check the weather from his point of view and I from mine. And only if we both agreed that it was safe, did we operate that day. This worked well, preventing false starts, so the days that were not suitable for operation could be used for other purposes.

The surface winds in that area are mostly onshore, while the coastal breezes blow onshore by day and offshore at night. So by day they add together, making a strong onshore wind, while at night it is often quite calm. But there is a lag in the system, so that the calm period starts late at night and ends around ten in the morning. And we took advantage of that, checking the weather early in the morning and leaving immediately if it was suitable for us to operate in.

Steaming out to sea, we would open the deckhouse roof and rig the sheave as we approached our assigned location and when we got there, we would drop a light anchor with 200 fathoms of nylon line to keep us from drifting out of position. Next we would let a floating line out astern of the ship, with a small life ring at its far end, and attach its near end to our antenna wire. Then Bill would come out and hover low over the water while his copilot dangled a large fish hook below the helicopter, snagged our line, drew it up and attached it to his bridle. And as soon as Bill got the signal that it was hanging clear below him, he would start to climb to his operating altitude.

That worked just as well as the old procedure, where June and I used to go out in the whaler to hook the wire onto the helicopter from below, and it was a great deal safer. But the subsequent operation was hard on the two pilots.

Essentially their problems were vertigo and fatigue. Sitting in the plastic bubble, high up several miles offshore, they would look down at the blue sea, up at the blue sky, and over toward the shore, blue in the distance. Circling as they had to over the ship, the whole view went round and round outside their cockpit, which is enough to make anyone dizzy. And even with two pilots, it was very tiring to maintain station over *Azara*, who they could hardly see. So we hung some dye markers in the water, leaving a large patch of yellow on the sea to guide them. But that led to another problem.

The captain of an airliner saw the dye, then looked at our gray decks and decided that we were a large airplane that had gone down in the sea. So he radioed in our location and out came the Coast Guard, looking for us. We had just finished operations for the day, so we offered to join them in the search and all through the afternoon we rushed around at our full 10 knots, busily looking for ourselves until it got dark and we gave up hope of finding us.

That really should not have happened, since there was a large poster at every airport in Florida, warning all pilots to stay well clear of us and our wire. It was printed in red and stressed the fact that there was One Million Volts in the wire, but in fact that was not the real danger, for the voltage would not have hurt them, with nowhere to go up there, but the innocent-looking wire would. It was only about an eighth of an inch in diameter but underneath its copper coating were seven strands of stainless steel that could have sliced the wing off an airplane like a bandsaw.

June and I had the job of searching the sky with binoculars all the time that the wire was aloft and letting Bill know if any aircraft came into the area. Usually the sightings were routine, on the lines of: "Target southeast, moving north. Looks like an airliner," followed a few seconds later by: "Okay, I've got him. Thanks." But a couple of times, one came so close that Bill had to drop the wire. The worst was a Sunday pilot in a National Guard jet fighter who seemed to be determined to get himself killed.

At first we thought that he would just go by but when he saw *Azara*, he decided to buzz her and swooping down, he whistled over her before Bill had time to drop the wire. By great good fortune he missed it, since it was hanging downwind of us, but when he banked around for another pass, Bill let it go. Then he put the helicopter into a steep dive, dropped several thousand feet and went straight at him head on, which scared him away for all time.

With two pilots aboard, plus the weight of the wire, the helicopter only had enough fuel for a couple of hours of operation, and by about eleven in the morning we were getting the anchor up, to steam back into port and spend the afternoon getting things ready for the next day. But even so, Bill's mechanic was having a hard time keeping the little machine going, day after day. And hearing of that, someone High Up sent us a balloon.

When Morris first mentioned it to me, it sounded insane. It was to be 96 feet long by 32 feet wide and filled with helium; it would have a static lift of 2,000 pounds, which meant that its wire had to be very heavy. And not only was I supposed to fly it from the schooner but I was also expected to dock her in the afternoon breeze with the thing flying from the top of her mast. But when I pointed out the technical problems to Morris, he arranged for a large, flat barge to carry it and a tugboat to pull the barge, which made a great deal more sense.

The balloon came with a crew of six men and was reputed to have cost the taxpayers over a quarter of a million dollars, including some helium to blow it up and a winch to haul it down. And for several days they were busy making preparations, while we continued to operate with the helicopter. But eventually it was ready and as soon as a calm day came along, it was scheduled to fly.

Spreading the silver cloth out in the open space behind the dock, its crew began to inflate it. Purposefully they moved around, adjusting its mooring lines as it got fatter and took on its proper shape, with a rounded nose and stabilizing fins near its tail. Then it lifted off the ground, went up a few feet and came to a stop, swaying gently from side to side. And suddenly it burst, to fall back down while its crew ran for cover.

And that was pretty much the story of its life. They would take it away to a basketball court, sew it up and bring it back. Then they would wait for a calm day and stage another fiasco.

It was all supposed to be a great secret, which was embarrassing because the local press reported each attempted flight with headlines such as BLIMP BLOOPS and BAG SAGS. But whoever thought of keeping a 96-foot balloon secret in a busy harbor was clearly the one who needed classifying, so we did not bother too much about it.

As time went on, it became evident that the balloon could not tolerate the slightest breeze while it was near the ground, for it would move with the air in the way that a ship will move with a body of water, and being both heavy and fragile, it would jerk against its mooring lines and burst. So they picked the calmest days for it and over a period of several weeks it flew for a total of three and one half hours, reaching an altitude of 3,000 feet before the fabric rotted in the sun and it was finished.

Meanwhile we were operating with the helicopter in the mornings but in the afternoons June and I started experimenting with kites, which seemed to us to be the logical vehicles to use for antenna support at sea, where there is usually plenty of wind available and if there is not enough, you can always run the ship to make some more.

Morris, in his usual generous manner, provided us with a shed on shore for a workroom and with time to build the kites. We in our turn bought any material we wanted. We started with paper, string and glue but soon progressed to more sophisticated designs that required more sophisticated materials.

Then he found a bigger shed for us, as our failures began to accumulate. We had kites of all shapes, sizes and colors hanging from the rafters. But our exhibit did demonstrate some progress and Morris continued to encourage us.

Not that Patrick could have been stopped at that stage. He entertained only one thought: to build a kite that would DO THE JOB.

Reading up on the subject in the local library, we found that box kites had been used by the military to support short wire antennae in the past, so we started off by building a big box kite. Finished, it was 16 feet long and we painted it red so that airplanes could more easily see and avoid it. But the only place we could think of to test it was Fort Pierce Airport.

Fortunately Ed Treat, who ran the airport, was a tolerant soul and when we showed up with the great kite, a thousand feet of wire and five scientists, he said we could go ahead and try it. The wind was out of the east, so we all went down to the western side of the field and laid out the wire on the ground, with the kite at one end of it and an axe handle at the other. Then June and two of the scientists held the kite up at an angle, while the rest of us took up the strain on the wire. And with a great deal of waving and shouting we went galloping through the grass, four of us on the axe handle, the rest running underneath the kite, exhorting us to go faster. But it only went up a hundred feet or so and as soon as we came to a panting halt at the other side of the field, it came gently back down.

We made a couple of more runs like that, until Ed came by in his car and said: "You know, we found 27 rattlesnakes in that grass last week." At which point we quit for the day.

The general opinion was that the kite would probably fly if we could only get it up higher, where the wind would be stronger. So the next day I went back to see Ed, who said we could borrow his fire truck to tow it with. That meant using the active runway but he had little traffic in the afternoon and would watch out for us, so that we would not be a menace to aviation. And off I went to fetch the kite and round up a crew.

Roaring down Runway 9 in the fire truck, heading into the easterly breeze, we watched the kite go straight up for five or six hundred feet but that was all, and when we stopped, it came down. Evidently it had plenty of stability but not nearly enough lift for our purposes, so reluctantly we gave Ed back his fire truck and went back to the ship.

When I tried to pay Ed for the use of his facilities, he would not take anything, which made me feel that at least I should buy something from him and the only thing he sold that I could use was flying lessons. So I took a few from him and later, not wanting to waste them, I got my pilot's license.

Meanwhile we obviously needed more hard information on kite design and I sent away to New York for transcripts of all the available material on the subject. There was not a great deal and it was fascinating reading, from the notes of Leonardo da Vinci to those of Thomas Edison. But the only serious work since World War II had been done by the Royal Air Force Experimental Establishment at Farnborough, England. And as we read, we built a series of kites.

Naturally our designs were influenced by what we were reading at the time and the first few were da Vinci types with long, curved wings, that swooped magnificently into the air and came rushing back down, straight into the ground. But those were smaller models, quickly made and flown off the dock with a borrowed fishing reel. And slowly we began to understand what the problems were.

It is easy to make a kite with good stability and poor lift, or the other way round. The trick is to find the best compromise between the two, for any given use. But the RAF reports were very helpful and eventually we developed a design that looked as though it would do the job. So we built several of them in four- to six-foot sizes and set about learning how to fly them.

The wind for the first 100 feet or so above the surface was usually turbulent but after that we had no more trouble until they got to 1,000 or 1,100 feet, where they would run into a layer of rough air about 50 feet thick. Then came a surprise, for the wind above that level was from an entirely different direction, so that as we paid out the line, it hung in a great curve. We had suspected that something like that was going on from the behavior of the wire when it was held up by the helicopter, but with the kite and the fish line, the whole thing became clear.

Evidently the prevailing southeasterly wind over Florida is only about 1,000 feet thick, while above it lies a turbulent shear, followed by a westerly air flow reaching up for another 4,000 feet or so to another shear. After which it might be in any direction, as far as we could tell. But at least we knew what to expect.

There were some incidents during those flights. One kite fetched up in the classic location at the top of a tree and another broke its line, to go sailing off across the town. Chasing it in a car, we spotted the line draped over a building and around behind it was the kite, lying in the middle of a railroad track, with a train about to run over it. Leaping out of the car, I ran to save it, but when I got to it, there was no time for me to stop and go back so I grabbed the kite on the fly and went on across the track to the other side, where I stood holding it while the train rumbled by and its driver looked me over with obvious distaste. But we got the information that we were after and could go ahead with the next stage of building the final kite.

The finished job looked much like a small airplane, with a wing span of 12 feet and a magnesium airframe, covered with red nylon and braced with aircraft cable. It had cost us $200.00 of our own money for materials and according to my calculations, it should fly. But we had no chance to find out until the balloon burst for the umpteenth time, the helicopter was down with supercharger trouble and *Azara* had an important operation to do. At which point the professor said: "All right, you can try your kite."

We were to work with Cape Canaveral that day and they were

holding up a rocket shot, waiting for us to get ready, so we put the kite aboard the ship and left immediately.

It was already late in the morning and there was a good breeze as we steamed down the channel, opening the deckhouse roof and leading the antenna wire aft as we went. As soon as we were a couple of miles offshore, I slowed right down and dropped three men off in the whaler, to hold the kite as we moved slowly away from them. When we had a thousand feet of wire out, we radioed to them to hold its nose up and Morris took up the tension on the wire with his winch, while I rammed *Azara*'s throttle open.

For an instant there was a scuffle in the far-off whaler, then the kite left it and went straight up, as we surged forward and the wire screeched out through the sheave above us. With just a faint curve from side to side it climbed, rapidly getting smaller in the blue sky until it reached 6,000 feet. Then we called Canaveral and told them that they could fire off their rocket as soon as they liked. We were ready.

Azara was slicing through the seas at flank speed, while the men in the whaler bounced along in hot pursuit. Morris was firing the generator, June was steering the ship and I was jumping up and down on the bridge shouting: "It works. It works."

With the kite in the upper air wind and the ship in the surface wind, the antenna wire led off to one side most of the time. But once in a while it would swing across and touch the aluminum mainmast, sending a million volts zapping down it as the generator fired. And where June was standing, the mast was touching her backside. So we posted a lookout to watch the wire and yell: "Tuck it in" to her when the wire got close to the mast.

As soon as the rocket had gone by, we slowed down to let the men in the whaler get back aboard the ship but the kite seemed to be quite happy where it was, so we left it up there and used the antenna for some other work before bringing it down later in the afternoon. When it was 200 feet above us, we cut the wire and it landed gently in the sea, to float on the surface until it was picked up by the whaler and brought back aboard the ship. Then we washed it with fresh water and by the time that we were back in port it was ready to use again. The next morning the helicopter was fixed and we went back to our routine operations.

A few days later we had some heavy equipment to load aboard *Azara* and since it might be dangerous, I ran the winch under our new loading boom. As it took up the strain there was a crack and without thinking I jumped aside, in time to see the boom break in half and spear its jagged end into the wooden deck where I had been standing. I could see at a glance that the people who made it had put in a miserable little collar at the joint, instead of the long one that I had told them to, so I went up to the foredeck and cursed them for about five minutes. And the same day, 200 miles away, the foundry burned to the ground.

You hardly find cursing like that nowadays but I did not hear about the fire until three weeks later and by then I had forgotten what I said. However the operations were successful and when we closed down, Morris announced that he was planning a new series, to take place in the Bahamas after the hurricane season, with our kites as the primary means of antenna support.

Morris always appeared on the first day of a project in a clean, tidy suit, a tie and white shirt, usually having just come from Washington and important meetings. Within minutes, he was deep in the engine room or the generator room, in a dirty, rumpled suit, a tie stuffed half into a pocket like a grease rag and a shirt not worth laundering.

When it came time for another important meeting in Washington, someone would take Morris to the local Sears store, outfit him, put him directly on the plane and hope for the best.

Alice, Morris's patient wife, could only shake her head and sigh. She tried so hard to keep things in some sort of order. She even vacuumed the generator, fastidiously dusting the huge capacitors and their intricate connections. After a rainy period she was always the first one to check the generator, keeping it as clean and dry as possible. But Alice couldn't leave her family to follow Morris on every trip and more often than not his clothing situation just got out of hand.

And Morris was quite well aware of it. Making a night run once, I walked onto the aft deck to find Morris sheepishly tossing mounds of clothes overboard. His wife was waiting for us at the next port. He looked at me and said: "Please don't tell Alice."

As soon as everyone was back aboard, we went down the

waterway to Palm Beach, where we anchored off the Coast Guard station to get our clearances. And while we were there, one of the scientists decided to check the marine radio by calling them. But getting no answer, he tried speaking louder and louder. And suddenly the Coast Guard came back, very loud indeed, saying that they could hardly hear him. For a moment we thought that the set had gone wrong, until someone pointed out that the microphone was not plugged in and he was shouting so loudly that they could hear him through their open window 100 yards away.

When we were ready to go, there was a strong southeasterly wind but leaving early in the morning with our sails sheeted hard in, we had a comfortable passage to Grand Bahama Island, where we put into West End. The harbor there is really for yachts and there was hardly room to get *Azara* into it, while to get her out in the morning, we had to turn her through 180 degrees, more or less in one spot. And as we started that maneuver, our big air horn decided to start blaring away.

All around the rectangular basin were motor boats, docked with the open ends of their deckhouses facing us, while their owners slept peacefully below. But not for long. As we swung slowly around, the entire output from our powerful horn would funnel into one boat after another. Inside, the noise must have been deafening and shortly after we came in line with each one, angry people would come out and shake their fists at us. But there was little that we could do about it, apart from waving and smiling politely, until someone cut off the horn's air and stopped it.

Leaving rather hurriedly, we were out of the harbor when we noticed that one man was missing and looking back, we saw him on the dock. Perhaps they were afraid that we would come back, but anyway someone brought him out in a speedboat and after that we had a pleasant day's run to Nassau, to enter the harbor just after dark and anchor in our usual spot off Paradise Island.

We had selected South Bight on Andros Island for those operations, where we would be clear of air traffic, but there was no chart of that remote harbor available and no one in Nassau knew the way through its rocky entrance. However one of the scientists had his light airplane with him and he flew John Robb and me over there to take a look at it. John was Morris's assistant and would share the rap if we goofed but circling low over the water, we could see the channel clearly and it did not take me five minutes to make a sketch chart of it, while John helped memorize the landmarks that we would need to go in there. Half an hour later we were back in Nassau and the next morning we set sail, to arrive off South Bight in the afternoon.

Lois, John Robb's wife, would join us from time to time. Thank goodness. She would fly out from St. Paul, all neat and tidy, with a bright smile, a keen wit and her monogrammed bowling ball. Somehow she and John managed to keep alive a sense of humor in spite of the constant trials aboard Azara. I think the bowling ball was Lois's secret. She would spend the afternoon in the nearest bowling alley, naming the ten pins and then sending them flying.

The water there is very deep and the strong onshore wind had built up quite a sea, so that *Azara* rolled and lurched heavily as we scanned the coastline for the entrance, but before taking her in, John and I went ahead in the whaler to lay our home-made navigation buoys. Those were three floats that we had rigged, each with a line and a sinker, to drop into the water at the points where the channel changed direction. And leaving June at the wheel of the ship, with instructions to take her to Nassau if we could not get back out to her, we felt our way cautiously inshore.

As we suspected, the seas got steeper as they came into the suddenly shallow water, but after a while they calmed down and by the time that we reached the channel, they were not bad at all, so that we had no trouble locating our turning points and laying our buoys. But the ride back out to the ship was interesting and once or twice I thought that the little whaler was going to flip end over end backwards before we got there.

After all that preparation, the run into the harbor in *Azara* went off very smoothly. For a while she wallowed in the following sea but soon she calmed down. One after another, our buoys came up ahead of us and before long we were anchored in the middle of the wide, shallow harbor, with nothing in sight but the distant shore line all around us and the bottom a few feet beneath our keel.

Behind a headland a mile or so away was the tiny village of Lisbon Creek and there we rented two local sailboats, a large one for our receiving equipment and a small one to supplement the whaler as a general runabout. When the tide turned, we took out a second anchor and dropped it astern of the ship, so that lying between the two, she was across the prevailing wind. And in the morning we were ready to operate.

Taking the kite out in the whaler, we ran downwind for 1,000 feet, stopped and held its nose up. Then John took up the tension on the wire with the winch, we released the kite and up it went, climbing away into the sky. With *Azara* anchored across the wind, the wire led clear of both masts and for the rest of the day the generator fired away as the experiments proceeded, until evening came and we brought the kite down. It was almost too easy.

On calm days we could not operate that way but we had three kites of different sizes and three wires of different weights, so that on most days we could find a suitable combination, and often we would fly the wire for 12 hours or more in a day, giving us a total flying time of 50 or 60 hours a week.

Dr. Larson, inventor of the electric organ, was receiving the signals and it was odd to see him step aboard the old native boat in the early dawn time and sail off to work. Anchored several miles away, he would dangle various loops and coils of wire in the water, then peer into his oscilloscope to see the result. And soon after sundown he would come gliding alongside *Azara* to have dinner and discuss the project late into the night.

So it went on, day after day until some people from *Life* magazine showed up in a chartered flying boat. We were expecting them and hauled the kite down to 600 feet so that they could make some pictures of it over the ship. Then the pilot came in to land. But approaching the ship against the wind, he did not notice that the current was going the other way. And as soon as he came under our lee, it carried him forward until he fetched up with his nose wedged firmly under *Azara*'s counter stern.

June ran and sat on the bulwarks, pushing him off with her feet while I took the whaler and pulled him away by the tail. His port engine was stopped with its propeller in the ship's life line but the starboard one was still running and as he swung around, he nearly got me with that. But I ducked and he swept clear, to discharge his passengers and fly away.

For several days the photographers lurked and muttered and clicked around the ship but after a while we got used to them and did not notice them any more, which was what they wanted. And as they went about their business, we went about ours.

We had a good supply of food aboard when we arrived in South Bight but we always seemed to need more, and one answer to the problem was fresh fish. The local fishermen came by nearly every day and as soon as we saw their sails, June would rush out to meet them in the whaler. Their boats were about 30 feet long and the two ends were watertight but the midship section in way of the fish hold had rows of holes in its bottom and was flooded to the waterline. Down there, the day's catch would be swimming around, and standing on deck, June would point out the ones that she wanted to buy.

Azara had plenty of space for all sorts of supplies. Her long freezer made it possible for us to carry plenty of good meat. But there are always things to get locally. Sweet fresh fruit in the islands. And beautiful fish. We always bought locally. It was fun to go into the different markets, fun to try the area foods and a good way to meet the people from the town.

Lisbon Creek sported a shop. A small wooden shack with a counter and a few shelves. I asked for eggs. Always a good start. The proprietor didn't have a dozen on hand but just a moment and he would see what he could do.

We walked from the store, down a dirt path that connected the few houses of the town to his house. The doors were open and we wandered through the tiny rooms, along with the chickens. Peeking in corners of chairs and under a bench, we found enough to get us through the day. Nine, as I remember it. We never seemed to find a dozen.

My other purchase was a box of paper napkins. Actually not a whole box. Some had been removed. Perhaps they were sold by the napkin. Anyway I took what was left.

The proprietor apologized for his low stocks. He sailed to Nassau from time to time and made his purchases. And there really wasn't much room in his little open sailboat for luxury items.

One evening we all went into Lisbon Creek and finding the only bar, we ordered drinks. The choice was rum and the brand was Red Tiger, on which you could have run an engine. The glasses on display were all chipped, so we asked for paper cups. But we had not figured that they would use them over and over. Mine was old and battered from long use, with cracks half an inch deep around its rim, and the others were about the same, but we did not feel that we could say anything without being rude, so we drank up and went back to the ship.

Later on, Morris began thinking about another operation that he was planning, which would require a relatively short antenna to be put up very quickly and last for a few seconds. So John decided to try out a Coast Guard line-throwing rocket. To find out how high it went, he planned to photograph it from the sailboat and the best time for that was at dawn. So one morning we all stood shivering on deck, while he fussed around the rocket and stood back.

Suddenly there was a noise like a jet airplane passing low overhead at full thrust. With afterburner. And two seconds later about 17 people were jammed tightly in the main hatch, trying to get away from the thing. But we need not have bothered, for it rose slowly into the air, no more than 10 feet, dropped back down and went wandering off under water at about five knots.

However, the rest of the rockets behaved better and John developed a neat rig by which they would carry up a fine steel wire that ran off the end of a spool, after the manner of a spinning reel, that was just what Morris needed. By this time the operations were completed and we sailed *Azara* back to Nassau.

There we dropped off some of the scientists, including Dr. Larson who took his leave saying: "You know, I shall remember you for hours." After which, we made a good passage to Palm Beach and went back up the waterway to leave the ship at Jacksonville. But already Morris was impatient to get on with his next project, and going up to the counter at the airport, he said: "I'd like a seat on the first plane out, please."

"Where to, sir?" the girl asked.

"Anywhere," he said.

15   MEHITABEL

Our yacht delivery business was increasing steadily, so that we had
to spend more time in the office, and while I made several short,
local trips to check out new people, I did not make a long one until
the next winter, when Arnie Gay of Annapolis sold his 36-foot
yawl *Mehitabel* to Lee McMillan of Corpus Christi, Texas, and we
got the job of taking her out there. Dick Vincent went along as
deckhand.

Sailing down the Chesapeake early in December was not as cold
as we had expected and motoring through the Intracoastal Waterway was quite pleasant, with the trees along the banks bare of
leaves and the docks almost deserted. But in Georgia a cold front
caught up with us and one morning we awoke to find a blizzard
outside.

We were lying to an anchor in a lonely marsh and a bitter
northwest wind was driving the snow almost horizontally across
the water, blotting out everything but the nearest bank. By the
time that we got the anchor aboard, we were chilled through,
so we took turns warming ourselves as best we could over the
galley stove, while the other one followed the winding river down
to St. Simon's Island, where we took a day off to let the front go
through.

*Some days I would be depressed at having been left behind but
then Pat would call in and tell me of the cold and the wet and the
long hours of sitting in the wind and the sun and I would be rather
glad to be sleeping in a warm, dry bed in clean sheets in a house that
didn't rock.*

The next few days were clear and with the biting wind in our
backs we made good progress down into Florida, following the

familiar route as far as Stuart. But there we left the main waterway to head westward toward Lake Okeechobee and soon we came to a lock.

Waiting for it to open, we noticed that the gates were curved instead of straight and in a moment we found out why. There was a rumbling noise and they opened a couple of feet apart, letting a column of water several feet high sluice through between them. Evidently the lock had no paddles to empty or fill it, but the gates, being curved, could be opened against the pressure of the water and served the same purpose. But what if they were opened the whole way? Surely the water would come surging forth in one wild rush. We never found out, for we were especially polite to the lock keeper and he let the water in gently for us, so that we had a smooth, easy ride up to the next level.

Farther along that canal you come to a vertical lift bridge that, when open, has a clearance of 46 feet above the water. And *Mehitabel*'s mast was 46 feet high. But it is a railroad bridge, so that its operator was in no hurry to close it, while the canal was calm and there was no traffic on the water. So we nosed the boat gently up to the shuttering beneath the bridge, to dock her against it with fenders amidships and lines fore and aft. Then we shut down the engine and walked her slowly through, clearing it by an inch or more, and off we went across Lake Okeechobee.

That is a fresh water lake, almost circular and about 30 miles across but scarcely more than six feet deep. It is above the level of the surrounding farm land, which is handy for irrigation but one year a hurricane blew all the water out of it, to go rushing across the countryside doing enormous damage, after which they built a high levee around it, with guard gates where the canals go through it. And from its western side, the Caloosahatchee River leads down to Fort Myers, where Joe Pelich joined us to sail as mate on the passage across the Gulf of Mexico.

After our experience in Georgia, I decided to sail southwest at first, then head west across the Gulf and finally go northwest up to Corpus Christi. That would be close to 900 miles but it would take us well south of the American coast and the cold fronts would have to cross a couple of hundred miles of warm Gulf water before they reached us, which should take some of the bite out of them.

And as soon as we had put fuel, water and food aboard, we motored down the river, past Sanibel Island and out to sea.

Sailing southwest in a light southeasterly wind, we soon drew away from the land and settled into the routine of life at sea. It would be Christmas before we reached Texas and Joe had bought a tree that he hoisted to the top of the mast in the traditional fashion. Then he put out a fish line, but during the night it got caught in the log line.

The next morning we noticed something odd following us that turned out to be a solid ball of line, for the log spinner had been going around, hour after hour, winding the two lines up into an unbelievable tangle that took the three of us half a day to sort out. After which we used a boathook as an outrigger to keep the fish line well clear of the log line.

Soon after we came onto our westerly heading, the wind went into the southwest but *Mehitabel* was a successful racing boat and she went well to windward, so that we continued to make good time until we were almost due south of New Orleans. Then the sky clouded over, the wind flew into the northwest and came on strong and cold, rising rapidly to gale force. A cold front had arrived.

We were 150 miles offshore, so we went through the routine of taking in all the sails, lashing the main boom down and securing everything on deck. Then leaving Dick on watch, Joe and I went below. To find the cabin full of smoke.

Fire at sea in a small boat is always serious but offshore in a storm it is more so. Usually you see them start, so that you can stop them before they get out of hand, but a cabin full of smoke with no obvious source calls for immediate action. Taking a side each, we searched rapidly in every locker, under every bunk.

It was all very dramatic, with the boat rolling and lurching as the seas caught her, the roar of the wind outside and the acrid smoke swirling around inside. As you opened a locker, the things in it would fly out, to roll and bang around your feet, while wisps of smoke would drift out of it. Or was it in? It was hard to tell, so you would stick your head inside and cough and wipe your eyes and try the next one.

Mehitabel had her companionway amidships, with a stateroom aft of it that was cut off from the cockpit, and there we found the fire, in a corner of a locker, centered on two thick black cables that ran from the engine to the battery. Quickly Joe got a wrench and took the cables off the battery, while I fetched an extinguisher to put out the fire, which was still quite small, for the smoke had been coming from the burning rubber and the wood around it had not yet caught. Then we tidied up the mess that we had made, checked the locker again and reviewed the situation.

The fire had broken out close to the gasoline engine and we did not feel like reconnecting the battery, in case there might be another fault in the wiring that we could not see. Which meant that we had no engine, no radio and no lights. But we were accustomed to sailing without those things, since they often went out in storms at sea. Two days later, when the front passed over us, we continued on our way.

For several days we had light winds and made good progress. It had been cold in the front but not really bitter and as the wind went back into the southwest, it warmed up again. Turning into the northwest brought the wind on our beam and by noon one day we were just under a hundred miles from Corpus Christi. By midnight we had less than 40 miles to go and making a good six knots in a smart breeze, we were looking forward to arriving in time for breakfast. But at three in the morning the wind died, clouds blotted out the stars ahead of us and the air suddenly turned cold.

Joe was on watch and, being from Texas, he knew what the signs meant. Calling Dick and me on deck, he set about getting all the sails down as quickly as possible and before we had finished, the wind was roaring out of the northwest. Another cold front had arrived.

Within minutes the temperature dropped from the 70's to the 30's and at dawn we looked out over a lime green sea, whose tops were being whipped off by the wind and flung across the surface in a layer of stinging spray. And about 20 miles away, straight up wind, was Corpus Christi.

It was exasperating not to be able to make those last few miles but there was no way that we could drive *Mehitabel* into that weather and all we could do was take turns keeping watch as it drove her relentlessly back down the Gulf. One man would crouch in the cockpit, shivering with the cold and peering with distaste at the world outside, while the other two tried to get warm in the cabin. And every two hours we would switch around.

Halfway through the night we noticed a sloshing noise and found that we had quite a bit of water in the bilges. But the only pump aboard was electric, so we had to bail it out. One of us would hold the flashlight while the other knelt on the floor, dipping cupfuls of oily seawater into a bucket, to be passed up through the hatch to the man on deck. Though actually we did not so much dip it as catch it as it went by, holding the cup in the right place to intercept a lump of water as it rushed across the boat, then trying to get it into the bucket without spilling it all.

Toward dawn, Joe and I were doing that when the hatch opened and Dick's face appeared above us. Stopping, we looked up and he said: "Which one of you guys called for a taxi?"

Before we could think of a suitable reply, the hatch closed. And as we continued to bail, we wondered what we were doing out there, trying to keep a leaking boat afloat with a teacup in a winter storm at sea. But in the afternoon of the third day, the wind eased and we were able to make sail again.

By then we were about 65 miles from Corpus Christi but it was no longer so cold and after a brisk night's sail we arrived off the harbor, to fall becalmed within sight of the entrance.

Being already four days late for breakfast, we were in no mood to tarry, so we dug out *Mehitabel*'s lightest sails and coaxed her across the last few miles of water, into the harbor and up to the nearest dock, where we secured her and set about fixing her electrical system. And while we were working, Lee came aboard.

He had seen the cold front go through and was worried about us, so he had arranged for some friends who lived on the beach to keep an eye out for us. But he was very happy to find *Mehitabel* in good shape and rode proudly with us over to the yacht club. And so ended another passage.

And perhaps there began Patrick's disenchantment with the sea. The passages had become routine. The discomfort, the exhaustion had become routine. How many icy waves do you take down your back in the cold, wet mornings, half asleep at the tiller, before you say: "No more"?

16 LIGHTNING BUGS

Next July we heard from Morris Newman. The Air Force wanted him to catch a natural lightning bolt and measure it, to provide information for the design of protective devices. And the best place to do that was at sea, where there would be nothing sticking up from the surface to confuse the picture. So *Azara* was to go on a lightning hunt.

August would be a good time for it, when the thunderstorms are thick off the east coast of Florida. That would be in the hurricane season, of course, but the Hurricane Warning Center in Miami would let us know if one was coming close. Morris would bring three of his people from Minneapolis and there were two more aboard the boat, while I was to bring a mate and two deckhands and meet him in Jacksonville.

The thunderstorms form over the west coast of Florida in the mornings and drift across the state, to arrive off the east coast in the afternoons, well-developed and full of lightning. They have very strong winds in them, so that it would pay us to catch them in the narrow strip of calm water between the coast and the Gulf Stream, but they are several miles high and we should see them in time to intercept them. The best port to work out of would be Fort Pierce and as we steamed down the waterway toward it, Morris and his people started their preparations.

All the way aft they set up a circular aluminum plate, five feet across, standing on long brown insulators like a tall table. That was to be the target for the lightning to strike and to encourage it, they mounted a rocket launcher on the plate, rigged to carry a thin steel wire up into the cloud. If all went well, the "leader" would come down the wire first, vaporizing it and leaving an ionized trail for the main charge to follow. And when that arrived, the idea was to measure it quickly and let it go.

Azara's bronze hull made an excellent ground, which was helpful, but I was a little concerned about two things. First, I felt that the lightning might fail to understand the procedure and come down the aluminum mainmast, to fetch up where Morris and I were standing. And second I wondered if we might be blown off the bridge by the blast, for the Russians had recently published a paper indicating that, at that distance, we might expect a puff of wind on the order of Mach 3 or 4.

When I mentioned those thoughts to Morris, he made it clear that (a) I was a sissy and (b) the Russians did not know how to do arithmetic. But to keep me happy, he let me set up an aluminum shield between the bridge and the target, with a plate overhead to deflect any lightning bolts that might come down the mast. And off we went to look for one.

Leaving the harbor about noon, we headed north up the coast and there were the thunderstorms, bearing down on us out of the west. But though they had plenty of electricity in them, it was concentrated in a few small cells that moved rapidly around.

To detect those, Morris had rigged a copper brush at the top of the mainmast, with a wire leading down to a meter on the bridge. That would measure the tiny flow of current that Benjamin Franklin had discovered in his famous experiment with the kite and the key. And when it told us that we were underneath a charged cell, we would fire our rocket.

What would happen then was open to discussion, for it had never been done before. If we succeeded in tapping a cell, it should discharge down to us and most likely the other cells in the same cloud would transfer their charges to the first one as it emptied, so that we would end up with a major stroke.

But first we had to get underneath a charged cell and that was not easy, for the meter would tell us when we were close to one but not which way to go after it. So we would steam under a dark gray cloud, through driving rain and confused seas. Overhead there would be bright patches in the cloud as lightning flashed to and fro within it and every now and then a stroke would crash into the sea nearby. But the meter would say "Not Yet" and we would keep on searching.

Morris and I stood on the bridge wearing Air Force helmets, dark glasses, ear plugs, foul weather gear and life jackets, while the rest of the crew stayed below decks, the scientific staff crouched over their instruments, the others prowling around with fire extinguishers. I handled the ship and Morris directed the proceedings with his usual enthusiasm. When a huge stroke of lightning curved across the sky, to hit the water half a mile away, he said: "Whee. That was a beauty. Let's go that way." And we went that way. But always the charged cells evaded us and at nightfall we headed back to Fort Pierce.

There we had a small problem, for our old berth was no longer available and we had to use another one, which was great for leaving in a hurry but tricky to get into in the dark. We had to take *Azara* between two docks, spin her around with a few feet to spare and lay her alongside, exactly on her fenders. So we developed a variation of the technique that we had used at Wingate on the Chesapeake and that worked every time. But day after day, the lightning continued to avoid us.

It is surprisingly hard to get struck by lightning. Every day we would go out as soon as the first thunderclouds appeared on the western horizon and steam underneath them, one after another. With nothing else sticking up above the surface for miles around, you would think that our two tall masts would attract a few accidental strikes but they never did. Hour after hour the crew stood at the ready as we bucked and rolled through storm after storm with lightning coming down all around us. But always the meter would tell us that we were not close enough and on the few occasions that we fired up a rocket nothing happened.

Morris fired the rockets by pulling on a rope that led from the launcher forward to the bridge. The two of us stood side by side under my shield, which was about the size of two telephone booths, and he would reach around outside it to pull the rope. With all our protective gear, we hardly heard the rocket go off. But when we looked back, it would be gone and we would have to put another one on the launcher.

Once as we were running into a storm, I noticed a bulge in Morris's pocket. It was a spare detonator that he was keeping dry. When I pointed out that it might go off, he stashed it away down below but I think that he felt I was being overly cautious.

Soon our time ran out. We only had a month to do the job and with two days left, we had not had a single strike. Perhaps it was not possible after all. But we kept on trying and just south of Cape Canaveral we found a big, black thunderstorm, piled high into the sky, with lightning shooting out of it. As we went underneath it, the wind came howling across the water, throwing a white blanket of spray across *Azara*'s high deckhouse and as we reached its center, the meter said "This is it."

Morris tugged the rope. There was a brilliant flash of white light and a noise like a three-inch gun. We had a strike.

He rushed below to see the results and a few minutes later he came back, looking very happy. Everything had worked. We had the volts, the amps, the blast, the wave form, all the facts and figures that the Air Force had asked for.

It is extraordinary in any research operation to have everything go right on the first try but clearly this was our day, so we put another rocket on the launcher and got a second strike. Just like that. The meter said "Fire" and we fired and down it came. With another complete set of data. Now we could go home.

Steaming north, we cleared the area of the thunderstorms and put in a radiotelephone call to the Air Force. Morris left the loudspeaker on so that we could hear both sides of the conversation and when he told them the results, the voice at the other end said: "Gee, that's wonderful." And so we steamed into Jacksonville, our mission completed.

That was *Azara*'s last trip. She was sold for the bronze in her hull and replaced by a bigger, more conventional ship. But it was not the same, for an era had ended. Gone were the days of the wild chances and the weird-looking rigs. But in all the trips that we made with her, *Azara* never failed to come back with the data that she went out to get.

17   ANTILLES

For some time we had been moving boats that were insured by Percy Chubb, and that fall he asked us to take his own yacht *Antilles* from Charleston to St. Thomas. The hurricane season ends at the first full moon in November and we left soon after that.

His captain was aboard when I arrived with Dave Putnam, Don Street and a deckhand, which gave us a strong crew, for Dave had taken his own yacht to Greenland and back, while Don ran a charter boat in the Caribbean and the deckhand had sailed in the America's Cup Races. Dave was the person for whom June and I had delivered *Orana* some years before, but most of the owners fetched up as friends of ours and it was not unusual for them to sail with us later as crew members.

Antilles was a fine yacht, 45 feet long, well built and maintained, that should not give us any trouble. But in the latitude of Charleston, we could expect cold fronts about once a week, while in that of St. Thomas the trade wind would be blowing strongly against us. So I laid our course via two imaginary points in the ocean that I called Able and Baker.

Point Able was 250 miles southeast of Charleston, on the far side of the Gulf Stream where the cold fronts would be much weaker and point Baker was just north of the trade wind belt, in a position from which we could sail down to St. Thomas in one tack. And from one point to the other, we would sail eastward in the slot between the cold northern weather and the trade wind.

We were delayed for a few days at the start while *Antilles'* diesel engine was fixed but after that the weather bureau gave us a good forecast and we sailed right away, to carry the fair weather across the Gulf Stream. And soon we were past point Able, heading out to the eastward in light, variable weather.

But such conditions do not last for long on a winter passage and as the barometer began to fall, the wind rose and the sky clouded over. Clearly a major storm was approaching.

Since it gave us plenty of warning, we had a good meal and checked the boat out thoroughly. Then as it got closer, we reduced sail until we were hove-to under the storm trysail, with the centerboard up and everything securely lashed down. And as the wind rose, the sea built up until we were in a full gale.

Soon after dark, the eye of the storm passed over us and the wind fell calm, leaving us banging and bouncing around in a steep, confused sea with nothing to steady us. The deckhand was on watch, while the rest of us stood in the cabin with our foul weather gear on, ready for any emergency. And as we were talking, I noticed the deckhand standing politely beside me, waiting to speak.

Turning to him, I said: "What is it?"

"There's a funnel outside," he replied.

Following him on deck, I got as far as the hatch when it hit us. The roar of the wind rose to a high screech, sending *Antilles* skidding sideways down into the trough between two seas and laying her flat on her side. Which was good, for we were sheltered to some extent in the trough and her bottom was facing the wind, deflecting it up and over us.

The deckhand was a sturdy 200-pound athlete and as he clung to the steel life line with both hands, his body waved like a flag in the wind, while I was wedged in the hatch, conveniently blocking it against incoming water.

The wind was very strong indeed. I have jumped out of military airplanes and fallen through the air at about 110 miles an hour and it was much stronger than that. But it did not last for long and as suddenly as it came, it left.

In silence *Antilles* heaved herself upright, the deckhand came down on deck, I scrambled out of the hatch and one by one, the others appeared. Getting used to the dark, they went all around the boat, looking for any signs of damage. But there were none.

We had come through it without a scratch.

At a time like that, you brew up a fresh pot of coffee and consider the matter. We were still in the eye of the storm, so we had better watch out, in case there were any more funnels around. For a while we peered out of portholes and sure enough, along came another one.

It was like a Grade B movie. People stood around, a cup of coffee in one hand, clinging on with the other as the boat heaved and lurched, the dim light reflected in their faces. And in quiet, clipped sentences they reported its progress. The funnel was clearly visible against the rest of the sky, though it was much wider than we expected a tornado to be. But in any case we wanted no part of it and when it passed by us, we were quite relieved.

Soon the eye of the storm moved away, leaving us back in a plain, ordinary gale and it was amazing how safe and peaceful it felt. For now we were dealing with something that we knew, something that we could easily handle.

For hundreds of years, the strength of the wind had been recorded on a scale running from 1 to 12, but a few months before, the range had been increased to 16. So I entered my first Force 16 in the log book and under "Remarks" I put "Draughty and Damp." Then just for fun, I tried the radiotelephone and in came Nassau, loud and clear. With no trouble I put a call through Miami to New York and June answered. It was Thanksgiving and she had friends in for dinner. And as we lay hove-to in the gale, far out in the Atlantic Ocean, I could hear the clatter of dishes and the sound of voices back at home.

We seldom had a turkey, or even a Christmas tree. There seemed no point when Pat was at sea more than he was at home.

When the wind decreased, we made sail again and worked our way out to point Baker. Then we stood down into the trade wind and fetched St. Thomas as planned, 14 days out of Charleston. And back in New York, I enquired about those funnels.

They are called "micro lows" and are not very common but are sometimes found in the eye of a large, rotating storm. When you do see one, there are often two of them and though they are not usually as intense as a tornado, they are in the same class and certainly have a lot more wind in them than you will ever need.

18   FLOATING ISLAND

The following summer, Peter and Nancy Mickles inherited a large houseboat in Canada and wanted her in New York to live on. She was ashore beside Lake St. Francis, so they got a bulldozer to push her into the water and a towboat to take her to a shipyard in Cornwall on the St. Lawrence River but there they ran into problems.

She was too wide to go through the Richelieu Canal and thence down Lake Champlain, but she had no engine and towing her by any other route would be too expensive. And anyway the yard said that she was unsound. So they came to us and I went up to inspect her.

Lying in a dry dock, she was a curious sight. Someone had taken two heavy steel tanks, each about 22 feet square, and built a frame of girders between them, so that they were some 20 feet apart and the whole structure was around 64 feet long. Then he had decked it over, with false sides between the tanks, and on top of it he had built a conventional wooden house.

It had a living room at one end and a dining room at the other, with a passageway between them, off which were four bedrooms, two bathrooms, a kitchen and a storeroom. There was a sun deck with an anchor on it at the living room end, so that must be the bow. At the other end was a smaller deck, with a huge pair of davits outside the dining room windows. And between the two was the white house, with its green pitched roof and a walkway along each side of it. Her name was *Floating Island*.

Examining the tanks, I found that they were pitted in places but there was plenty of metal left to last for several years and when I explained to the yard that she could go down to New York via Oswego and the Barge Canal, they agreed that they could fix her up for the journey.

That left the problem of how to move her but after some calculation, I found that the most economical way was to lease a pair of big outboard engines and motor her down. And when I went over the details with Peter, he told the yard to get her ready.

A couple of weeks later, June drove Paul Stabler and me up to Cornwall in our old station wagon with two 75-horsepower engines in the back. Afloat, the bow tank was deeper in the water than the stern one and she would never steer that way, so I had the engines put on that end and called the other end the bow. Then we set six 50-gallon drums of gasoline on the deck, piped three of them to each motor and the engine room was complete.

Good friends, the Langs in Mamaroneck, gave us the ancient Buick station wagon. They thought they might as well, we borrowed her so often. And a good car she was. We slid the huge outboards for Floating Island *in through her back door. And without a complaint she delivered them to Canada, winding her way through the back country roads.*

She drove like a Sherman tank and it was a job keeping her on the twisting roads through the Upper New York State mountains. But we made the trip back home the same day, she and I.

Her body was rusting away and there were lichens growing in the cracks of her wooden upperworks but every year we would give her a fresh coat of rustproof paint — lichens and all. It seemed to hold her together and give her courage to withstand another year of our abuse.

Next we led cables around pulleys to the new bow and set up a steering position there, with a striped awning over it. Then we ran a fish line under the eaves of the house to a bell at the other end, by which I could signal to Paul to start or stop the engines. Meanwhile Peter and Nan arrived with some friends of theirs and early one morning we got under way.

For the first few miles up river from Cornwall the current runs strongly against you, so we got a work boat to tow us past that section, after which she turned us loose, Paul cranked up our engines and we went ahead on our own.

With the two big outboards roaring away, the noise at Paul's end was so loud that you could not hear yourself think but he did not seem to mind and settled down in a deck chair to sunbathe, while at my end of the house it was so quiet that you could not be sure if the engines were running, except by putting your foot on a certain spot on the deck where you could feel a slight vibration. And a faint chuckle of water across the bow told us that we were moving forward through the water.

Trying out the steering, I found that it was tricky. For sitting right in the bow, you could not tell which way you were going. So the tendency was to oversteer wildly from side to side. Looking back down the passage, I found that I could keep her more or less straight by getting a feature on the bank in line with something in the living room but that was not entirely satisfactory as a navigational system. And then I remembered the Great Lakes ships.

They always have a pole sticking out in front of the pilot house, and when we rigged one of those, we could tell where we were going and the steering was much easier. It was still weird, because the slightest breeze would send her wandering across the water sideways but now we could tell what was going wrong in time to do something about it. And when we got her going straight, we measured her speed.

In calm water with no head wind, she was making one and a quarter knots through the water. But the current was running against us at half a knot, so that we were making three quarters of a knot over the bottom. And so we crept silently up the St. Lawrence.

Coming to a dock, we put in to top up our gas tanks and when we stepped ashore, we had trouble finding our way back again. The houseboat looked like a part of the dock and it was hard to tell where it was from the shore. But soon we were under way again and relaxing; we began to enjoy the ride.

Moving at that speed, you can dive overboard and swim around the boat, to climb back aboard with no trouble. There was an aluminum boat with a 14-horsepower engine in which people would go ahead and visit shops or museums, to meet us a mile or two farther up the river. And in the evening we anchored in a quiet bay, where she felt solid and secure, with no sign of motion.

Her name *Floating Island* was well chosen, for that is exactly what she felt like. Inside the house, you might as well have been ashore, except that the view from the windows changed a little over the course of the day. But not so fast that you could not read a page of a book and look up and know that you have not missed anything. And at night, silent on the dark, still water, she was quite enchanting. A house poised for a moment in a special place, where it had never been before and would never be again.

And so we crusied through the Thousand Islands, past quaint old vacation homes in every imaginable style. In one section the current runs rather strongly and for a while our speed over the ground was no more than a quarter of a knot, as we worked our way close along the bank in the slackest water. But once we were in the wider reach above it, we made good time to Cape Vincent where the river ends and Lake Ontario begins.

There we had to cross the 60 miles of open water to Oswego, the only unsheltered part of the trip, and at our speed it would have taken us two days and nights, during which time the weather would most probably have turned sour on us. So we found a man with an old landing craft to give us a tow across the lake and the weather forecast being good, we left right away.

With his powerful engine, we made a good four knots and as darkness fell we swept past the offlying islands out onto the lake, but he did not know how to navigate and had no instruments, not even a compass. So I rode with him and navigated with my protractor.

It was a calm, clear night and I would place the protractor against the side of his pilot house, which ran fore and aft, and sight over it, to measure the angle between it and the Pole Star. Then I would direct him to steer to the left or right until he was on the proper heading and he would follow whatever star was ahead of him for the next quarter of an hour, when we would repeat the procedure. Just before dawn we picked up the lights of Oswego and by breakfast time we were safely in port, while he went off, following the shore line back home.

After clearing with the customs people, we set off up the Barge Canal and right away we came to the first lock. We had already discovered that we had no stopping power at all, since when Paul reversed his engines, their propeller wash bounced back from the steel tank and pushed us forward. But we had a row of old tires along each side that would make good brakes. So we slowed down to half speed and I asked Nan to bring the small boat and secure it across our bow.

As we entered the lock, I rang for Paul to stop his engines and put the steering hard over, so that the engines were facing across the boat. Then I stood at the corner of the house, where I could see along the side and signal with the bell to Paul or by hand to Nan. As our momentum carried us slowly ahead, we used the engines to move the bow or stern left or right. And when we got to the middle of the lock, we pressed the boat sideways against the concrete wall and the tires brought her to a stop.

It worked out well and we soon found that you could do all kinds of maneuvers that way. We would arrive at a dock sideways and leave it sideways. If necessary, we could pirouette around in our own length. And before long we came to Three River Point, where we joined the canal that runs from Buffalo to Troy.

Going east, we came to Oneida Lake, which is 22 miles long. It took us all day, from before dawn until after dark, to cross it but the day was calm and sunny, with infinite visibility and we had plenty of time to admire the countryside around it. As we went down the Mohawk River, we picked up the fair current which increased our speed to a solid two knots, but I had to get back to the office, so Tom Kelly took over at Palladian Bridge to complete the canal section and take her down the Hudson River.

There the current runs faster than they could go, so they sailed on the tide in the manner of the old sailing barges. For six hours they would sweep down the river, making good time, then they would pull over to the side and anchor while the current went the other way. And so on, day and night, down to New York.

They had to pass through the Harlem River and Hell Gate, so I joined them and took the small boat ahead to check the currents. It was dark as they approached the swing bridge that leads from the Hudson into the Harlem and the current was running at an angle underneath it, but forewarned, Tom brought her through without any trouble and reaching the other end, we moored her to an old dock, just before Hell Gate.

Early the next morning, before the tide was due to turn, I was out there in the small boat, watching the flow of the water. As it slowed down, I went back to get the houseboat and when she arrived there, it was calm and still, with the current just beginning to go in our direction.

I joined the crew for the ride to City Island. By that time, Patrick was well aware of the behavior of the barge. He was able to maneuver her through the masses of small boats moored off the island, as if he were driving down a highway. I stood with heart in mouth waiting for the corners to catch on someone's pride and joy. But it didn't happen.

So *Floating Island* arrived safely at City Island, where Peter and Nan lived aboard her for several years, anchored off in the summer and moored to a dock in the winter. And often as we went by, we would see her out there, lying serenely on the calm water within sight of New York City.

19   SOME OTHERS

By then we had moved our business to Larchmont, a few miles from Mamaroneck, and for the next five years June and I spent most of our time there but I still went out once in a while to keep my hand in. Sometimes they were routine jobs, like taking a new 57-foot Chris Craft from the factory at Algonac, Michigan, to a dealer in New York or a 45-foot Matthews from Port Clinton, Ohio, to the Chesapeake. But more often I would pick the unusual boats, that were more interesting.

Expanding from a one-man show to a professional service proved to be difficult but it was a stage we had to go through. Many yacht owners wanted only Patrick and we lost jobs as Pat held his ground and refused to sail himself.

One was *Black Hawk*, a 50-foot schooner built in Washington, North Carolina, and bought by Julius Payne. She was a real character yacht, dripping with glamor, and we both slipped away to help him take her around to Mississippi.

Sailing across the Gulf of Mexico on a beautiful night with a light southeasterly wind, we had everything set, including the big fisherman's staysail that only a schooner can carry. Her sails were new and glistened white in the moonlight as she heeled gently to the breeze and slid over the calm sea, far from the land. The yellow light of an oil lamp came from the cabin and there was a feeling about her that you do not get in modern boats.

Of course she was highly inefficient as a sailing machine and a pig to handle in bad weather but when things were right, she had great charm. And if you take the view that the purpose of a yacht is to give pleasure, she was entirely valid.

Another interesting boat was a Magnum that I took from the factory in Miami to her owner in New York. She was 35 feet long, with two large and thirsty gasoline engines and very limited accommodations, but she did go. We were running in her engines and kept her speed down but still she made an easy 25 knots and left a wake behind her with six separate elements to it.

It was impractical to steer her from inside, so my deckhand and I had to sit on the flying bridge and the motion was so jumpy that it was hard to read a chart or do anything except hang on, but still it was fun. We would slow right down and creep past a sailboat, to have them ask us to go back and make a high speed pass. Which we could do, for in fact her wake was mostly spray when she was going fast, though it was horrendous at intermediate speeds. And going up the Chesapeake in her was a revelation.

The red small craft warning flags fluttered tautly against a gray, overcast sky as we left Norfolk and headed up the bay. There was a moderate sea running but she went straight through it without slowing down and soon we left the bad weather behind us, to cross the mouth of the Potomac in a flat calm. Off Annapolis we ran into some thunderstorms but again we left those behind and arrived at the Chesapeake & Delaware Canal in clear, sunny weather, eight hours after we started.

The next day, as we ran down the Delaware, there was a strong southwesterly wind, and approaching Cape May in a following sea, she nearly put her bow under water a couple of times, which would never do at that speed, so I took her through the Intracoastal Waterway as far as Atlantic City.

Going through the narrow, winding creeks at high speed, we found that full rudder was not enough to bring her around some of the sharper turns, but she had electrically operated trim tabs on each side and by using these, we could bank her around the corners without slowing down. And north of Atlantic City, the wind was off the shore, so we ran up the beach as far as Sandy Hook, to rush across New York Harbor in the lowering dusk, less than a week out of Miami.

As the crew grew, we expanded our services. My time was spent running from boat yard to boat yard, picking up crews, delivering them to airports, working out ticketing with agents, getting spare parts as needed and a dozen other tiny details. Marge McKenna joined us, much to the delight of the accountant for I had never acquired the art of bookkeeping. But I could work as a translator between the crew and the office. I knew about rubbing strakes and turnbuckles and the way to Apalachicola by that time. And with Marge's help the office began to shape up.

The following month I was bound up out of Florida for the Chesapeake in a big old Trumpy houseboat that was just the opposite of the Magnum. Slow and quiet and comfortable, she was so heavy that you could stop her a few feet off a dock and leave the pilot house while you spoke to the dockmaster. And she would sit there without moving until you were ready to leave.

Her cabins were large and airy, her engine room had seven feet of headroom and everything about her was on a generous scale. She was not suitable for offshore work but she was never designed to be and in sheltered waters she rumbled and splashed along with the air and dignity of a ship. A pleasant, civilized yacht.

By then we were getting a fair number of "gold platers," yachts built and maintained for people who could afford the best. We took *Antilles* to and from St. Thomas several times, while Gabby Gianini's 50-foot yawl *Pacifica* went out to the West Coast.

From New York she sailed down past Florida and carried the trade wind across the Caribbean Sea to the Panama Canal, but in the Pacific Ocean she ran into calms and had to motor for about 2,000 miles, past Central America and Mexico to Baja California, where she ran into head winds and storms for the last thousand miles to San Diego. And that was a typical westbound passage.

Another "gold plater" was Don Haskell's 70-foot cutter *Chubasco* that we delivered from Los Angeles to the East Coast and back. The eastbound passage was easier at first, since she had a fair wind to Mexico, but after the Panama Canal she had a hard beat against the trade wind until she reached Haiti. So those trips always took a long time and while we made several of them in different boats, I was never able to go on one. But we had attracted some remarkable people who handled them.

Steve Lang came to us as a young man from a family that had

always had boats, and sailed as deckhand and mate before starting as skipper, to become one of the best in the business. And when he took *Chubasco* to California, he arrived within 15 minutes of his estimated time.

Basil Mosenthal was a well known ocean-racing navigator before retiring from the British navy with the rank of commander and coming to America to join us, while Richard Ensor spent World War II sailing around the Pacific in native boats for an organization that shall be nameless and eventually found his way to us.

Tom Follett took time off from working with us to sail *Cheers* single-handed across the Atlantic Ocean from St. Croix to England, then race her to Rhode Island and sail her back to St. Croix. And walked into our office exactly on schedule.

David Humphreys was navigating officer in the *Empress of Britain* and sailed in several ocean races off Australia before coming to America and joining us. And one year, he took time off to lead the Humphreys Expedition to Greenland, which resulted in a major revision of the geography of that continent.

We also had some younger skippers who did the easier jobs, plus people sailing as mates and deckhands to gain experience, so that we could fill just about any order that came our way.

Most of our work was for the yacht brokers, taking boats from one place to another as they were bought and sold but we got an occasional commercial vessel, such as the ferry boat *Caneel Bay II* that we took from New York to the Virgin Islands, and once in a while we ran a charter yacht like the 100-foot *Sea Panther* for a few weeks while her owner found a permanent crew for her.

Basil handled that one and on the first day he had a party to pick up on the Hudson River and no dock for the boat. So he chartered a seaplane and flew up the river until he found one, then landed to make the arrangements and flew back to bring the ship up, just in time to meet them. But we used light airplanes quite often and things did not always work out that smoothly.

On one occasion, Steve was flying from St. Thomas to San Juan and noticed that they were heading east. But San Juan is west of St. Thomas, so he mentioned it to the pilot, who muttered something and turned the airplane around. And when they landed, both fuel gauges were reading "Empty."

Another time, I was taking off from Annapolis on a calm night when we met an airplane landing on the same runway in the opposite direction. But more impressive was taking off from Kennedy Airport for San Juan in a four-engined jet airliner. As we climbed out, I saw a stream of liquid going past my window that looked like jet fuel, so I rang for the steward and showed it to him. Telling me that it was condensation, he went straight to the flight deck and immediately the left wing went way down as we started a tight turn back to the airport, to land and change airplanes.

But flying was a part of our lives all those years, for almost every job started or finished with a flight, and as with most things, one forgets the scary moments and remembers rising through the billowing clouds into the bright sunshine over Chicago or watching the lights along the coast of Florida twinkle 30,000 feet below, with three weeks' work behind us and home only a few hours away.

In our office, Marge McKenna kept the books and as much else as she could in order but sometimes there were technicalities that baffled her. One of our crews found a life buoy floating in Chesapeake Bay and since it had *Palawan* written on it, they gave it to Marge to send to Tom Watson. But it had a light attached to it that went on when you turned it right way up, so they left it upside down. And if she knew nothing else about marine gadgets, Marge could tell when something was upside down, so she turned it over.

It promptly started flashing, brightly and busily, while she hunted for the switch to turn it off. And finding none, she got more and more exasperated until finally she solved the problem by shutting it in a closet until we came back from lunch.

Of all the boats that we handled, the most comfortable at sea was *Criterion*, a 77-foot motorsailer designed by Philip Rhodes and owned by James Moffett. She had a permanent crew of three men, but Jim was his own skipper and when she made a passage without him aboard, one of us would take her. Her single engine gave her about eight knots and was very quiet, but with her ketch rig, she could do much better than that and generally we used both.

My first trip in her was from Charleston, South Carolina, to Montauk, New York, and we made it in less than three days with no fuss at all. Rounding Cape Hatteras in a seven-foot sea, she was so steady that I could stand in the bathtub and take a shower without holding onto anything, then sit down to a leisurely breakfast without having to worry about spilling my coffee.

Patrick claims that the greatest advance that has been made in yacht design and construction in this century has been the introduction of the hot shower. He is probably right. Unfortunately, I sailed during the "a man who would go to sea for pleasure would go to Hell for a pastime" era.

Another time, we were southbound near Palm Beach under full sail in a fresh breeze, having dinner while the autopilot steered *Criterion* and one man kept a lookout. It was a black old night and he did not notice a squall bearing down on us until the wind was over 40 miles an hour on the meter, but we did not feel like going out in the rain to ease her sheets and, heeling slightly, she sailed straight through it. A truly remarkable sea boat.

The strongest wind I ever saw was on the St. Clair River. We were approaching Port Huron in a 42-foot Hatteras called *Happy Talk* when a cold front came through. The line of clouds was black and straight, with lightning in it and a dark curtain of driving rain beneath it. And as it swept across the river, a tornado dipped out of it, heading straight for us.

We were cruising at 17 knots and as I pushed the throttles wide open, the little boat darted forward. For a moment we thought that it would still hit us fair and square but it went howling across our stern, slapping us with a blast of air as we shot into the wall of rain. There we lost sight of it, so we kept going at full speed, rushing up the river for another minute in rain so hard that we could barely see our bow, steering by the compass and hoping that we would not run into anything. Then we slowed her down and checked for damage.

Both windshield wipers had been bent away from the glass but no glass was broken. My pipe had been taken from the ashtray two feet in front of me and flung overboard, but nothing else was missing. And the only way we could figure it was that tiny jets of air moving at very high speeds had done those things. So tiny that they did not break the glass but moving fast enough to bend a heavy windshield wiper almost double. In which case, we had come as close to the tornado as I would ever care to.

As we became better known, people would come to us for advice on fitting out their boats for long passages. Count Theo Rossi had a 140-foot schooner with a permanent crew of 14 men under a former submarine captain and when he was planning to bring her across the Atlantic Ocean, he came to us. He wanted his yacht inspected and a report prepared, telling him what should be done to get her ready for the trip, what spare parts should be carried, how to rig her for the trade wind passage and so on. But it had to be done tactfully, so we arranged for Tom Follett to sail as a guest aboard her on a three-week cruise in the Mediterranean.

The other guests included such notables as the Archduke of Austria and the whole cruise was splendidly run, with a couple of the Count's cars waiting at every port of call in case they might be needed. And having made four transatlantic passages, Tom was able to give him all the information that he wanted.

Working in the office, we enjoyed doing things that people thought were impossible, as when one of our skippers telephoned us from Charleston, South Carolina, at a quarter to four on a Friday afternoon, to say that he needed a spare part for a foreign diesel that the yard there could not get in less than 10 days. Phoning the importer in Boston, we got the names of his dealers and checking with them, we located the part. As it was being wrapped, we had a girl on the way to them and when she got there, we told her which office to go to at the airport, where the clerk was waiting for her. Within minutes after she arrived, the part was airborne and when it landed in Charleston, our skipper was there to get it, less than three hours after he had asked for it.

Another time, a man telephoned us from Cape Cod, distressed because he was all alone and needed help with his boat. But one of our skippers had just finished a job five miles away, so we told the man to stay where he was and within 20 minutes our skipper walked up to him, with his gear and ready to go.

But as time went on, June and I got into other things, like designing equipment for research, selling electronic navigational instruments and building a restaurant in a Vermont ski area. And the yacht delivery business was a demanding one, requiring constant attention, so in the summer of 1969 we sold it to David Humphreys and went off to pursue our other interests.

20   SWAN SONG

Two years later we took a vacation and delivered a yacht for our old firm, as skipper and deckhand. She was a new 40-foot motor-sailer, built on the lines of a trawler, out of Huntington, New York, for Naples, Florida. Frank Lualdi who owned her sailed with us for the first few days and on a clear, calm morning we set out down Long Island Sound toward New York City.

Frank had never been through the city by boat before, so we showed him the sights as we ran down the East River and across the harbor to The Narrows, where the new bridge was finished. It had taken a long while to build and month by month we had noted its progress, watching the tiny men at work high overhead as we passed underneath it. But completed, it had changed the appearance of New York Harbor forever.

Before, you came in from the sea, between the high bluffs of The Narrows, to a natural harbor. On your right were some red brick apartments and in the distance you could sometimes see the sky-scrapers of Manhattan but to your left were the wooded hills of Staten Island and ahead lay the Hudson River, wide and deep, flowing unobstructed into the Atlantic Ocean.

Now all that had changed, for the bridge made it clear that you had entered an area that man had taken over, where nature must take second place to his needs and abide by his rules. And if you knew the harbor before, there was a sense of loss.

When first we sailed those waters, there were fish traps along the

Jersey coast, so close inshore that you had to stay within 100 yards of the beach to clear them, but now they were all gone and we had an easy run to Manasquan, where we stopped to lower our mast before continuing down Barnegat Bay.

There was a time when we could take a sailboat through that waterway with her mast up, for there was a full six feet of water and plenty of clearance overhead but now there were low, fixed bridges and scant four feet of water. We were told that the bridges cost so much, there was no money left for dredging. Still, when we anchored for the night, it was peaceful and quiet on the water, even in the heart of bustling New Jersey.

Following the ship channel up the Delaware, we remembered the days when we had to take the "overland passage," skirting behind Dead Man's Shoal in six or seven feet of water, dodging between oyster stakes to bring a tired, old boat safely through in a north-easterly gale, and trying to find a buoy that was hidden among the tall, thin stakes with their bushy tops.

The Chesapeake & Delaware Canal was being straightened and the dock where we had so often spent the night was gone but Chesapeake Bay looked the same as ever and the old, familiar headlands came up, one after another, all the way to Norfolk.

On the way down Chesapeake Bay a little storm came over and we sought shelter for a day in a quiet cove.

It's a good feeling, when a gale is overhead, to know the anchor is holding and the trees around the water's edge are breaking the greater part of the wind.

The boat will swing on her anchor as winds and tides change. She will bounce unhappily when the two forces are at odds with each other. But then she quiets down again and you hear only the high-pitched screech of the wind in the rigging and the slap of the choppy water against the hull. It's a time to be glad you aren't at sea.

There Frank had to leave, while we carried on to Pamlico Sound. Often we had taken boats through there in the dead of winter, when the buoys were white with ice and our decks were like skating rinks. And once, bringing a sailboat in to a dock, we had both lost our footing, so that she scraped along the pilings. We were sure that her paint must be damaged but when we checked it, we found she had ice a quarter of an inch thick all along her topsides and had slid in on that without taking a scratch.

But in fine weather with a good, modern boat it was almost too easy, and heading down the long stretches past Morehead City, we wondered what would happen next. We had seen Lake Erie go from a huge reservoir of clear drinking water to a gigantic cesspool within 10 years. We had seen waterways closed off by bridges so that people could rush faster from place to place in their cars. Everywhere it seemed that things were being made easier and dirtier and uglier, with little thought for the consequences.

On Wind Song, years before, we spotted an orange crate awash in the sea. It was the first sign of "civilization" since leaving St. Thomas about two weeks earlier. The crate meant that we were near shipping lanes. And that meant that the navigator was probably right: We were fast closing in to the American shore.

Now friends tell us that the Sargasso Sea herself is just a huge oil slick with bits of debris caught in her spongy carpets of weed. And I feel guilty for tossing garbage overboard almost 20 years ago.

Already pollution was receiving serious attention, though so late that the cost of repairing the damage already done would be enormous. But what about the problem of noise? It only takes one noisy engine to shatter the peace of a quiet river or a silent wood, destroying its value as an antidote to the stresses of modern living. We could only hope that it would be tackled before it also resulted in untold harm to the human race.

Going quietly along at 10 knots, we had time to look around us, and sitting high up on the flying bridge, we could see things that we had never seen before. In river sections we could see far out across the marshes, while going through narrow land cuts we could look over the banks, to find fields and houses in what we had thought to be desolate areas. And so we came into Florida and took the waterway across to Lake Okeechobee.

At one time we did the waterway run so often that I would notice a new lamp shade in a house window along the 800-mile stretch.

After a few years of absence, we saw only the tremendous increase of buildings along the route. Where there had been a half dozen modest dwellings, there were now dozens of suburban houses, many sporting at least one outboard boat. The summer cabins were giving way to year-round residences. The old fishing docks selling bait and beer were changing their names to So-and-so's Marina and painting the old pilings white. And bridges, new bridges were now everywhere, connecting the once inaccessible sandy coastal islands to the mainland.

There the water level was down and we were driven below by bugs. They swarmed over us in their hundreds until we abandoned the flying bridge to steer from the saloon, with all the windows firmly closed and the air-conditioner going. But as we approached Fort Meyers, a thunderstorm cleaned them off for us.

The next morning we went down the river to the Gulf of Mexico and along the low, sandy coast to Naples, where we secured the boat and cleaned her, finally mopping our way off her decks and taking a taxi to the airport. It had been fun to be afloat again for a little while, but we had had more than our share of yachting and there were so many other things that we wanted to do before we got too old.

And so we stepped aboard the airplane, to take off for new places and different things, leaving our life at sea behind us, with fondness but without regret.

EPILOG

After we left the sea, we decided to try travelling over land and had a truck built, smaller than most cars but equipped to carry 500 miles' fuel and a week's food, water and ice, plus our gear and its spare parts for half a year.

There is a large tent for fine weather and a bunk in the truck for emergencies, a galley and a work bench, everything we need. And we call it *Minim*, a small thing of no importance.

To check it out, we spent three months in Baja California and the next winter we cruised the mountains of Guatemala. And we found it to be much like ocean voyaging, presenting the same sort of problems and offering similar rewards.

So now we have come full circle, back to the days before this book started, when we were wondering how far we might go on the sea. And what we would find when we got there.

THE BUSINESS SIDE

When first we started delivering yachts, there were no organizations that we could find specializing in that kind of work. Instead, there were a number of individuals in every port who called at the offices of the yards and brokers each day, offering their services as yacht captains.

But we were told that the best ones already had full-time jobs aboard the larger yachts and since there were no recognized criteria by which they could be evaluated (other than a Coast Guard license that was easily obtainable by any 18-year-old boy with minimal knowlege of boat operation) the remainder tended to be viewed with considerable doubt by the yacht owners.

And in fact anyone could call himself a yacht captain, if he wished, regardless of what training or experience he had.

So the owner who wanted his boat taken from one port to another would seek the advice of someone at the yard where she lay, or perhaps of his yacht broker or naval architect, in the hope of finding a reliable crew that he could engage on a short-term basis. But few of the brokers and almost none of the people who worked in the yards had any experience of delivery passages, outside their immediate areas. And the result was that it became a matter of reputation.

If a man was known to have taken a motor boat down the Intracoastal Waterway from New York to Florida without damaging her, it was assumed that he could be trusted to do so again. And some of the brokers kept lists of such people, who might be available when a client required them.

But if she were a sailboat out of St. Thomas for New York, such men could not handle her. And that was where we came in, for in a case like that, the owner would go to his naval architect and in those circles we were soon quite well known.

So we got our real start, not with the easy jobs, but with the difficult ones; not following a line of markers from dock to dock down a calm, protected waterway but strugging to keep an old wooden boat from sinking, a hundred miles offshore.

We were fortunate, of course, in having the background of training and experience to handle the problems that we ran into ashore, for I already knew my way around most of the ports from Trinidad to Miami and we had both been in management.

So when people told us that something could not be done, we showed them how to do it. When the parts or tools were not available, we searched them out or had them made. And when the bills came in, we were able to convince the owner of each yacht that they were fair and reasonable.

For delivering a yacht was not merely a matter of aiming her from one port to another. There was the crew to be selected and trained. There were mechanics (who might not speak English) to be shown how to get her machinery in shape for the passage; sailmakers and shipwrights to be found and instructed and paid before the provisions were put aboard and the passage started.

Then there was the accounting, at the end of the passage, when the books had to be balanced (sometimes in three or four different currencies) and the owner made to understand that he had received proper value for his money; that none was wasted but everything that should be done, in his best interests and for the safety of the vessel, was done.

It was not enough that he pay his bill. He must be sure he had been fairly treated because there were only a few owners in the market for deliveries of that kind and they tended to know each other, so that his goodwill was vital to us.

And after that, we would start looking for the next job: making calls, writing letters and minding the telephone, ready at any moment to give a detailed estimate of the cost of taking a yacht to Chicago or to drop everything and fly to Bermuda.

Even the passage-making part was not easy. The owner of an ocean racer would spend months getting her in perfect shape for the Bermuda Race, put a crew of nine men aboard and make the three or four day passage (under the supervision of Coast Guard cutters and aircraft) to arrive with his men exhausted and the boat in shambles. Then we would take her back with three men and hand her over in better condition than when we started.

But we survived, as this book tells, and as our reputation grew, we had enough work to keep two or three men busy.

That was a difficult period, since it required that we maintain a full-time office, staffed by someone who really knew the business, yet there was not enough income to support it.

When the phone rang, it was essential that whoever picked it up be able to answer all the caller's questions in the kind of detail that only comes from first-hand experience, to convince him that he could safely entrust his yacht to us.

So either June or I had to be there all the time and we only survived by not spending money. We lived in a tiny apartment that was also our office, ate two meals a day, and even though we moved out of New York City after a year or so, we went without a car for the first seven years.

To help support our yacht delivery business, we also did other things. One winter we designed a midget (dinghy-sized) ice boat, built a dozen of them, took a stand at the Winter Sports Show and sold them. For a while I worked as chief engineer for a nuclear research company, designing equipment for them at a drawing board in my own office. And so on.

But as our business grew, it became more efficient. With several crews, we could nearly always fill a client's order. With a good flow of orders, we could usually give our people as much work as they wanted. And with two dozen men out in several different boats, we began to get the "airline effect."

Each crew would report anything unusual to the office. If a shoal spot developed in the Intracoastal Waterway, we knew it. If a boat yard in Wisconsin was especially helpful, we were told. If there was a problem with the officials in Central America, we heard of it. And the information was used in briefing the crews when they came to the office at the start of each job.

By then we had a suite of offices in Larchmont with four telephone lines: one reserved for incoming calls from clients, another (unlisted) kept open for the crews to reach us, and two more for outgoing traffic. The clients' line had an extension at our house in Mamaroneck, plus an answering machine in case we were out. And in emergencies, the crews could use that.

So it was no nine-to-five operation but a 24-hour-a-day service with good communications, located by a railroad station (35 minutes from New York) and the New England Thruway, with at least one car and driver always available to take people to the boat yards or the airports.

In the first room, Marge McKenna kept the books and typed the letters while across from her was the Schedule Board, eight feet long, where June kept track of each job, making sure that the right people were in the right places at the right times.

Next came the Skippers' Room, where they made out their reports and balanced their accounts (with Marge's help) after a passage or consulted the charts, weather data and route information for the next one. And the third was for the manager.

Sometimes that would be one of our skippers, running the office while I was at sea, but more often it was myself, talking to clients on the phone, figuring estimates, briefing crews about to leave and interviewing people.

On average, 70 people came to see about working with us each year but only four percent made it. That is, one in five was invited to take a trial run after the interview and of those, one in five was asked to stay on.

It was not that we did not need more people but so few of them were really suitable for our kind of operation.

For our clients had come to expect men from us who could not only handle a boat very well but who could be relied upon to look after their interests in far places. And it was that quality of reliability, of commitment to the idea of putting the client's interests above one's own, that we were after.

Skills we could teach a man, if he knew enough to start as deckhand (we required three seasons' experience), and some of our best skippers came up that way. For sailing as deckhand and later as mate, they spent more time at sea in more different boats in a year than most owners did in a lifetime. And sailing with different skippers, all of whom were highly competent but each of whom had his own techniques, they learned fast.

So the first thing I tried to find out in an interview was not what the applicant could do for us but what he wanted for himself. What were his objectives? Why did he want to do this kind of work and what did he expect of it?

If his primary interest was money, I would advise him to try something else because few people indeed make anything like as much money in the service areas of the yacht business as they could in almost any other line of work.

The reason is simple. It offers a good life, in terms of one's surroundings and the people one meets, and it therefore attracts people who can afford it: those with private incomes or rich wives, or those who are willing to trade off the money for other things that they consider more important.

What could be more important? Working at what they liked doing. The freedom to set their own hours and plan their own lives. Learning the yacht business; getting to know the boats and the waters, the yards and the brokers. Travelling, perhaps, and meeting civilized people. If those were the things that he wanted (at least, at that time) we could proceed.

The next thing I sought to find out was his attitude toward the world around him. If he believed that it was divided into "them" and "us," the rich and the poor, the masters and the servants, I would advise him to try the uniform companies that served as clearing houses for full-time employees aboard the larger yachts. For such a man would never be able to see things from the point of view of the owner of a yacht.

In fact after several years I could spot most of the men who would not be suitable as they walked in the door.

If a man wore khaki (or a funny hat) or called himself Captain or presented worn references, he would never work out and I would continue the interview, not with the idea of taking him on but of helping him find work elsewhere.

But if I felt that his objectives and his attitude were in line with ours, then I would go on to describe our business and what we were trying to achieve, in more detail.

Technically we were marine contractors but since there was no precedent for a corporation formed to deliver yachts, we followed that of the firms that delivered airplanes, modified as necessary to comply with marine law.

And we limited our objectives to selecting and training people, then supplying them to clients on a short-term basis for specific purposes. Which means that we never agreed to move a boat anywhere but only to supply her with crew members as required, for the purpose of making a passage.

We charged the owner for our fees, based on the number of men and their ranks (skippers, mates and deckhands) for each day they were at his disposal, plus the expenses incurred by the vessel for fuel, provisioning, dockage, etcetera, and our men's transportation to and from the boat.

For we had discovered that a flat-rate contract favors the old boat, the "clunker" that breaks down and takes longer, while the daily rate favors the good, modern yacht that makes a smart passage, and those were the ones that we wanted.

And it was our policy to give the best possible service, while charging the client about the same rates as anyone else, so that it would always be in his best interest to come to us. Which worked out well, since in periods of recession, the clients who were concerned with economy cut back on their yachting activities, while those who demanded the best were able to carry on as usual and our business was scarcely affected.

Each man who worked with us was technically a self-employed sub-contractor, engaged on a short-term basis by each vessel in which he served. And that had several advantages.

From his point of view, it meant that he was free to take any job we offered him, or turn it down. If he wanted a month off, he merely called in and told us when he would be available again. And from our point of view, it greatly reduced the paper work, while avoiding the relationship of employer to employee, that we felt was inappropriate.

For we preferred to regard those who worked with us as friends and equals, representing us aboard our clients' yachts and handling them as we would, if we could be there.

Our basic policies were spelled out in the Agreement that each man signed when he started with us: We never drank at sea, or 12 hours before going to sea. We never accepted "kick-backs" from yards or marinas. If we were weatherbound in port, we did something for the vessel (like paint her) or declared a "rest day" that was not charged to the owner. And so on.

There was also an Order Form which the owner was asked to sign, that gave the necessary details of his yacht (such as her fuel consumption and overhead clearance) and included our terms of business: The money for expenses was due at the start of the job and our fees were due at the end of it. Our men's travelling time was chargeable, going to the vessel but not coming back. The owner could send the men back whenever he liked but they need not sail in his yacht if her condition or that of the weather made it unsafe. Etcetera.

In theory, the Order Form and the Agreement between them protected the owner, the crew and our firm by setting forth all the rights and responsibilities of each party. But in real life, things were not that simple.

To get enough business to operate economically, we had to take orders from owners all over America. And in most cases, they were busy men who placed their orders by telephone and expected us to act upon them immediately. So it would be quite normal for a man to call us from Las Vegas, tell us that his yacht was in Nassau and ask us to fly a crew down there, to take her to Rhode Island in time for a race.

If the call came in the morning, we would often have the crew assembled, briefed and on their way that afternoon, for that was the kind of service we were selling. Then we would send the owner our Order Form by way of confirmation. And just as he trusted us to take his yacht, we would trust him to pay his bill, in due course.

But every now and then, an owner would let us complete the job, stalling for time by having his secretary say he was away on business for a few days and then simply not pay us.

And though we fought and won several lawsuits, including one that went to the Supreme Court of the State of New York, we never did collect on those accounts.

Of course we went through all the normal collection procedures, but the plain fact is that a very rich man a thousand or more miles away who does not want to pay you can make it impractical, if not impossible, for you to collect.

But the great majority of the owners were decent, honest people and rather than offend them by prying into their affairs before a job, we simply included three percent in our calculations, when figuring our rates, to take care of such matters.

Of course we had to convince them that any extra expenditure was justified. For example, when we arrived aboard *Fair Weather*, her owner was in Hong Kong and he believed that she was not only fit to go to sea but in suitable condition to be offered for sale in America, while in fact she was totally unfit to go to sea and worthless in the market, as she was.

So first we borrowed a typewriter and wrote a detailed report of her condition, backed up by color photographs, that we sent him by air mail. Then we considered the alternatives and decided that the best way to cut his losses would be to fix her up in Jamaica and take her to America to be sold. So we got estimates and came up with the figures and telephoned him in Hong Kong: It would cost so much to fix her up and she might then be worth so much in the market. What did he want?

Naturally he was unhappy with the situation but the color pictures told the story clearly and he gave us the okay to go ahead, while he provided the funds and it all worked out.

But it was a grown-up world, not a place for ninnies who thought they could hide behind pieces of paper. For the risks were far more serious than the mere loss of money.

Almost every year, a few people we knew would die making the kind of passages that we took on as routine operations. And with the volume of work that we handled, we felt the odds must be piling up against us. So we were very careful.

No man, however qualified, was allowed to sail as skipper under our flag without first making a trial passage as deckhand. We had to be sure, to see for ourselves that he really was good at handling boats and that he was temperamentally suited to our kind of work. That he would not treat it as a dull job or as a chance to goof off but as a serious profession. That he would constantly take the greatest care of the boat and her crew. And that he would neither dawdle nor push the boat too hard, but set a sober, sensible pace that would get her to her destination in the best time consistent with absolute safety.

So what did we do for kicks? We were precise. We enjoyed delivering a yacht with the quiet competence of the crew of an airliner: arriving at our destination exactly on schedule, in perfect condition and docking her without a word spoken. And it was men who understood such things that we wanted.

Of course people made mistakes occasionally, like leaving a fender on deck where it could fall overboard, and in those cases we would ask the owner to replace it and send us the bill, which the firm would split with the man who did it. But more often than not, the owner never did charge us, so that the cost of such mistakes over the years was negligible.

And in all the years that we ran the business, the total value of items we were told were missing from yachts and might have been taken by our men was less than $50.00.

Every yacht that we handled was insured, since a man just does not shell out a hundred grand for something that can sink and forget to insure it. But after 10 years of operation, we finally managed to get additional insurance, which we paid for, to take over where the yacht's insurance left off.

When we sold the business, we had never made a claim on that insurance but it was nice to have and a nice thing to be able to give the people who worked with us. But we never heard of any other organization that was able to get such insurance for yacht delivery work, and the individual who worked on his own would never had been able to afford it.

Nor could he afford the advertising that we did, to keep our name before the people who might need our service, for that alone cost thousands of dollars every year, while our telephone bill ran into hundreds of dollars a month.

Clearly, if we were to charge the client the same rates as anyone else, yet pay out those additional expenses, we had to give our people less, per day, than they might get in the open market for the same kind of work. But from the man's point of view, there were several advantages.

For a start, his annual income would be greater working with us because he need spend little time between jobs and none hunting for work. Then he had the advantage of our reputation, that brought the best owners and the best boats to us. And when he went off on a job, he had our backup.

If he needed a part in St. Thomas, he had only to call us and it would be on the next plane. If a crew member fell sick in Acapulco, we would fly in a replacement (at our own expense if it was the man's fault) and so on.

The same backup was of course a great plus for the owner, since at no extra cost he got our complete service, which minimized the chances of expensive delays in far places. Which made him tell his friends about us. Which meant more jobs for our people.

So we had a stable business, based not on a "hard sell" but on the fact that intelligent people can be relied upon to do what is in their own best interests. And it was in the best interests both of the owners and of the crew members to come to us for yacht delivery work. When I finished explaining our operation to an applicant, I would invite his questions and those would tell me more about him. If he thought we were an agency, he was not very bright. If he asked who would pay his fare back, when a boat was unfit for sea, he had failed to understand our outlook.

For in such a case it was up to the skipper to evaluate the situation from the owner's point of view and decide whether it was better for the crew to stay and do the necessary work, or to return while the local yard handled it. Then he should report to us and we would consult the owner.

So the decision whether to have the men stay aboard or go back would lie with the owner and if he sent them back, we would pay their fares and include them in his bill.

There were no hard-and-fast rules, followed by everyone who delivered yachts, but that was the way we did things and as far as we knew, we were the leaders in the field.

Many owners of well-known yachts came back to us, year after year and our skippers would maintain contact with the yards and brokers who might recommend our service by visiting them at the end of each trip. But we could not afford to lose an order by being slow to respond or sloppy in our work at the office, because the market was still limited.

Yachts below 35 feet could be moved more economically by other means and over 65 feet they nearly always had full-time crews, while most of those in between never went farther than their owners could take them on their vacations.

The easy jobs, like taking a 57-foot Chris Craft down the Intra-coastal Waterway to Florida, were still taken by the men who were available at the docks where the boats lay.

From time to time, other firms would spring up, in competition with ours, though they never seemed to last very long. And as yachting became more popular, more individuals who could sail a boat offered their services for yacht delivery, which tended to offset the effect of the growth of the industry.

So I doubt if it will ever be an easy business but it is an interesting one, far from the daily grind that most men put up with, and if anyone who has read this book still wants to go into it, I would advise him to give it a try.

But I would suggest that he join an established firm if he can, rather than try to start his own, for the first seven years or so can be quite hard.